THE PSYCHOBIOLOGY OF
HUMAN FOOD SELECTION

THE PSYCHOBIOLOGY OF HUMAN FOOD SELECTION

edited by
Lewis M. Barker, Ph.D.
Department of Psychology
Baylor University
Waco, Texas

AVI PUBLISHING COMPANY, INC.
Westport, Connecticut

©Copyright 1982 by
THE AVI PUBLISHING COMPANY, INC.
Westport, Connecticut

Second Printing   1983

Library of Congress Cataloging in Publication Data
Main entry under title:

The Psychobiology of human food selection.
    Includes bibliographical references and index.
    1. Diet.   2. Food preferences.   3. Food habits.
I. Barker, Lewis M., 1942–
TX357.P88   1982   641'.01'9   82-1140
ISBN 0-87055-409-3

Printed in the United States of America

Contents

List of Contributors   ix

Preface   xi

Introduction   xv

PART I BIOLOGICAL ASPECTS OF HUMAN FOOD
SELECTION   1

1 **Biological Basis of Food Selection**   3
Lloyd M. Beidler

   Evolution of Chemical Sensing   3
   Dominant Role of Taste in Body Wisdom   6
   The Study of Human Taste   9
   The Chemistry of Sweetness   10
   References   14

2 **Diet, Performance, and Their Interaction**   17
Per-Olof Åstrand

   A Brief History   17
   Fuel for Muscular Work   18
   Energy Balance   23
   Gaining Weight   24
   Appetite for Energy   27
   References   31

3 **Brain Mechanisms Involved in Feeding**   33
Edmund T. Rolls and Barbara J. Rolls

   Feeding and Satiety Centers in the Brain   34
   Direct Neurophysiological Evidence on the Role of the Lateral
     Hypothalamus in Feeding   35
   Effect of Learning on the Responses of Hypothalamic Neurons
     to Food   41
   Role of Hypothalamic Neurons in Feeding   42
   Responses to Food Reward and to Brain-Stimulation Reward in
     the Lateral Hypothalamus   44
   Role of the Ventromedial Hypothalamus in Feeding   45
   The Neural Control of Eating in Man   48
   The Role of Catecholamine Pathways in Feeding   49
   The Role of the Amygdala in Feeding and Food Selection   51

The Role of the Orbitofrontal Cortex in Feeding and Food Selection   54
Conclusions   57
References   58

PART II PSYCHOLOGICAL DETERMINANTS OF FOOD CHOICES   63

4 How Nutritional Effects of Foods Can Influence People's Dietary Choices   67
D.A. Booth

Understanding the Process of Food Selection: Analysis and
   Synthesis   68
Hedonic Conditioning by Effects of Nutrient Ingestion   70
Other Sources of Appetite and Satiation   76
Integration and Conflict between Biology and Culture   78
References   80

5 Building Memories for Foods   85
Lewis M. Barker

Information Processing Models of Memory   86
Memories for Flavors   89
Laboratory Studies of Flavor Memory   92
Concluding Remarks   98
References   99

6 The Influence of Variety on Human Food Selection and Intake   101
Barbara J. Rolls, Edmund T. Rolls, and Edward A. Rowe

Sensory Specific Satiety and Dietary Selection   101
The Influence of Variety on Feeding   109
Variety, Monotony, and Obesity   117
Conclusions   120
References   120

7 The Synergistic Properties of Pairs of Sweeteners   123
James C. Smith, David F. Foster, and Linda M. Bartoshuk

Polydipsia for a Saccharin/Glucose Mixture in the Laboratory Rat   123
The Human Subject   134
The Bitterness of Saccharin   136
References   138

8 Social Determinants in Human Food Selection   139
M. Krondl and D. Lau

Introduction   139
Relationship of Price, Convenience and Prestige to Food Use   141
The Relationship of Perceived Health Belief, Cognition, and Flavor
   to Food Use   146
"Fixed" and Changing Food Habits   148
Conclusion   149
References   149

PART III SOCIOCULTURAL FACTORS IN HUMAN FEEDING BEHAVIOR   153

9 Choice and Occasion: Sweet Moments   157
Sidney W. Mintz

Choice and Occasion   158
Sugar Usage   162
Concluding Remarks   168
References   168

10 Food, Behavior and Biocultural Evolution   171
Solomon H. Katz

Maize and Biocultural Evolution   171
Fava Beans, G-6-PD Deficiency, and Malaria   176
Bitter Manioc   179
The Origins of Soybeans in China   180
Conclusions   185
References   187

11 The Structure of Cuisine   189
Elisabeth Rozin

Culinary Behavior   189
Cuisine   190
Manipulative Techniques   191
Flavoring Foods: Flavoring Principles   194
Sources of Variation in Cuisine   199
Cuisine as a Cultural System   201
References   203

12 Geography and Genetics as Factors in the Psychobiology of Human Food Selection   205
Frederick J. Simoons

Culture Defines Food Choices   207
Religion and Food Selection   208
Human Usage of Milk   210
Lactose Malabsorption   213
Human Ecogenetics   216
References   221

13 Human Food Selection: The Interaction of Biology, Culture, and Individual Experience   225
Paul Rozin

Introduction   226
Transformation or Amplification of Biological Tendencies by Culture: Sugar versus Flavor Principles   228
Representation of Nutritional Adaptive Function in the Minds of Contemporary Individuals: Manioc versus Corn   232
Amplifying or Reversing Biological Biases: Sugar versus Chili Pepper   236

Biology to Culture and Culture to Biology: Cultured Milk versus
    Raw Milk   240
Affective or Cognitive Bases for Acquisition of Culture: Poisonous
    Mushrooms versus Insects   243
Multiple or Unitary Pathways to Enculturation: Chili Pepper
    versus Tobacco or Coffee   246
Two Persistent Problems   249
References   252

Index   **255**

List of Contributors

PER-OLAF ÅSTRAND, Department of Physiology III, Karolinska Institute, Lidingov. 1, S-11433, Stockholm, Sweden

LEWIS M. BARKER, Department of Psychology, Baylor University, Waco, Texas

LINDA M. BARTOSHUK, John B. Pierce Foundation Laboratory, New Haven, Connecticut

LLOYD M. BEIDLER, Department of Biological Science, Florida State University, Tallahassee, Florida

DAVID A. BOOTH, Department of Psychology, University of Birmingham, Birmingham, England

DAVID F. FOSTER, Department of Psychology, Florida State University, Tallahassee, Florida

SOLOMON H. KATZ, Department of Anthropology, University of Pennsylvania, Philadelphia, Pennsylvania

M. KRONDL, Department of Nutritional Sciences, Faculty of Medicine, University of Toronto, Toronto, Ontario, Canada

D. LAU, Department of Nutritional Sciences, University of Toronto, Toronto, Ontario, Canada

SIDNEY W. MINTZ, Department of Anthropology, The Johns Hopkins University, Baltimore, Maryland

BARBARA J. ROLLS, Department of Experimental Psychology, University of Oxford, Oxford, England

EDMUND T. ROLLS, Department of Experimental Psychology, University of Oxford, Oxford, England

EDWARD A. ROWE, Department of Experimental Psychology, University of Oxford, Oxford, England

ELISABETH ROZIN, 672 S. Highland Avenue, Merion, Pennsylvania

PAUL ROZIN, Department of Psychology, University of Pennsylvania, Philadelphia, Pennsylvania

FREDRICK J. SIMOONS, Department of Geography, University of California at Davis, Davis, California

JAMES C. SMITH, Department of Psychology, Florida State University, Tallahassee, Florida

Preface

The psychobiology of human food selection is primarily the study of what determines the choice of the foods we eat. It is also, however, the study of the behavioral control of nutrition, for there are consequences not only to what we choose to ingest, but also to the foods we avoid. In addition, food selection is the study of pleasure and pain, preference and aversion, likes and dislikes—indeed, hedonic experience.

The symposium reported here is directly concerned with the determinants of food selection, but it also opens doors to our thinking about nutrition and hedonic experience. The theme of the symposium is built around three classes of factors which control the selection of food.

1. Biological factors, those innate, hard-wired factors which are present at birth or unfold during development. Some are typical of the species, such as the positive response to sweet taste. Some are matters of genetic individuality, such as the "blindness" some people have to bitter tastes (e.g., phenylthiocarbamide). Others are concerned with the kind of postingestional machinery we inherit, such as whether we have the enzymes to digest milk sugar, for example (cf. lactose intolerance—see Simoons, Chapter 12).

2. Individual experience, such as the development of aversion to foods that make one sick. Or conversely, the development of an idiosyncratic preference for a food, whether it be a life-long appreciation of the particular flavor of "mom's apple pie" or habits in the use of salt or other seasonings or spices.

3. Cultural factors, also the result of learning and experience, but shared with virtually everyone else in the "community." Examples would be the aversion to eating the pig in Jewish and Moslem cultures or the Mexican preference for hot chili peppers in their food in quantities that are highly aversive to people from other cultures and even to young Mexican children until they are "acculturated."

All three classes of factors work together to determine the food choices an individual makes at any instant. This interaction of factors is accomplished through the brain, which is the final common path for all behavior. Examples of these interactions abound. A particular taste or odor codes a message to the brain, not only that a food quality has been sensed, but that it has a particular hedonic tone, based either on how it is "hard-wired" or on what experience is associated with it or both. Memories about food are stored in the brain. The brain also senses the internal environment of the body and assesses blood sugar or insulin levels or whether the body is sodium deficient or not. If it is sodium deficient, for example, then there is a strong craving for salt, so the brain's sensitivity to its internal environment gets transformed into motivated behavior.

We still do not know how the brain accomplishes feats such as these, but we are exposed to some new insights here. For example, there are nerve cells in the lateral hypothalamus that discharge nerve impulses only when the organism is stimulated by the sight or smell of food, and then only when it is hungry! (see E. Rolls and B. Rolls, Chapter 3) We also learn that while taste and smell are the first determinants of food preference and aversion throughout the animal kingdom, postingestional consequences of foods are important, too, for example, in learning aversions as a consequence of getting sick on certain foods. Another variable is exercise, an important factor in the role metabolism plays in the control of food intake, but also contributing because the more active a person, the more foods he eats, and the better chance he has of getting a balanced diet (P.-O. Åstrand, Chapter 2).

A number of factors are described that determine how much we eat of a given food. Palatability is one such factor, and this is shown to operate dramatically in the greatly increased ingestion of sweet solutions when saccharin and glucose are mixed, compared to the ingestion of each substance alone. Variety is also conducive to increased eating as reported in the experiments by Barbara Rolls (Chapter 6). Memory of foods should also determine what is eaten and how much, but at the present time, we are only beginning to develop a theoretical conception of how food memories are built into the organism. Human food choices are also based on social and economic factors which are important determinants of nutrition in the aged, for example.

Like the rat, humans are omnivores and they sample widely in their food environment, but they must also be cautious in their sampling to avoid poisonous foods, hence, the neophobia or fear of new foods that both rats and humans display, priming them for the learning of food aversions. On the other hand, preferences may arise because culture provides a means of "marking" safe foods and making a wide variety of them familiar by means of cuisine that prescribes ethnic flavors and consistent techniques of food preparation and cooking. Remarkably, both the preferences and aversions that are inculcated by culture have strong hedonic qualities and form the basis of strong likes and dislikes, often characterized as great pleasures and intense disgusts.

The chapters in this volume abound with new ideas of how biological and cultural factors go together to determine the food choices that yield both good nutrition and pleasure in eating. As a consequence, new insights into the principles underlying food selection, the behavioral control of nutrition, cuisine, and the acceptability of food products await the readers of this volume.

Eliot Stellar
University of Pennsylvania School of Medicine
Philadelphia, Pennsylvania

Introduction

You inch forward in the cafeteria line, anticipating the pleasures of the *smorgasbord*. Maddening arrays of fruits and vegetable salads appear. Each dish is enticingly prepared to enhance colors, shapes, and textures. Some of the foods are comfortably familiar. You are intrigued by the novelty of others, and their aromas promising unusual flavors. Steaming pumpernickel, corn-on-the-cob, and prime rib of beef beckon you.

Now you are hungry. Your pace slows perceptibly as the decision process begins. The saliva flowing in your mouth is a measure of the eagerness to accomplish the task before you—to select foods in your characteristic manner. You begin to compose a meal to satisfy your palate as well as your hunger.

How do you choose? Which items will you select? In what quantities? What flavors and food combinations will provide the most satisfaction? Which the most healthful? Which yield the most food energy? In short, what are the factors that help determine your food selections?

Cafeteria lines merely accentuate our day-to-day task of choosing foods. Most of us accomplish this without much thought or effort. We get hungry periodically (often at "mealtime") and we eat and are satisfied several times a day throughout a lifetime. Only occasionally is our attention directed to one or another of the quite remarkable aspects of this process. Consider the following instances: You have a craving for something but you are not sure what it is, and then you find just the right thing. How did you do that? From literally thousands of possibilities you select specific foods in a supermarket to last for two weeks (approximately 40 meals), and in doing so you attempt to satisfy the nutrient needs as well as the palates of a family of four individuals. (Without a computer!) You are empathetic in trying to please a finicky eater because you had the flu recently and you know how unappealing even the tastiest of foods can be. (However, how can someone be hungry and finicky at the same time?) Finally, the bathroom scales confirm that you are gaining weight. You don't understand this because for years you remained at the same weight without constant attention to the foods you selected. (Is your weight gain due to reduced physical activity, or have your tastes and food selections and appetite changed over the years?)

A group of scientists knowledgable in one or more areas of human food selection were brought together to exchange ideas and to discuss and provide answers to these questions. This book represents the cumulative wisdom of these individuals. Perhaps because scientists tend to specialize in selected sub-areas of complex problems, they often hesitate to address outright the more global interests of the public they serve. In this book the experts have been encouraged to make "educated guesses" in those areas where our knowledge is limited—to questions in which the public has high interest. The scientists were also asked to avoid jargon as much as possible and to write for a general audience.

Sixteen individuals expert in anthropology, biology, food science, geography, physiology, and psychology received a list of six questions. They were asked to consider as many of these six as they felt competent to discuss. The questions were as follows:

1. Why do we choose particular foods, in specific amounts, at certain times of the day?
2. Can we identify the physiological, ecological, psychological, and sociocultural factors underlying our feeding behavior?
3. To what degree are our food choices "fixed" (e.g., by biology and heredity) and alternatively, to what extent are our food selection patterns determined by sociocultural factors?
4. What are the evolutionary origins of our appetites? Can cultural variability give us insight into these origins?
5. Are sweet and salty flavor preferences innate or acquired and to what extent is there cultural variability in their relative acceptance?
6. Is there evidence that each of us has an innate wisdom governing the selection of appropriate foods (cf. "body wisdom" and "nutritional wisdom")?

The contributors bring to this volume more than their specialized knowledge in responding to these six questions and others related to food selection. Indeed, this book is more than a compilation of the collective results of their thinking, reasoning, and experimenting. Each individual is genuinely interested in selecting and eating foods. Jean Soler (1979)[1] has described this fascination with foods as follows:

[1]SOLER, J. 1979. The dietary prohibitions of the Hebrews. *The New York Review of Books*, June 14, 1979, p. 24.

Man knows that the food he ingests in order to live will become assimilated into his being—will become himself. There must be, therefore, a relationship between the idea he has formed of specific items of food and the image he has of himself and his place in the Universe. There is a link between a people's dietary habits and its perception of the world.

This book is about man's relationship with his foods. Each chapter represents curiosity, creativity, and effort. Each contributor is not only expert in his or her particular area of investigation, but like you, each is also a human being who makes decisions about food selection on a daily basis. Join them in spirit and enjoy the fruits of their labor.

Lewis M. Barker

Related AVI Books

ALCOHOL AND THE DIET
  Roe
CONSUMER BEHAVIOR
  Redman
DRUG-INDUCED NUTRITIONAL DEFICIENCIES
  Roe
FOOD AND ECONOMICS
  Hungate and Sherman
FOOD AND THE CONSUMER
  Revised Edition   *Kramer*
FOOD FOR THOUGHT
  2nd Edition   *Labuza and Sloan*
FOOD, PEOPLE AND NUTRITION
  Eckstein
MENU PLANNING
  2nd Edition   *Eckstein*
NUTRITION AND MEDICAL PRACTICE
  Barness, Coble, MacDonald and Christakis

Part I

Biological Aspects of Human Food Selection

The scientific investigation of human food selection can be characterized in many ways. As a starting point we can conceptualize levels of analysis which extend from molecular to molar concerns. Consider the following examples. Molecular investigations would include the study of nutrient needs of a tissue such as muscle, and the relationship of firing patterns of neurons in the brain in the presence of tasty foods. More molar studies of food selection might involve an experiment in which humans are asked to choose the more preferred of two flavors, and how economic and political factors influence the availability and cost (and ultimate selection) of meat at the supermarket.

This book is organized in a manner which takes the reader from molecular explanations (biological) to higher levels of analysis (psychological and sociocultural). The composite of this knowledge at present comprises our best answers to general questions about food selection— even if these answers are incomplete, confusing, contradictory, and not well integrated. The above scheme based on levels of analysis would work fairly well if each investigator remained within his or her well-specified realm of inquiry and knowledge. This is seldom the case, however. Biologists want to talk about learning and memory and cultural differences, and anthropologists now commonly use genetics to explain many of their findings (see Part III). Nevertheless, in broad outline we can begin by looking at tissue needs and the responses of taste buds and certain neurons in the brain which are important in food selection.

In this first part there are contributions from a biologist (more specifically, a molecular biophysicist), an exercise physiologist, and two experimental psychologists specializing in neurophysiology. These individuals have addressed a wide range of issues within a biological framework. Taken together this section provides an analysis of the body's equipment used for detecting, selecting, and assimilating nutrients from the environment. In the first chapter ("Biological Basis of Food Selection") Lloyd Beidler presents the argument that we, like other living organisms, inherit an innate sensitivity to foodstuffs, and use basic taste and olfactory sensitivity to predict which objects in our environment are suitable for ingestion. Our bodies, moreover, are energy consuming machines which perform more or less optimally as a result of the appropriateness of our food selections, in intimate interaction with energy expenditure levels (Åstrand, "Diet, Performance, and their Interaction").

The human brain regulates and ultimately controls the processes of food detection, selection, and ingestion in ways that neuroscientists are only now beginning to understand. One approach to the study of brain mechanisms is presented in a chapter by Ed and Barbara Rolls ("Brain Mechanisms Involved in Feeding"). Monkeys are presented with the sight and flavor of palatable or aversive foods and the activity of various parts of the brain is measured.

A consistent theme emerges in these three biologically oriented chapters. The complexity of human food selection is immediately apparent. A complete understanding of nutrient repletion, tissue needs, and energy demands, and an intimate knowledge of brain wave patterns associated with food selection, however, leaves us with a frightfully limited understanding of the reasons we choose the foods we do. The biologists tell us at the outset that experiential factors of learning, socialization, and acculturation have critically modified the innate sensing and regulatory mechanisms that successfully guided our feeding behavior in the past. This interaction of biology with culture reemerges in ensuing chapters.

1

Biological Basis
of Food Selection

Lloyd M. Beidler

It is the thesis of this paper that both our selection and ingestion of food have a strong biological basis that is reflected in our eating behavior. This behavior is not unique but rather is shared in one form or another with most animals, from unicellular to primates. Since it can be considered as a rather primitive biological drive, alteration of eating behavior is often difficult—as most dieters know. An outline of this thesis will now be considered.

EVOLUTION OF CHEMICAL SENSING

Cells. All cells are responsive to changes in their chemical environment. Unicellular organisms that move toward or away from chemical stimulants (chemotaxis) show high discriminative ability for a large number of substances (Hazelbauer 1978). The food seeking behavior of amebas is perhaps the best known. The white blood cells (leukocytes) of man also show locomotion to remove damaged cells and tissues by engulfing them. How do they distinguish normal from damaged cells? They respond to gradients of chemicals released by the cells. This is nicely demonstrated by the ability of leukocytes to consume old red cells without disturbing the younger and normal cells. Bessis (1973) used a laser beam to damage a single red cell and observed that the white cells immediately moved toward the injured cell. Proteins, amino acids, and lipids, but no sugars, have been shown to stimulate leukocytes. Some tripeptides produce responses at a 10^{-10} M concentration. Stimulus stereospecificity is present. The activation of the locomotion response is mediated by changes in the membrane of the leukocytes.

Bacteria.   The membrane changes that lead to chemotaxis is better understood in bacteria that move by their flagella. The bacterium *Escherichia coli* is attracted by many sugars and amino acids that are involved in its nutrition. On the other hand, the same bacterium is repelled by many harmful molecules. The sensory processes that allow the detection of trace levels of chemicals to control the bacterial migration are not completely known (Adler 1969). It has been shown, however, that nine or more polypeptides are active in the transduction mechanism in addition to the initial receptor protein to which the stimulus binds and two or more additional membrane proteins of 60,000 molecular weight (Stock and Koshland 1978). One of these membrane proteins is methylated when the bacterium is chemically stimulated by an attractant and demethylated when repellents are present. Several of the polypeptides are involved in the enzymatic reactions that control the methylation and thus bacteria migration. Our understanding of bacteria chemotaxis is aided by genetic studies of strains containing deficient mutants. This allows the determination of function of specific gene products.

Sensory Receptors

As animals evolved further, so did their sensory receptors. Indeed, special cellular structures appeared that were specific for chemical detection. Stimulation of these receptors often leads to acceptive or aversive reflexes. These receptors are often specific for certain groups of stimuli.

Insects.   The world of insects offers a large number of examples of chemical detection by receptor systems. Many insects imbibe sugars obtained from plants, and it is therefore not surprising that such insects may have sugar receptors on their feet, legs, and mouthparts. The receptors of several species of flies have been studied extensively. The flies' detection threshold for over 200 different molecules have been determined. Two sugar receptor types were found: one responds to glucoselike molecules and the other to fructoselike molecules (Shimada and Morita 1974). Other receptors respond to a variety of salts, with potassium salts very effective. Water receptors are also present.

Many blood-sucking insects, including mosquitoes, fleas and black flies have receptors that respond to nucleotides (Hansen 1978). Sucking commences when the receptors are stimulated by adenosine tri-, di-, and monophosphates (ATP, ADP, AMP), etc., which are released by blood platelets as the insect's stylet penetrates the blood vessel. It is interesting to note that some nucleotides are utilized as taste enhancers in foods for humans.

Aquatic Animals. Aquatic animals such as fish, crustaceans and mollusks are particularly sensitive to amino acids, peptides, nucleotides, and in some cases, proteins associated with prey. The taste and olfactory receptors of the catfish, for example, can detect certain amino acids at a 10^{-10} M concentration (Caprio 1978). Some of the receptors are highly specific and respond primarily to arginine. Other receptors in the population are generalists and respond to a wide variety of amino acids.

Mammals. Mammals, including man, have receptors that respond to most of the molecules mentioned above. Furthermore, the resultant behavior is similar. Sugars are accepted and bitters are rejected. Amino acids, peptides and certain proteins stimulate the receptors. Other receptors respond to a variety of salts and acids.

Sweet Sense in Man

One may conclude that chemical detection is an attribute of all animals. Furthermore, reflexive behavior to substances such as sugars and bitters evolved early and remains even with primates, including man. Thus, a biological basis for sweet ingestion and bitter avoidance appears to be well founded. Let us consider this in more detail for man.

Taste Buds. The taste buds of man are very similar to those of the catfish. In fact, they were discovered in fish a number of years before they were found in man. They appear in the human fetus about $5-6$ months before birth. At this time they also appear to be functional since injection of saccharin into the mother's amniotic fluid increases the rate of sucking by the fetus (De Snoo 1937). Laboratory studies of fetal sheep indicate that their taste nerves are functional well before birth and suggest that human taste nerves may develop similarly (Bradley and Mistretta 1971).

Infant Preferences. Immediately after birth, the human infant already prefers sweet solutions, and feeding sugar water to newborns is quite common. Bitter and sour solutions produce aversion. Infants born without a cortex show a similar behavior to the same taste stimuli (Steiner 1977). Thus, the sweet preference by human babies may be innate and only involve the lower nervous centers. Indeed, Keverne (1978) suggests that "Neocortical processing may provide us with our esthetic pleasures while the emphasis may be on survival value from the subcortical processing."

Adult Preferences.   As the infant grows, selection of sweets may be modified by cultural and economic factors. However, it appears that people of many nations and cultures continue to eat sweets if available. There is good agreement between sugar availability and sugar consumption, with people of countries with high per capita income consuming large quantities of sugar (Cantor 1975). This is evident in Japan where pastry shops are becoming as common as in Europe. It is of interest that per capita sugar consumption in the United States has remained reasonably constant for several decades, contrary to what many believe. The question then remains, "how much of our taste behavior is a reflection of our evolutionary development?"

DOMINANT ROLE OF TASTE IN BODY WISDOM

Although I have emphasized an almost stereotyped behavior of animals in response to chemical stimulation, much of man's response is a result of learned behavior. The early work of Richter (1942) and others on the ability of rats to self-select their diet in response to imposed specific deficiencies is now explained on the basis of learning. In fact, learned behavior (cultural, religious, economic, etc.) is now thought to determine most of man's food preferences.

Self-Selection.   Some instances of self-selection by humans still need clarification, however. It has been observed, for example, that some people with deficiencies of the adrenal cortex increase their consumption of salt much like adrenalectomized rats, while others consume large quantities of licorice candy (Baron 1973). Natural licorice contains the sweetener, glycyrrhizin, which has the structure shown in Fig. 1.1. It has been noted that this substance has a corticoid action and

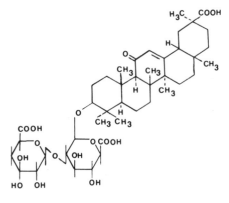

FIG. 1.1.   THE LICORICE FLAVOR IS DUE TO GLYCYRRHIZIN, THE SALT OF GLYCYRRHIZIC ACID

therefore would help to maintain mineral and water balance in those individuals with adrenal insufficiencies. The problem remains, "how do children relate licorice intake with its pharmacological action?" Since most known physiological actions occur at a time much later than that of the intake of glycyrrhizin, it is not clear how a person could learn the association between licorice ingestion and symptom relief.

Learned Food Aversions

The sensory qualities associated with taste, odors and other sensations that form a composite referred to as flavor are well known. They play a great role in food preference and food intake. Their hedonic value, however, can be dramatically changed by visceral feedback, and aversions to formerly highly preferred foods can be observed. It is well known that humans associate a digestive upset with any unusual foods recently eaten (Garb and Stunkard 1974). This emphasizes the fact that taste plays a dominant role in formulating eating behavior that protects animals, including man, from foods that are found unfit for the digestive system. Thus, taste and visceral reflexes are closely related and at times combine to form a strong biological basis for aversions to specific foods.

The effect is so pronounced that taste aversions can be produced by single trial conditioning. Garcia and colleagues first studied such taste aversions using a single association with X-ray irradiation (Garcia and Kimeldorf 1957). These studies were followed by others using a single application of any of a whole series of chemicals thought to produce sickness associated with changes of the viscera and thus nausea (Barker et al. 1977; Milgram et al. 1977).

Specific Food Preferences

Exactly what foods does man prefer? Data on this subject are quite limited. About 3900 males in the Armed Forces, most being white and under 25 years of age, were surveyed concerning preference of 378 food items (Meiselman and Waterman 1978). Both hedonic scores and frequency of selection were scaled. Some of these scores are shown in Table 1.1. Note the large variations of specific items within a food category and also the variety of highly scored food categories. Unfortunately, green vegetables and soups were scored very low. However, salads were highly preferred and milk as a beverage was well liked. Not surprisingly, this population also preferred hamburgers, pizza and cola. If variety is offered, however, it appears that the diet of these young men would fare quite well.

TABLE 1.1.   SURVEY OF FOOD PREFERENCES

	Relative hedonic score	Relative frequency score
Beer	19.78	7.26
Eggs	16.57	6.98
Hot beverages	13.68	5.88
Green salads	13.37	6.57
Milk products	13.35	6.19
Fresh fruits	12.61	6.76
Ice cream	12.14	6.78
Fruit drinks and iced tea	11.39	6.48
Carbonated beverages	11.26	5.80
Breakfast cereals	9.83	5.60
Sandwiches	9.61	6.34
Fish and seafood	9.20	6.22
Potatoes	9.03	5.99
Meats	9.03	6.24
Yellow vegetables	8.50	5.67
Cakes	8.45	6.10
Pies	8.34	5.90
Puddings	7.97	5.71
Cookies	7.94	5.67
Fruit salads	7.67	5.45
Vegetable salads	7.30	5.12
Green vegetables	7.41	5.22
Soups	7.13	5.33

[1] Selected from Meiselman and Waterman 1978.

My personal experience in teaching the basis of food intake and digestion to 600–1000 young college students indicates that not all young people select their food as well as the above men in the Armed Forces. Perhaps this is due to a more limited option of foods normally available. This is particularly true of young women who are on a diet. For many of them, all meals are eliminated, and when hungry, they nibble. The nibbling often does not include those items that are usual components of a normal four food group meal. Sweetened items are frequently high on their list. Again we can ask, "why is this so?"

Sweets.   As shown earlier, there is a biological origin for our strong preference for sweet foods. Carbohydrates have fewer calories per pound than either proteins or fat. What, then, is bad about eating sweets? The answer is that they taste too good! Our consumption, therefore, is often too great and at the expense of protein or foods with vitamins and minerals. In addition, sugars are the main culprits in the widespread occurrence of tooth decay. It should also be mentioned that glucose enters the blood stream rapidly and thus quickly elevates the blood glucose level. This is not always beneficial for man. Starches would be a better choice of carbohydrates, since the entrance into the blood stream of the resultant monosaccharides would be slower and over a greater period of time and thus the blood glucose level would not reach as high a level. Thus, sugar consumption should be moderate and the unusual attractivenss of sweetness controlled. The obvious answer is to diet and change our eating habits. However, changing habits is difficult, particularly if our eating habits have been maintained over long periods of time. How can the study of taste help? Let us first examine the taste system of mammals, including man.

THE STUDY OF HUMAN TASTE

Thousands of taste buds are scattered unevenly over the surface of the tongue. Taste buds are also evident on the palate and to a lesser degree elsewhere in the oral cavity. Each taste bud contains 40−50 cells with microvilli extending from their apical end into the saliva covering the tongue. These cells are continually renewed, each living about 10 days, although the integrity of the bud is always maintained. Taste nerve fibers enter the base of the taste bud and innervate the taste cells with one fiber connected to many cells.

Methods

The taste system and its functioning in food intake is usually studied by one of three methods.

1. Electrophysiology. The changes in electrical potential of the taste cells or the frequency of nerve impulses of the taste nerve fibers can be recorded in response to tastants flowed over the tongue. This offers objective and quantitative data useful in the study of the sensory receptors and nerves but is of limited usefulness in application to the knowledge of sensations elicited by foods.

2. Psychophysics. Psychophysical measurements of such parameters as threshold, intensity, quality, etc., of tastants can be obtained for man and to some extent for other animals. Most, but not all, of these studies have been limited to pure chemicals rather than complex foods.

3. Behavioral Studies. The relative preference of foods taken two at a time in choice tests provide useful information for both man and animals. Other behavioral studies, such as amount of food consumed, can be used as a measure of food preference. This is of particular interest to those studying the taste behavior of animals other than man. A special type of behavioral study is the consumer testing of new food products. Consumer testing offers little information as to how the taste buds function but is useful for those interested in how man reacts to a product.

The choice of method of testing depends on the question that is asked. Sometimes, however, an understanding of the results of a consumer survey can only be found in knowledge of how the taste bud functions! Thus, it is important that scientists using any of the above methods of studies be acquainted with the results obtained by those using the other methods.

Taste Nerve Impulses

A study of the electrical properties of the taste system has revealed that the chemical stimulus is probably adsorbed to the microvilli of the taste cells. The binding strength is about 1−2 kcal/mole. Electrostatic interactions are dominant for salts and acids, while hydrogen bonding and hydrophobic interactions are important for sweeteners and bitters (Beidler 1971).

Adsorption of the tastant molecule to the taste receptor eventually leads to an increase in permeability of sodium, calcium, or other ions at the membrane near the base of the cell where the nerve connects. This then leads to nerve stimulation followed by a series of nerve impulses that travel toward the brain. The frequency of nerve impulses is related to the magnitude of taste sensation.

Not all the taste cells are alike. In fact, each reacts a little differently toward a series of chemical stimuli. One may be very reactive to sugars and less so to other stimuli. Others are more reactive to other tastants. The activities of a number of taste fibers are necessary for the brain to be able to determine the exact quality of a taste sensation.

THE CHEMISTRY OF SWEETNESS

A study of molecular structure has been most useful in our understanding of sweeteners. Both electrophysiological and psychophysical measurements have been used to measure the magnitude of taste response to a series of molecules. Shallenberger and Acree (1967) noted that all sweeteners have two sites 3Å apart that can hydrogen bond to the receptor site. In many sweeteners there is also a third site where the molecule can bind to the receptor membrane with hydrophobic bonds (Kier 1972). This third bond may be related to the intrinsic activity of the stimulus that is responsible for the ultimate membrane depolarization (see Fig. 1.2).

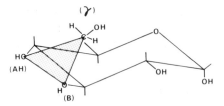

From Shallenberger and Lindley 1977

FIG. 1.2.   TWO D-GLUCOSE HYDROGEN BOND SITES (AH,B) ARE SHOWN. A THIRD HYDROPHOBIC OR LIPOPHILIC SITE (γ) EXISTS NEAR THE CARBON ATOM SHOWN

Artificial Sweeteners

These bits of information concerning the nature of those molecules that evoke sweet sensations are useful in designing new sweet tastants. Unfortunately, scientists have not been too successful in the quest, but new sweeteners are still being discovered by accident. This was true for saccharin, cyclamate and even the recently found aspartame. However, even aspartame appears to follow the hydrogen bonding and lipophilic characteristics of the other sweeteners. An intense study of the aspartame dipeptide molecule revealed its three-dimensional structure (see Fig. 1.3) and gave an insight as to the nature of the receptor site with which it interacts (Temussi *et al.* 1978). Note the two hydrogen bonds at

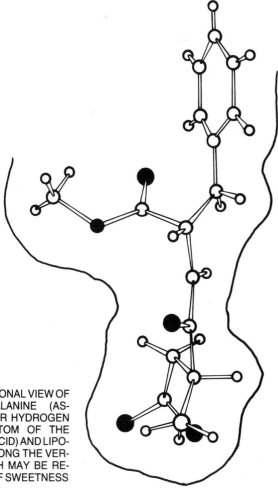

FIG. 1.3. A TWO-DIMENSIONAL VIEW OF α-L-ASPARTYL-L-PHENYLALANINE (AS-PARTAME). AH-B SITE FOR HYDROGEN BONDING AT THE BOTTOM OF THE STRUCTURE (ASPARTIC ACID) AND LIPO-PHILIC INTERACTIONS ALONG THE VER-TICAL DIMENSION, WHICH MAY BE RE-LATED TO THE DEGREE OF SWEETNESS

the aspartic acid end and the lipophilic bonding at the phenyl group above. The more we understand the nature of the stimulus receptor, the greater the opportunity of designing new sweeteners that are both intensely sweet and noncaloric.

Natural Sweeteners

Most chemicals that can serve as taste stimuli can also interact with other cells. Thus, some of these stimuli have been found to have deleterious effects, such as being carcinogenic. For this reason, other naturally occurring sweeteners of low threshold, particularly proteins, have been studied. The first protein was miraculin, the active ingredient of a berry found in Nigeria. The molecule is a glycoprotein of 44,000 molecular weight (Kurihara and Beidler 1968; Pintauro 1977). When placed in the mouth for about 30 seconds, the normal sour taste is changed to one with a high magnitude of sweetness. Thus, lemons taste sweet with a sour component. This modification of the taste sensation may last for over an hour (see Fig. 1.4).

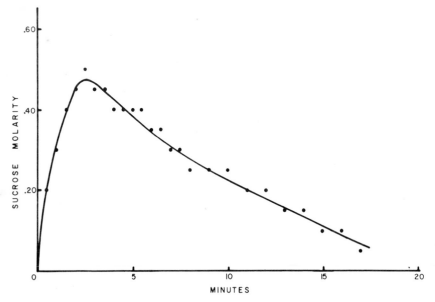

FIG. 1.4.   THE VERY SOUR 0.01 M CITRIC ACID TASTES VERY SWEET AFTER MIRACLE FRUIT IS PLACED INTO THE MOUTH. THE CONCENTRATION OF SUCROSE EQUIVALENT IN SWEETNESS TO THE CITRIC ACID DECREASES WITH TIME

Sour to Sweet.   It is thought that the miraculin protein is a sweetener that is only activated at low pH. Thus, any sour sensation will be modified to one that is primarily sweet. Since miraculin threshold is about 10^{-7} M and since its effect only decreases slowly, it affords an excellent opportunity to turn sweetness on or off by merely changing the pH of the fluid in the oral cavity. Lemon chiffon pie baked without sugar becomes sweet as does unsugared iced tea with lemon juice. Miraculin also enhances the natural sweetness of many fruits. It can be used effectively to control the diet without loss of the highly desired sweetness.

Since miraculin was discovered, several other proteins have been found to be sweet and have a rather low threshold (Cagen 1973). However, these proteins need to be added to each food that is to be sweetened in a manner similar to the use of saccharin. All of the sweet proteins behave like most other proteins and their activities are destroyed by high temperature or enzymatic action. For this reason they are stored in a dry state to maintain their activity.

Counteracting Sweetness through Chemistry

It may be beneficial to inhibit temporarily the normal sweet sensation of those who eat too many sweets. For this purpose one may consider taste modifiers that depress sweetness. The best known taste modifier of this type is gymnemic acid (see Fig. 1.5.) It is a triterpene derivative found in a plant grown in India called *Gymnema sylvestre*. It, like miraculin, has a rather long lasting period of taste modification (Kurihara 1969). Shortly after being placed on the tongue, all normally sweet stimuli no longer elicit a sweet sensation. Thus, table sugar tastes like grains of sand, gritty and tasteless. After application of gymnemic acid, Coca Cola tastes awful, many chocolates are creamy, hard candies are undesirable, etc. This taste modification effect can persist for several hours. For example, 130 minutes after application of gymnemic acid, the saccharin threshold remains elevated by a factor of 2.5 (Kiesow

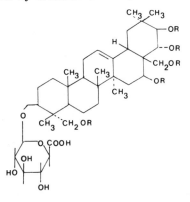

FIG. 1.5. GYMNEMIC ACID IS A TRITERPENE DERIVATIVE WITH AN ATTACHED GLUCURON IC ACID. IT IS ESTERIFIED WITH THREE OR FOUR DIFFERENT ORGANIC ACIDS

1894). Thus, the taste world of those desiring sweetness now crumbles. The gymnemic acid molecule is quite stable and can be heated and stored with undiminished activity remaining. A tea made from the leaves of *Gymnema sylvestre* can be used to form a candy that will act as a taste modifier. Its natural taste is similar to that of the hoar hound candy in New England.

The above are just a few known examples of taste modifiers whose actions may be useful to control the ingestion of high caloric sweet foods. A more complete knowledge of taste physiology, biophysics and chemistry may help in the formulation of taste modifiers with properties more desirable for use by the food industry and for diet control.

REFERENCES

ADLER, J. 1969. Chemoreceptors in bacteria. Science *166*, 1588–1597.

BARKER, L.M., BEST, M.R., and DOMJAN, M. (Editors). 1977. Learning Mechanisms in Food Selection. Baylor University Press, Waco, Texas.

BARRON, J.H. 1973. Glycyrrhizophilia. Lancet, Feb. 17, 383.

BEIDLER, L.M. 1971. Taste receptor stimulation with salts and acids. *In* Handbook of Sensory Physiology IV, Vol. 2, Taste. L.M. Beidler (Editor). Springer-Verlag, Berlin and New York.

BESSIS, M. 1973. Necrotaxis-chemotaxis towards an injured cell. Nouv. Rev. Fr. Hematol. *13*, 887–888.

BRADLEY, R.M. and MISTRETTA, C.M. 1971. Chorda tympani responses to lingual application of taste stimuli in foetal sheep. J. Physiol. *218*, 104P.

CAGAN, R.H. 1973. Chemostimulatory protein: A new type of taste stimulus. Science *181*, 32–35.

CANTOR, S.M. 1975. Patterns and use. *In* Sweeteners: Issues and Uncertainties. National Academy of Sciences, Washington, DC.

CAPRIO, J. 1978. Olfaction and taste in the channel catfish: An electrophysiological study of the responses to amino acids and derivatives. J. Comp. Physiol. *123*, 357–371.

DE SNOO, K. 1937. Sucking behavior in the human fetus. Monatsschr. Geburtshilfe *105*, 88–97. (German).

GARB, J.L., and STUNKARD, A.J. 1974. Taste aversions in man. Am. J. Psychiat. *131*, 1204–1207.

GARCIA, J., and KIMELDORF, D.J. 1957. Temporal relationship within the conditioning of a saccharin aversion through radiation exposure. J. Comp. Physiol. Psychol. *50*, 180–183.

HANSEN, K. 1978. Insect chemoreception. *In* Taxis and Behavior. G.L. Hazelbauer (Editor). John Wiley and Sons, New York.

HAZELBAUER, G.L. (Editor). 1978. Taxis and Behavior. John Wiley and Sons. New York.

KEVERNE, E.B.   1978.   Olfaction and taste: Dual systems for sensory processing.   Trends Neurosci. *1*, 32–34.

KIER, L.B.   1972.   A molecular theory of sweet taste.   J. Pharm. Sci. *61*, 1394–1397.

KIESOW, F.   1894.   Effects of the application of cola and gymnemic acid to the mucous membrane of the tongue and oral cavity.   Philos. Stud. Leipzig *9*, 510–527. (German).

KURIHARA, Y.   1969.   Antisweet activity of gymnemic acid A_1 and its derivatives.   Life Sci. *8*, 537–543.

KURIHARA, K. and BEIDLER, L.M.   1968.   Taste-modifying protein from miracle fruit.   Science *161*, 1241–1243.

MEISELMAN, H.L., and WATERMAN, D.   1978.   Food preferences of enlisted personnel in the armed forces.   J. Am. Diet. Assoc. *73*, 621.

MILGRAM, N.W., KRAMES, L., and ALLOWAY, T.M. (Editors).   1977.   Food Aversion Learning.   Plenum Press, New York.

PINTAURO, N.D.   1977.   Sweeteners and Enhancers.   Noyes Data Corp., Park Ridge, New Jersey.

RICHTER, C.P.   1942.   Total self-regulatory functions in animals and human beings.   Harvey Lect. Ser. *38*, 63–103.

SHALLENBERGER, R.S., and ACREE, T.E.   1967.   Molecular theory of sweet taste.   Nature *216*, 480–482.

SHALLENBERGER, R.S., and LINDLEY, M.G.   1977.   A lipophilic-hydrophobic attribute and component in the stereochemistry of sweetness.   Food Chem. *2*, 145–153.

SHIMADA, S., and MORITA, K.   1974.   Separation of two receptor sites in a single labellar sugar receptor of the flesh-fly by treatment with p-chloromercuribenzoate.   J. Insect Physiol. *20*, 605–621.

STEINER, J.E.   1977.   Facial expressions of the neonate infant indicating the hedonics of food-related chemical stimuli.   *In* Taste and Development: The Genesis of Sweet Preference.   J.M. Weiffenbach (Editor). Publ. No. NIH 77-1068, U.S. Department of Health, Education, and Welfare, Bethesda, Maryland.

STOCK, J., and KOSHLAND, D. Jr.   1978.   A protein methylesterase involved in bacterial sensing.   Proc. Nat. Acad. Sci. *75*, 3659–3663.

TEMUSSI, P.A., LELJ, F., and TANCREDI, T.   1978.   Three-dimensional mapping of the sweet-taste receptor site.   J. Med. Chem. *21*, 1154–1158.

Diet, Performance and Their Interaction

Per-Olof Åstrand

The purpose of this volume is to integrate different scientific subjects of a broad analysis of human food selection. I will view foods as fuel for energy, describe the energy balance problem, and finally, relate this to appetite (Åstrand and Rodahl 1977; Åstrand 1979).

A BRIEF HISTORY

In the 1930s Christensen and Hansen (1939) studied in a systematic way how diet, training, and other factors influenced the choice of substrate for exercising muscle and the effect on physical performance. As a tool they applied the value for the respiratory quotient (R or RQ). Based on their data, Fig. 2.1 illustrates schematically how under normal conditions carbohydrate and fat, respectively, contribute to the energy yields at various rates of work.

In the 1950s techniques were developed for a percutaneous introduction of catheters into blood vessels and the arteriovenous difference of substrates, substrate precursors, gases, etc., could be determined over exercising and resting skeletal muscles, liver, and fatty tissue. Regional blood flow could also be quantified. The use of isotope labeled atoms made it possible to study in more detail the exchange of nutrients and substances between blood and tissues. In my opinion there was often too much emphasis on the importance of free fatty acids as substrate for the muscles. Surely the muscular uptake of glucose was limited but the contribution of stored glycogen was "hidden."

In the 1960s the muscle needle biopsy technique was introduced by Bergstrom (1962). That opened the door for more detailed studies of what was going on within the *human* skeletal muscle during exercise, and the picture of the metabolic events became clearer. Essen (1978) developed the technique to analyze enzyme activity and glycogen content in pools of type I and II muscle fibers (including subgroups, respectively).

FUEL FOR MUSCULAR WORK

From various studies we can conclude the following relationships between fuel utilization and muscular work.

Protein or Carbohydrate?   Protein is *not* used as a fuel for exercising muscles to any appreciable extent when the supply of energy is adequate. At least, nitrogen excretion in the urine does not rise significantly following vigorous cross-country skiing over long distances. The choice of fuel for the muscles is, therefore, limited to carbohydrate and fat. (It is certainly a wise arrangement that the muscles do not in a cannibalistic manner consume themselves.)

Exercise Intensity and Carbohydrate Utilization.   With an increase in the intensity of exercise there is a gradual switch toward a proportionally greater share of energy yield from carbohydrates (see Fig. 2.1).

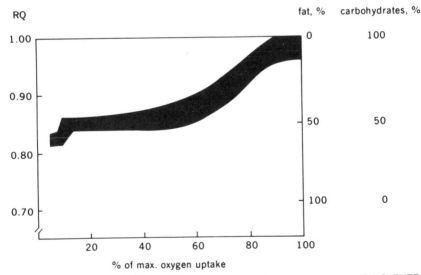

FIG. 2.1.   NONPROTEIN RESPIRATORY QUOTIENT AT REST AND DURING EXERCISE, RELATED TO THE OXYGEN UPTAKE IN PERCENT OF THE SUBJECT'S MAXIMAL OXYGEN UPTAKE. TO THE RIGHT, THE PERCENTAGE CONTRIBUTION TO THE ENERGY YIELD OF FAT AND CARBOHYDRATE. PROLONGED EXERCISE AND DIET CAN MARKEDLY MODIFY THE METABOLIC RESPONSE

From a teleological viewpoint that is efficient. One liter of oxygen can, in the respiration chain, oxidize glycogen and yield energy for a regeneration of about 6.5 moles of adenosine triphosphate (ATP). When fatty acids are oxidized, the ATP formation is reduced to 5.6 mole/liter of oxygen consumed.

Prolonged exercise and free fatty acids. In prolonged exercise of moderate intensity there is a gradual increase in the metabolism of free fatty acids replacing some of the carbohydrate oxidation. Figure 2.2 illustrates this point. A hypoglycemic may limit the performance due to exhaustion of the liver's glycogen store (see Pruett 1971). When exercising at a level demanding about 75% or more of the individual's maximal aerobic power there is not such a shift in fuel utilization. The carbohydrate metabolism is maintained at a high level as long as glycogen and/or glucose is available. At exhaustion the muscle glycogen store is usually emptied (in well-motivated subjects). When carbohydrate is not available as substrate, the subject must stop or reduce the rate of work (see Hedman 1957; Bergstrom *et al.* 1967).

Training Effects

O₂ Uptake and FFA. A very important effect of *training* is certainly the induced increase in maximal oxygen uptake. Another positive effect is the increase in the oxidation of free fatty acids (FFA) and the reduced energy yield from glycogen. This modification in fuel utilization is not only evident at a given metabolic rate, but also when working at a given percentage of the maximal aerobic power. Table 2.1 presents data that can explain the improved endurance after a period of training. The enhanced FFA utilization is glycogen saving, and it takes a longer time to empty a given glycogen store. In this example 350 g of glycogen permitted the trained individual to prolong the standardized exercise for an additional 40 minutes when his untrained companion finished after 145 minutes. Note the difference in demand on the carbohydrate metabolism in the two subjects.

Fat and Carbohydrate Metabolism. How can we explain this effect of physical training on the fat and carbohydrate metabolism? A high lactate concentration will suppress the mobilization of FFA from the adipose tissue. Training will reduce the lactate production during submaximal exercise, and thereby the plasma FFA level may increase. Such an increase is always followed by an increased rate of FFA utilization (see Paul 1975). Also, local factors affected by training will influence the FFA utilization: One leg was trained prior to standardized

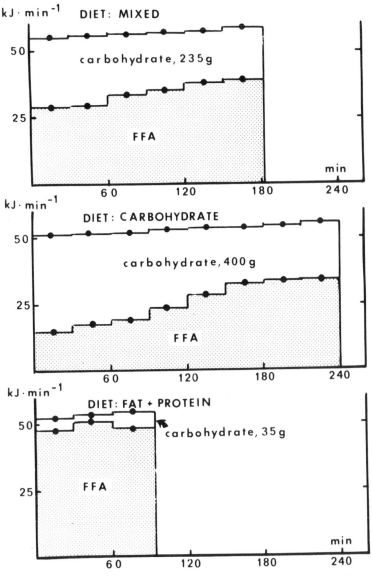

Data from Christensen and Hansen 1939

FIG. 2.2. INCREASE IN FREE FATTY ACID METABOLISM IN PROLONGED EXERCISE
One well-trained subject exercised on a cycle ergometer at 183 W after a mixed diet, then at 176 W after a carbohydrate-rich diet for 3 days. In another experiment 176 W preceded by a 3-day period on fat and protein, excluding the carbohydrate from the diet. The subject worked until exhausted. The total energy output was calculated from the measured oxygen uptake and respiratory quotient (RQ) during 15 minute periods; the energy yield from carbohydrate and free fatty acids (FFA), respectively, was estimated from the RQ values. The calculated total carbohydrate consumption (g) is presented. Note how working time and the diet affects the choice of substrate. At the given rate of work the endurance time varied from 93 to 240 minutes depending on the diet. (The subject's maximal oxygen uptake was not determined.)

TABLE 2.1. ENDURANCE OF TWO SUBJECTS TO PROLONGED EXERCISE[1]

| Subject | Oxygen uptake (liter/min) | | RQ | (kJ/min) | Carbohydrate metabolism | | Work time on 350 g glycogen (min) |
	Max	80%			(%)	(g/min)	
Untrained	3.0	2.4	0.95	50.1	83	2.4	145
Trained	3.0	2.4	0.90	49.5	66	1.9	184

[1]Two subjects with the same maximal oxygen uptake were working at 80% of this maximum until exhaustion. For the calculations an eventual protein metabolism was not considered.

two-leg exercise. That gave an increased utilization of FFA in the trained leg when compared with the untrained leg. Certainly, the arterial FFA concentration was identical in the two legs (Henriksson 1977).

Other Training Effects. The modification in the mitochondrial enzyme profile (including the succinate dehydrogenase activity) induced in trained muscles may also be of importance. A reduction in the diffusion distance between capillaries and the interior of the muscle cells will facilitate the FFA uptake. Training does increase the capillary density in the muscles. An increased oxidation of FFA will elevate the concentration of citrate which in turn will inhibit the activity of the enzyme phosphofructokinase, retarding the glycogenolysis and lactate formation. All this means that the endurance-trained individual can work closer to the maximal aerobic power for longer periods of time than the untrained person (see Åstrand and Rodahl 1977). If trained and untrained individuals are on similar diets, the glycogen stores in the skeletal muscles are not different.

Diet and Performance

As illustrated by Fig. 2.2, the *diet* during the days before prolonged, vigorous exercise can markedly affect the endurance. Issekutz *et al.* (1963) point out that it is the carbohydrate intake rather than the amount of fat in the diet that determines whether the preferred fuel is FFA or carbohydrate. However, the factors behind this dependence of diet for the choice of substrate for the organisms is, as far as I know, not revealed.

"Glycogen Loading." Bergstrom and Hultman (1966) performed a now classical experiment in which one of them worked with his left leg and the other worked with his right leg on the same cycle ergometer. After several hours' exercise the exercising legs were almost depleted of glycogen while the resting leg still had a normal glycogen content. The experimenters then went on a carbohydrate-rich diet for 3 days. This regime gave a small elevation in the glycogen depots of the resting limb, but in the previously "emptied" legs there was a dramatic increase in the glycogen content until the values were about twice as high as those in the nonexercised legs (see Fig. 2.3). It is not known how this local enhancement of the resynthesis of glycogen is operating. If the glycogen content in the previously exhausted muscles is maintained at a low level for a few days by excluding carbohydrate from the diet, there is an additional increase in their glycogen stores. Many marathon runners and cross-country skiers have successfully applied such programs when preparing for endurance events of long duration. (For details and additional view points on the athletes' diet, see Åstrand and Rodahl 1977, Chapter 14.)

Glycogen Stores.   It should be emphasized that the liver's store of glycogen is limited (less than 100 g). During prolonged exercise there is an enhanced hepatic gluconeogenesis from various glucose precursors, e.g., alanine and glycerol (see Wahren *et al.* 1975). A consumption of a sugar solution during prolonged exercise will improve the performance, for it can prevent a drop in the blood glucose level, and there will be a reduced demand on the glycogen stores. Dehydration can also reduce the physical performance. When glycogen is metabolized water is liberated. From a theoretical point of view, evaporation of that water (as sweat) from the skin can take care of up to 50% of the heat production from that metabolism. (About 2.7 g of water is bound per gram of glycogen stored. Therefore, a reduction in body weight after a prolonged, vigorous exercise does not reflect the degree of dehydration.)

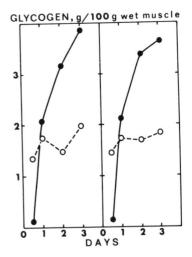

GLYCOGEN, g/100 g wet muscle

Modified from Bergstrom and Hultman 1966

FIG 2.3.   GLYCOGEN LOADING
Two subjects were exercised on the same cycle ergometer, one on each side working with one leg, while the other leg rested (dashed line). After working to exhaustion, the subjects' glycogen content was analyzed in specimens from the lateral portion of the quadriceps muscle. Thereafter, a carbohydrate-rich diet was followed for 3 days. Note that the glycogen content increased markedly in the leg that had been previously emptied of its glycogen content.

DAYS

ENERGY BALANCE

Energy Output

Our resting metabolic rate is relatively high. For a person with a body weight of 75 kg the 24-hr value may be about 7 MJ (1700 kcal). As a comparison, the extra energy demand for walking 35 to 40 km would be on the same level. Therefore, it is not relevant always to express the energy content of Danish pastry, beer, chocolate, etc., in terms of how many kilometers the consumer must walk in order to spend the energy! However, as mentioned later, it is difficult to choose food that for a day supplies this modest energy content and also provides all essential nutrients needed.

Energy Needs of Muscle and Nerve. No cells are able to vary their metabolism to the same extent that skeletal muscles do. During maximal exercise muscles consume up to 100 times as much energy as at rest. Metabolic rate, then, measured per gram of tissue, is not greater than for nerve cells. However, nerve cells are always at a high metabolic level whether a person is asleep or engaged in intensive mental efforts. It is estimated that the central nervous system continuously "works" at a power of about 15 W. In top male skiers all skeletal muscles have an energy output of about 40 W at rest but can attain a 2000 W level during intensive skiing (and all muscles are still not utilizing their full potential; the figures only include the aerobic power, not the anaerobic energy yield).

Exercise. We can conclude that the only factor that to a significant degree can increase the basal metabolic rate is muscular activity. The energy requirements of occupational activities is in most cases very modest, and they rarely demand a 24-hour energy output exceeding 12 MJ (3000 kcal). Leisure time engagements in various sports will therefore be relatively decisive for the total energy output. On the extreme, it was estimated that a 300 km bicycle race brought the 24-hr energy output up to about 50 MJ or 12,000 kcal (Olsson 1970). Those who participate in the famous Swedish "Vasalopp" which is an 86 km cross-country skiing race, need about 30 MJ (7000 kcal) that particular day if the energy output is to be covered (Hedman 1957). For two athletes running 251.5 and 234.5 km, respectively, during a 24-hr period, the energy cose was estimated to be 77.8 MJ or 18,600 kcal (Davies and Thompson 1979).

Energy Intake

Out appetites are mainly geared to secure an adequate energy intake, but we are not directly aware of lack of essential nutrients. Within a wide range of energy expenditures through various degrees of physical activity, there is an accurate balance between energy output and intake so that the body weight is maintained constant. If the daily activity is very intensive and prolonged, the spontaneous energy intake is often less than the output, with a reduction in body weight as a result. A daily energy expenditure *below* a threshold level often leads to an energy surplus and consequently obesity. In this case satiety is not reached until more energy has been taken in than has been expended (compare results from the classical experiments on rats by Mayer *et al.* 1954). A person easily consumes one ton of food and fluid per year. With that figure in mind one may say that the energy intake is remarkably well regulated according to the energy demand.

The Balancing Act

We know virtually nothing about the control of food intake in man. As pointed out by Garrow (1974) the long-term energy balance may be more of a nonphysiological control than physiological. The factors that determine energy intake are the habitual diet, modified by social pressure and to a lesser extent the sensation of hunger, appetite, and satiety. Apparently, habitual diet balances fairly well the habitual energy expenditures within a few percent. Over long periods of time those few percentages may, however, markedly modify the body weight. Of those individuals who maintain a reasonably accurate energy balance while they are physically active, there will be many who will become obese when they exercise less. The decreased exercise can no longer be fully compensated by an increase in the variable component of resting metabolism.

GAINING WEIGHT

It can be easily calculated that a daily energy intake of 400 kJ (100 kcal) in excess of the energy demand has the potential to increase the adipose tissue with about 5.5 kg after one year—or 55 kg (120 lb) after 10 years! (400 kJ/100 kcal is the approximate energy demand of a 2 km walk or the energy content of 12 g of butter or margarine.)

Nonlinear Weight Gain. However, there are experimental evidences showing that a weight gain will be less than theory would predict on the assumption that all the excess energy were stored as adipose tissue. Widdowson (1951, as reported by Garrow 1974) noticed that the weight gain in a group of 19 undernourished Germans provided with unlimited food for 8 weeks was 10.3 kg per man. Their energy intake was about 25 MJ (6000 kcal). Assuming their requirements were about

12.5 MJ (3000 kcal) per day, which is probably an overestimate, there should have been about another 12.5 MJ (3000 kcal) available for a daily storage. With an energy density of 27 MJ (6.500 kcal) of each kilogram adipose tissue, one might predict a weight gain of 26 kg for the 8 weeks or in average 3.4 kg per week. But, as mentioned, the actual increase in body weight was just 10.3 kg. The average weekly weight gain was 2.5 kg for the first week but only a few 100 g during the last weeks (see Fig. 2.4). In other words, after a few weeks of excessive energy intake there is a discrepancy between the predicted and observed gain in body weight and some of the dietary energy seems to have been lost (see Garrow 1974, p. 214).

Metabolic Adapatation? Apparently there is a metabolic adaptation increasing the metabolic rate thus "burning" some of the extra energy. Certainly the energy cost of moving the body increases as there is a weight gain, but also the resting metabolism must become elevated. This assumption is further supported by observations that the weight loss of obese individuals is much greater at the beginning of a period of reduced energy intake than at a later stage of the slimming program. (This holds true even if we disregard the first few days with a probable reduction in glycogen stores and water content of the body). As can be seen in the lower portion of Fig 2.4, obese subjects submitted to a daily energy intake of only 0.8 MJ (200 kcal) lost about 5 kg of body weight the first week, 2.5–3.0 kg for the following weeks, but only 1.5 kg the last two weeks of a 7 week program (Rooth and Carlstrom 1970).

Energy Balance Measurement

Unfortunately, our methods to measure accurately the *energy output* over long periods of time are very uncertain and loaded with inaccuracies. For that matter precise methods to establish the *energy intake* (and intake of various nutrients) are very time-consuming and complicated in their application. One problem is to make sure that the subjects maintain their habitual food intake and energy output during the period they are studied. An error in the methods of a few percentages may seem insignificant, but when calculating the energy balance over a longer period of time it complicates the calculations of energy balance! A 5% systematic discrepancy in the figures for energy intake and output, respectively, at a 10 MJ (2500 kcal) level of a daily metabolic rate will after one month build up a difference of 15 MJ (3600 kcal). That corresponds to the energy content of about 500 g of adipose tissue.

Measuring Energy Stores. Another problem is the measurement of the energy stored in the body. The variation in body weight due to water

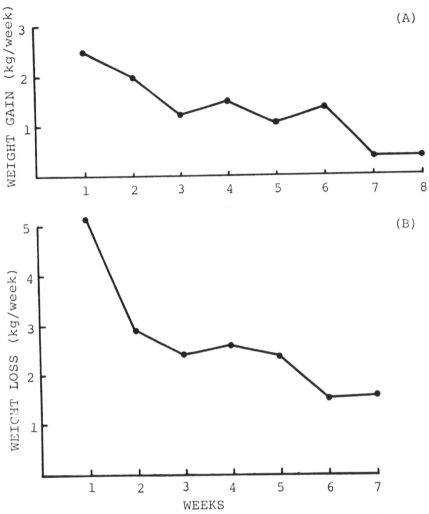

From Garrow 1974

FIG. 2.4.   CHANGE IN BODY WEIGHT WITH PROLONGED ENERGY IMBALANCE.
(A) Average for 19 undernourished men fed 6000 kcal (25 MJ) per day (data of Widdowson 1951). (B) Average for 3 obese patients fed 200 kcal (0.8 MJ) per day (data of Rooth and Carlstrom 1970). Note that both in the case of overfeeding thin men, and underfeeding obese patients the rate of change in weight decreases over several weeks.

shifts are quite pronounced and the difference between one day and the next is, in 5% of the measurements, about 1 kg or more. The available energy content of 1 kg of water is, of course, 0 MJ but if this kilogram were adipose tissue it would contain 25–29 MJ (6000 to 7000 kcal)! One kilogram of glycogen gives when metabolized aerobically an energy yield of about 17 MJ (4100 kcal); when stored in the body it will in addition bind about 2.7 kg of water.

Tegelman (personal communication) applied different methods in an effort to determine the energy output over a week: (1) by measurements of energy intake and body weight; (2) by estimation of energy output from standard tables and nomograms applied for reported activities; (3) by continuous recording of heart rate and prediction of energy output from heart rate—oxygen uptake curves observed on the individual subject during standardized activities; (4) by combining methods (2) and (3). Due to evident fluctuations in water content in the body during the period of observations it was impossible to establish the true level of energy output. It was noticed that during one week of reduced physical activity the energy intake was not reduced to prevent an increase in weight. (For a detailed discussion of methods for measurements of energy balance, see Garrow 1974.)

APPETITE FOR ENERGY

It is pointed out by Garrow (1974) that the rat has an astonishing ability to regulate its energy intake in accordance with the energy output over long periods of time, but it only applies if the food available is relatively monotonous, if the rat has been fed *ad libitum* with this diet, and if flavoring agents, especially sweeteners, are excluded. These conditions are *not* relevant for modern man. In contrast, for the primitive man there was available a relatively small selection of naturally occurring animal and plant foods. For periods of times the food was probably quite monotonous!

Energy Demands of Modern Man

Homo sapiens until *very* recently were hunters and food collectors. They were stone-age people. They were high energy consumers. Biological and psychological properties, which promoted this life style, were favored and selected (see Beidler, this volume, Chapter 1). It would take thousands of years to modify our genetic code to adapt to our, in many ways, very artificial and biologically hostile environment, created by the very capable but "unresponsable" human brain. For instance, appetite, which may at one time (and a long time!) have been a reliable guide to a correctly balanced diet, is now merely a sensation that can be manipulated in many ways by food manufacturers. At specific situations eating and drinking have always played an important social and cultural role in human life, but today eating and drinking are a daily entertainment! Man of today is facing two aspects of this modern society: (1) a food industry and social and cultural impacts favoring a relatively large energy intake, and (2) a reduced energy demand in jobs and during leisure time (including the negative aspects of carts carrying the American golf player!). It is no surprise that we see so many obese people around. For evident reasons, the social factors that predispose to obesity are increasing rather than decreasing. I will not discuss the various aspects of obesity. Inactivity may certainly contribute but it is probably not the main cause (see Garrow 1974).

Diet and Exercise

As often as possible I try to sell the "diet and exercise" message. With the exception of children during growth, women during pregnancy, and sometimes convalescents, the energy intake should not exceed the energy expenditure. The energy requirements vary naturally with the individual's physical activity. On the other hand, the need for most of the nutrients is comparatively independent of the individual's activity level; therefore the less active the individual the higher is the content of the essential nutrients required per energy unit in order to obtain the desired optimal nutritional level (Wretlind 1967).

Getting Essential Nutrients. In a homogenous population, a dietary tradition is usually quite similar. Blix (1965) found that a linear relation exists between daily energy supply of many nutrients (protein, calcium, vitamin A, thiamin, iron). This is schematically illustrated in Fig. 2.5. Through the centuries people obtained their choice of food to an energy output of 12.5 MJ (3000 kcal) or more, which also gave all the nutrients needed. For many of the nutrients mentioned, the energy intake should actually exceed about 10.5 MJ (2500 kcal) to ensure an adequate supply. In other words, the diet in Sweden, and no doubt in many other countries, seems to be adjusted to persons with an energy requirement of a least 10.5 MJ (2500 to 3000 kcal) (Wretlind 1967). This diet, however, is not suitable for the large number of "low energy consumers" who actually do exist. This unsuitability may explain the rather common disturbances in the state of health and well-being associated with malnutrition even in countries with plenty of food available. Is it possible that some of our "modern" diseases including iron deficiency anemia, atherosclerosis, metabolic disorders, diabetes, and constipation may at least partly be consequences of a chronic malnutrition?

Low Energy Consumers. There are two general ways of improving the nutritional conditions of the low energy consumers. (1) Change their food habits so that their diet consists of a higher content of essential nutrients per energy unit than it does now. A dietary habit should be developed so that the requirements of those who consume only 6.3–8.4 MJ (1500 to 2000 kcal) per day can be satisfied. (2) Low energy con-

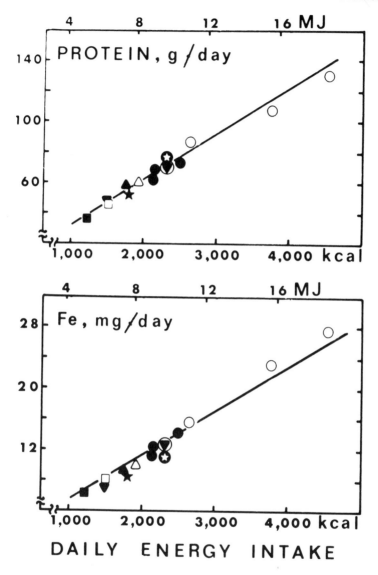

FIG. 2.5. THE SUPPLY OF MOST ESSENTIAL NUTRIENTS IS ROUGHLY LINEAR IN RELATION TO THE DAILY ENERGY INTAKE
The demand for such nutrients remains constant. ○ Lumberjacks (4500 kcal), metal workers (3760 kcal), clerks (2640 kcal); △ elderly men, two cooked meals daily; ▲ elderly women, two cooked meals daily; ✪ female clerks, 16–20 years, two cooked meals daily; ▲ female clerks, 21–34 years, two cooked meals daily; ● wives of lumber jacks (2500 kcal), of metal workers (2160 kcal), of clerks (2150 kcal); □ elderly men, one cooked meal daily; ■ elderly women, one cooked meal daily; ★ female clerks, 16–20 years, one cooked meal daily; ▼ female clerks, 21–34 years, one cooked meal daily (from Blix 1965). The risk for malnutrition is minimal among high energy consumers, i.e., the physically active person.

sumers should be stimulated to become high energy consumers by taking part in regular physical activity in one form or another. By an increase in energy output, they can, without the risk of obesity, eat more and automatically get a greater supply of essential nutrients.

Exercise More, Eat More. As mentioned, our appetite is mainly geared to secure an adequate energy intake, but we are not directly aware of a lack of essential nutrients. With large meals there is a better chance that the consumer gets enough nutrients. Being a low energy consumer with a diet that has a preponderance of foods with a low density of essential nutrients, which is the case if it is rich in fats and sugar (sweets, snacks, cookies, and cakes), the risk of malnutrition and disease does certainly increase. With this discussion in mind, one could say that a mild obesity had some advantages. As pointed out, an extra energy intake will increase the metabolic rate. The obese person is potentially a high energy consumer and that might secure an adequate intake of essential nutrients.

Advice for Exercise

Regular physical activity is essential for the optimal function of many vital organs and tissues and for general function (Åstrand and Rodahl 1977). I think that this is part of our biological inheritance. The positive effects from a nutritional point of view should be evident. My present prescriptions for exercise are as follows.

Daily: At least 60 minutes of physical activity, not necessarily vigorous, and not all at the same time is recommended. During your daily routine, moving, walking, climbing stairs, etc., whether for 1 minute 60 times per day, 12 minutes 5 times per day, or any combination totalling 60 minutes, you will burn up approximately 1.2 MJ (330 kcal). This is advantageous from a nutritional point of view; see Fig. 2.5.

Weekly: At least two or three periods of 30 minutes of sustained activity (brisk walking, jogging, cycling, swimming, cross-country skiing, etc.) are necessary for maintaining good cardiovascular fitness, and will consume an additional 3 MJ (750 kcal) per week. This routine improves the potential and quality of the oxygen transport system.

To conclude, food intake and energy output is a less precarious balancing act for the habitually active person than for sedentary man.

REFERENCES

ÅSTRAND, P.O. 1979. Nutrition and physical performance. *In* Nutrition and the World Food Problem. M. Rechcigl (Editor). S. Karger, Basel, Switzerland.

ÅSTRAND, P.O., and RODAHL, K. 1977. Textbook of Work Physiology. 2nd edition. McGraw-Hill, New York.

BERGSTROM, J. 1962. Muscle electrolytes in man. Scand. J. Clin. Lab. Immunol., Suppl. 68.

BERGSTROM, J., HERMANSEN, L., HULTMAN, E., and SALTIN, B. 1967. Diet, muscle glycogen, and physical performance. Acta Physiol. Scand. *71*, 140.

BERGSTROM, J., and HULTMAN, E. 1966. Muscle glycogen synthesis after exercise: An enhancing factor localized to the muscle cells in man. Nature *210*, 309.

BLIX, G. 1965. A study on the relation between total calories and single nutrients in Swedish food. Acta Soc. Med. Ups. *70*, 117.

CHRISTENSEN, E.H., and HANSEN, O. 1939. Work capacity and diet. Scand. Arch. Physiol. *81*, 160 (Swedish).

DAVIES, C.T.M., and THOMPSON, M.W. 1979. Estimated aerobic performance and energy cost of severe exercise of 24 hours duration. Ergonomics *22*, 1249.

ESSÉN, B. 1978. Studies on the regulation of metabolism in human skeletal muscle using intermittent exercise as an experimental model. Acta Physiol. Scand. Suppl. 454.

GARROW, J.S. 1974. Energy Balance and Obesity in Man. Elsevier North-Holland Inc., New York.

HEDMAN, R. 1957. The available glycogen in man and the connection between rate of oxygen intake and carbohydrate usage. Acta Physiol. Scand. *40*, 305.

HENRIKSONN, J. 1977. Training induced adaptation of skeletal muscle and metabolism during submaximal exercise. J. Physiol. *270*, 661.

ISSEKUTZ, B., BIRKHEAD, N.C., and RODAHL, K. 1963. Effect of diet on work metabolism. J. Nutr. *79*, 109.

MAYER, J. *et al.* 1954. Exercise, food intake, and body weight in normal rats and genetically obese adult mice. Am. J. Physiol. 177, 544.

OLSSON, K.E. 1970. Total body water and water exchange during prolonged physical work. Foersvarsmedicin *6*, 221.

PAUL, P. 1975. Effects of long lasting physical exercise and training on lipid metabolism. *In* Metabolic Adaptation to Prolonged Physical Exercise. H. Howald and J.R. Poortmans (Editors). Birkhäuser Verlag, Basel, Switzerland.

PRUETT, E.D.R. 1971. Fat and carbohydrate metabolism in exercise and recovery, and its dependence upon work load severity. M.S. Thesis. Institute of Work Physiology, Oslo, Norway.

ROOTH, G., and CARLSTRÖM, S. 1970. Therapeutic fasting. Acta Med. Scand. 187, 455.

WAHREN, J. et al. 1975. Splanchnic and leg metabolism of glucose, free fatty acids, and amino acids during prolonged exercise in man. In Metabolic Adaptation to Prolonged Physical Exercise. H. Howald and J.R. Poortmans (Editors). Birkhäuser Verlag, Basel, Switzerland.

WIDDOWSON, E.M. 1951. The response to unlimited food. In Studies in Undernutrition. Wuppertal 1946–1949. Spec. Rep. No. 375. Ser. Medical Research Council, London.

WRETLIND, A. 1967. Nutrition problems in healthy adults with low activity and low caloric consumption. In Nutrition and Physical Activity. G. Blix (Editor). Almqvist and Wiksell, Uppsala, Sweden.

3

Brain Mechanisms Involved in Feeding

Edmund T. Rolls and Barbara J. Rolls

Since the early part of this century there has been evidence that implicates certain parts of the brain in the control of feeding in man. It was known, for example, that damage to the base of the brain in man could lead to overeating and obesity (Grossman 1967). In order to better understand how our brain controls feeding, and the disorders in feeding produced by brain damage, investigations into the neural controls of feeding have been conducted in animals. For example, identification of the brain regions involved in animals' feeding responses has been determined using localized damage in particular parts of the brain produced by experimental lesions. Following this, the activity of single neurons (i.e., single brain cells) in these regions has been recorded to determine how they are involved in the control of feeding.

In this article, investigations of this type into brain mechanisms involved in feeding are discussed. To ensure that the discussion is as relevant as possible to the neural control of feeding in man, studies on nonhuman primates are given particular consideration. Evidence from man is considered when possible. Also, studies on the activity of neurons in different brain regions during feeding are given prominence. This is because such studies provide information on how the brain actually processes sensory inputs produced by the sight and taste of food, as well as on sensory-specific satiety, learning, and other factors that influence which food is selected for ingestion.

FEEDING AND SATIETY CENTERS IN THE BRAIN

From clinical evidence it has been known since early this century that damage to the base of the brain in or near the hypothalamus can lead to overeating and obesity in man. Later, it was demonstrated that the critical region is in the ventromedial hypothalamic region. Bilateral lesions in this area led to hyperphagia and obesity in animals (Grossman 1967, 1973). Then, Anand and Brobeck (1951) discovered that bilateral lesions of the lateral hypothalamus lead to a failure to eat, or aphagia. Conversely, electrical stimulation of the lateral hypothalamus can lead to eating, whereas electrical stimulation of the ventromedial hypothalamus can stop ongoing eating behavior (see Fig. 3.1). Evidence of this type led in the 1950s and 1960s to the view that food intake is

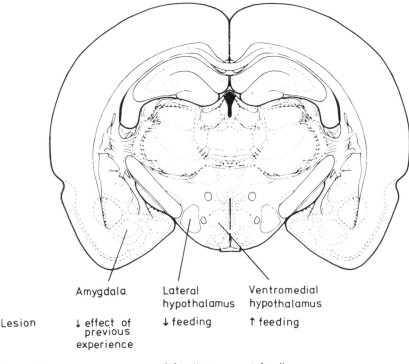

	Amygdala	Lateral hypothalamus	Ventromedial hypothalamus
Lesion	↓ effect of previous experience	↓ feeding	↑ feeding
Stimulation		↑ feeding	↓ feeding

FIG. 3.1.   TRANSVERSE SECTION OF THE RAT BRAIN AT THE LEVEL OF THE LATERAL HYPOTHALAMUS

Bilateral lesions of the lateral hypothalamus decrease food intake and of the ventromedial hypothalamus increase food intake. Electrical stimulation of the lateral hypothalamus may elicit feeding, and of the ventromedial hypothalamus may stop feeding. These observations formed part of the evidence for the dual center hypothesis of the control of feeding, according to which the lateral hypothalamus is a feeding center and the ventromedial hypothalamus a satiety center.

regulated by two interacting hypothalamic "centers": a feeding center in the lateral hypothalamus and a satiety center in the ventromedial hypothalamus (Stellar *et al.* 1954; Grossman, 1967, 1973).

Problems with the "Dual-Center" Hypothesis

Soon, problems with the dual-center hypothesis appeared. Morgane (1961A,B,C) showed that the lateral hypothalamic lesions that were particularly effective in producing aphagia were far lateral and damaged pallidofugal fiber pathways. Damage to these pathways *outside* the lateral hypothalamus could also produce aphagia. Thus the possibility arose that "lateral hypothalamic" aphagia was due to damage to fiber pathways that merely coursed near the hypothalamus.

Marshall *et al.* (1974) showed further that the dopaminergic nigrostriatal bundle near the far lateral hypothalamic region was also damaged by lateral hypothalamic lesions, which produced aphagia, and that damage to *this* pathway outside the hypothalamus could also produce aphagia. The damage was associated with a complex sensorimotor dysfunction in which the rats could not orient correctly to visual or somatosensory stimuli, including food. It was suggested that this sensorimotor disturbance at least partly accounted for the aphagia produced by lateral hypothalamic lesions. Consistent with this view that lateral hypothalamic lesions impair feeding by some nonspecific sensorimotor impairment is the finding that lateral hypothalamic lesions impair drinking as well as feeding.

Thus, by the middle 1970s it was clear that the lesion evidence for a lateral hypothalamic feeding center could not be taken at its face value. At least part of the effect of the lesion was due to damage to fibers of passage traveling through or near the lateral hypothalamus, and it was therefore not at all clear from the lesion evidence what role the lateral hypothalamic neurons themselves might have in feeding (Stricker and Zigmond 1976). In this situation a more direct type of evidence on the role of the lateral hypothalamus itself in feeding was needed. This evidence comes from neurophysiological investigations in which the activity of single lateral hypothalamic neurons are recorded during feeding.

DIRECT NEUROPHYSIOLOGICAL EVIDENCE ON THE ROLE OF THE LATERAL HYPOTHALAMUS IN FEEDING

Using the neurophysiological approach to complement and add to the lesion evidence, it has been established by a number of investigators that the firing rates of some lateral hypothalamic neurons alter during

(Hamburg 1971; Oomura *et al.* 1969; Oomura 1973) or immediately before (Olds *et al.*1969; Rolls *et al.* 1976) feeding in the rat, cat and monkey. These changes could be related to a number of factors, some of which have now been investigated in the monkey. Some neurons had activity related to movements made by the monkey, or to touch (Rolls *et al.* 1976; E.T. Rolls *et al.* 1980; Rolls and Rolls 1977; Rolls 1980, 1981). Other lateral hypothalamic neurons had activity more specifically related to feeding as described later, and interestingly these neurons extended out lateral to the lateral hypothalamus into the substantia innominata.

Responses Associated with the Taste of Food

The activity of some neurons in the lateral hypothalamus and substantia innominata of the hungry monkey is associated with the taste of food (E.T. Rolls *et al.* 1980; Burton *et al.* 1976). That is, these neurons respond when *some* solutions or foods are tasted and ingested, but not when *other* solutions are tasted and ingested, even though similar movements are made to drink the different solutions. In a sample of 764 neurons in the monkey lateral hypothalamus and substantia innominata, 33 neurons responded in association with the taste of food, and 19 of these also responded in association with the sight of food (see next section). Gustatory responses to water, glucose and saline have also been found in the rat lateral hypothalamus (Norgren 1970).

Responses Associated with the Sight of Food

In the hungry monkey, we found that some neurons in the lateral hypothalamus and substantia innominata responded immediately before feeding, that is, as soon as the monkey saw the food, and while he looked at the food (Rolls *et al.* 1976). The foods to which these neurons responded most were the monkey's most preferred foods, and comparable responses did not occur when the monkey looked at or reached for nonfood objects. These neurons did not respond, furthermore, if the monkey smelled, grasped, and then tasted and ate the food in the dark. The results of these and other tests suggest that the responses of these neurons are associated with the sight of food and are not due to olfactory, gustatory, or motor responses associated with feeding, or to anticipatory responses, such as salivation.

Modulation by Hunger of the Responses of Lateral Hypothalamic Neurons to the Sight and Taste of Food

These neurons in the lateral hypothalamus and substantia innominata, which respond when food is seen and/or tasted if the monkey is hungry, do not respond if he is satiated (Burton *et al.* 1976). The responses of these neurons associated with food diminish in intensity as satiety, measured by whether the food is rejected, progresses. It is very interesting that the spontaneous baseline firing rate of these neurons is little affected by the transition from hunger to satiety. Rather it is the sensitivity of these neurons to their visual and/or taste inputs that is modulated by satiety.

These experiments indicate the following principle: at the hypothalamic stage of processing, visual and gustatory responses to food-related sensory inputs are modulated by the hunger (or need, in terms of physiological variables, or motivational state) of the animal. This modulation by hunger of responsiveness to food-related sensory inputs, suggests that these hypothalamic neurons could mediate the responses which occur in the hungry animal to food. These responses include autonomic and endocrine as well as feeding responses to the sight (or taste) of food.

Sensory-Specific Modulation of the Responsiveness of Lateral Hypothalamic Neurons and Appetite

While we were performing these experiments on the effects of hunger on the responsiveness of lateral hypothalamic neurons to food, we (E.T. Rolls and M.J. Burton) made the following discovery, reported here for the first time. In one satiety experiment, we were recording from a neuron with a spontaneous firing rate of approximately 21 spikes/sec. This neuron responded to the sight of a syringe containing 20% sucrose solution from which the monkey was fed by mouth, by decreasing its firing rate to 6–9 spikes/sec.

The neuron also responded to the sight of other foods, such as a peanut (Fig. 3.2). On each trial of the satiety experiment the monkey was fed 2 ml of the sucrose solution. Over trials 20–35 the response of the neuron to the sight of the sucrose solution diminished (there was little deviation from the spontaneous rate). This was the period in which satiety was developing, as shown by the increase in the rejections by the monkey of the sucrose solution (by using his hand, or closing his mouth and not swallowing). However, after trial 35, when the monkey was apparently completely satiated, as shown by rejection of the sucrose on 100% of the trials, the neuron responded strongly by decreasing its firing rate when he was shown the peanut. The strong response of the neuron to the sight of the peanut at the end of the satiety experiment surprised us, and we then gave the peanut to the monkey, and found that not only did his lateral hypothalamus respond to the sight of the nut, but also he accepted the nut (and many more on repeated tests), and ate it very readily (Fig. 3.2). Nevertheless, it was shown that the lateral hypo-

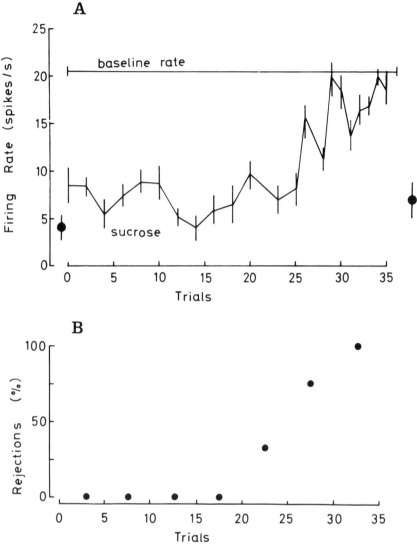

FIG 3.2. SATIETY PRODUCED BY SUCROSE
(A) Effect of the sight of a syringe from which the squirrel monkey was fed 2 ml of 20% sucrose solution on the firing rate of a hypothalamic single unit. The rate decreased below the spontaneous baseline rate (the mean and SEM are shown) at the start of the experiment when the monkey was hungry, but not at the end of the experiment when the monkey was satiated. The firing rate and its standard error were measured over a 5 sec period during which the monkey was looking at the syringe. The monkey drank the sucrose subsequently. On some trials (not shown) different stimuli were shown, and the monkey was not fed. The neuron responded by decreasing its firing rate to the sight of a peanut (filled circle, ●) at the start of the experiment, and also responded to the peanut at the end of the experiment, after the monkey was satiated with sucrose. (B) The time-course of the satiety of the monkey in the same experiment. For each block of trials, the percentage of trials on which the monkey rejected the sucrose solution is shown. Rejection was measured by the animal's turning its head away from the syringe and failing to reach for the syringe.

thalamic neuron still failed to respond to the sight of the sucrose-containing syringe, and the monkey still rejected the sucrose. This experiment was performed on a squirrel monkey, and the same effect was found in the rhesus monkey.

Thus, these lateral hypothalamic neurons ceased to respond to a food on which the monkey had been fed to satiety, but continued to respond to another food with which he had not been satiated. Perhaps because we were measuring digital pulses (the spikes from the neurons), and the objective measure of their mean firing rate altered so convincingly, we were led to appreciate that the animal's satiety was in some way specific. In fact, his appetite (measured by his willingness to reach for and accept a food) for a food on which he was fed fell to zero, yet his appetite for other foods at least partly remained. This finding may be called sensory-specific satiety (Le Magnen 1967), in that appetite can diminish following ingestion of one food (such as sucrose) which produces one form of sensory input (in terms of sight, taste, smell and texture) when consumed, yet remain for another food (such as a nut) which produces a different type of sensory input when consumed.

Sensory-Specific Satiety for the Taste of Food. We have also observed a similar phenomenon for hypothalamic neurons with responses associated with the taste of food in the monkey. An example is shown in Fig. 3.3. This neuron responded while the monkey was drinking glucose solution or blackcurrant juice, but not while it drank isotonic saline. Thus, the responses of the neuron were not associated with mouth movements, and other nonspecific effects (and indeed did not occur during touch to the mouth and mouth movements). Rather, the responses were classified as being associated with taste.

Further evidence for this is shown in Fig. 3.3a, in which it is evident that the firing rate of the neuron depended on the concentration of the glucose solution in the mouth. The effect of satiety on the responses of the neuron to the taste of the 20% glucose solution is shown in Fig 3.3b. At the start of the experiment, when the rhesus monkey was food deprived for 18 hr, the neuron responded to the taste of the 20% glucose solution (Pre) and the taste of the blackcurrant juice, by decreasing its firing rate below the spontaneous rate of approximately 22 spikes/sec. On each trial of the satiety experiment (Fig. 3.3b) the monkey was fed 10 ml of the 20% glucose solution. The firing rate decreased when the glucose was tasted on the early trials in which the monkey was still hungry (as shown by acceptance, see lower part of Fig. 3.3b), but as the monkey became satiated (as shown by rejection) due to drinking of the glucose (trials 5–15), the response when the glucose was tasted diminished to nil. However, at the end of the satiety experiment the neuron still responded when the monkey drank the fruit juice (see Fig. 3.3b),

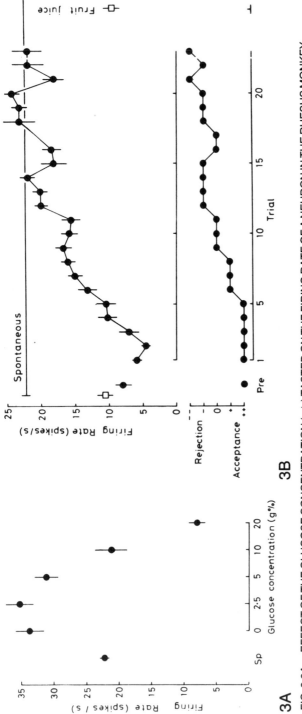

3A

FIG. 3.3A.   EFFECT OF THE GLUCOSE CONCENTRATION (w/v) TASTED ON THE FIRING RATE OF A NEURON IN THE RHESUS MONKEY LATERAL HYPOTHALAMUS

The firing rate (mean ± SEM) was measured in a 7–10 sec period during which the monkey was drinking 2 ml of the solution from a syringe. 0% represents drinking water. Sp–spontaneous firing rate.

FIG. 3.3B.   SENSORY-SPECIFIC SATIETY IN THE NEURON SHOWN IN FIG. 3.3A

The firing rate was measured on each trial in a 7–10 sec period in which the monkey drank 10 ml of 20% glucose solution. At the start of the experiment the neuron also responded while the monkey drank blackcurrant juice (□). The firing rate (mean ± SEM) decreased when the glucose was tasted on the early trials of the satiety experiment in which the monkey was still hungry, but as the monkey became satiated because of drinking the glucose (trials 5–15), the response when the glucose was tasted diminished to nil (for further details see Rolls et al. 1980). However, at the end of the experiment, the neuron still responded when the monkey drank the blackcurrant juice.

and the monkey accepted the fruit juice, even though it still rejected the glucose solution. Thus neurons with responses associated with the taste of food can also show an effect of sensory-specific satiety, in that they cease responding to a food on which the monkey has been fed to satiety, but may still respond to the taste of other foods.

Satiety in Humans. These neurophysiological and behavioral investigations led us to consider the notion of sensory-specific satiety further, and its implications for food selection and the control of food intake in humans. A series of experiments revealed that the human appetite, as measured by the rating of how pleasant foods taste, is reduced for the food eaten, but much less for other foods, at least partly in a sensory-specific manner (Rolls and Rolls 1977; B.J. Rolls *et al.* 1980; see also B.J. Rolls *et al.* this volume, Chapter 6). When running these experiments it is clear that this satiety effect is not completely specific, for eating meat (e.g., sausages or beef) may produce some depression in the pleasantness of other meats (e.g., chicken), and can in fact elevate the pleasantness of sweet foods (see Fig. 6.1). Each food thus appears to produce its own pattern of appetite reductions for other foods, producing greater reductions for "similar" foods. Exactly how broad the generalization is to other foods from a particular food is open to further investigation. So far we have shown that the ingestion of calories is not essential for the effect in experiments with meat extracts vs. low calorie orange juice. Also, sensory factors such as similarity of flavor and texture are often relatively more important than metabolic equivalence in terms of protein, carbohydrate and fat content.

EFFECT OF LEARNING ON THE RESPONSES OF HYPOTHALAMIC NEURONS TO FOOD

In the course of the recordings in the monkey hypothalamus, it was observed that the neurons responded to a variety of foods and food-associated objects when the animal looked at foods. These foods include the sight of oranges, grapes, nuts, bananas, and even the sight of a black syringe from which the animal was fed glucose. Thus, it seemed unlikely that these neurons responded innately to the sight of these different stimuli and probable that the responses of these neurons could change as a result of learning.

Visual Discrimination Experiments

To test this proposition, a formal visual discrimination task was set for the monkey while recordings were made from these single units. For example, it was found that these neurons came to respond to a black syringe from which the animal was fed glucose solution, but not to a white syringe from which the animal was fed an aversive (5%) saline solution (Mora *et al.* 1976). Over the same period, the monkey learned to accept the black syringe and to reject the white syringe. The significance of the colors was then reversed, so that white was now associated with food, and black with saline. In this visual discrimination reversal, the responses of the lateral hypothalamic neurons also reversed, so that the responses of the neurons came as a result of learning to respond again to the food-related stimulus.

Another example of this learning was seen when the responses of these hypothalamic neurons disappeared when a visual stimulus was no longer associated with food. This occurred, for example, when a visual stimulus (such as the sight of a banana or a nut) which formerly meant food was either repeatedly shown but not given to the monkey to eat, or was made aversive by adulteration with saline (Mora *et al.* 1976).

Neurons Reflect Learning. Thus, as a result of learning, the responses of these lateral hypothalamic neurons become associated with the sight of food as contrasted with nonfood-related visual stimuli. This type of learning is essential if the hungry animal must recognize foods and respond with appropriate food-seeking and ingestive behavior and with appropriate autonomic and endocrine responses only to food-related visual stimuli. The neurophysiological evidence thus implicates the responses of hypothalamic neurons in these processes. It is quite likely that the actual learning takes place in a structure that sends projections to the hypothalamus, perhaps in the amygdala (see next section). As the responses of these neurons are modulated by learning, it is possible that when animals, including man, learn to reduce the intake of a flavor associated with a high calorie food, the responses of these hypothalamic neurons are also modulated by this type of learning. This conditioning contributes to the satiety for each food (Booth 1977; this volume, Chapter 4).

Clearly, then, the responses of these hypothalamic neurons to different foods are influenced by learning. This indicates that these neurons at least receive information about which visual stimuli are food-related and therefore about which stimuli are selected for ingestion. The exact role these neurons have in the responses of animals to food is considered next.

ROLE OF HYPOTHALAMIC NEURONS IN FEEDING

The experiments described above show that some lateral hypothalamic neurons (13.4% in one sample of 764 neurons) respond to the sight and/or taste of food, responding most to the most preferred foods. These responses only occur if the monkey is hungry, and in fact are modulated by sensory-specific satiety. These neurons only respond, moreover, to foods for which an appetite can be demonstrated, and the visual responses occur only to objects the animal has learned are foods.

Neurons Implicated in Animals' Feeding Responses

It has been shown that these neurons respond to food-related visual stimuli with latencies that are relatively short (150–200 msec) compared with the animals' feeding responses to the same stimuli (300–400 msec) (see Fig. 3.4). Therefore, these neuronal responses could be involved in the responses of the hungry animal to food. These responses include autonomic and endocrine responses (such as the release of insulin) as well as feeding responses to the sight (or taste) of food. Some role in the autonomic and endocrine responses is likely, for there are hypothalamic neurons that project toward brainstem systems that control these systems (Saper *et al.* 1979A,B; Jones *et al.* 1976). Moreover, hypothalamic lesions and stimulation do influence autonomic and endocrine function (see below). Some role in the feeding responses is also

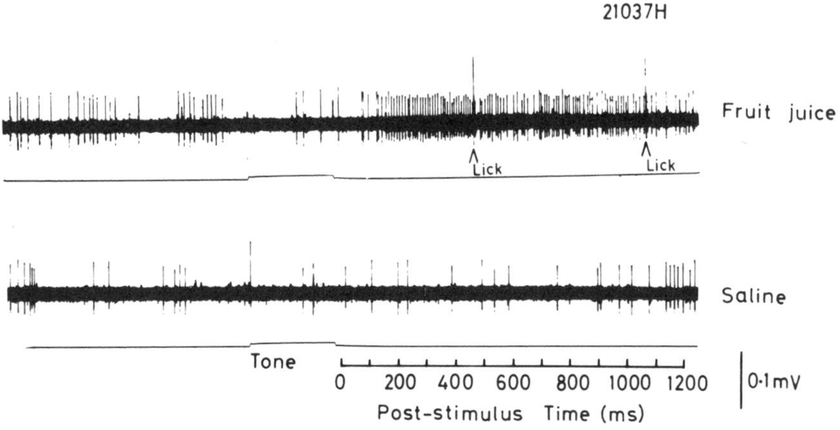

21037H

Fruit juice

Saline

Tone   0   200   400   600   800   1000   1200   0·1mV

Post-stimulus   Time (ms)

From Rolls et al. (1979A)

FIG. 3.4.   ACTIVITY OF A NEURON WITH FOOD-RELATED ACTIVITY IN THE SUBSTANTIA INNOMINATA DURING A VISUAL DISCRIMINATION FOR FOOD
The monkey saw either a food-associated stimulus (food trial) or a nonfood associated stimulus. *(Top trace)* Food trial. At the end of the signal tone the shutter opened at time 0 to reveal a food-associated visual stimulus: the unit responded to the stimulus with a latency of 150 msec and the monkey licked the tube in front of his mouth at approximately 470 msec to obtain fruit juice. *(Lower trace)* Nonfood trial. When the shutter opened it revealed a saline-associated visual stimulus, and correctly the monkey did not lick the tube, or he would have obtained hypertonic saline.

possible, for not only do the responses of these hypothalamic neurons show the food-related, appetite-related, and learning-related responses described above, but in the visual discrimination illustrated in Fig. 3.3 their responses precede and predict the responses of the hungry monkey to food (Rolls *et al.* 1979A).

Consistent with this possibility is recent evidence that damage to the lateral hypothalamus with kainic acid injections (which spare fibers of passage) leads to some aphagia and adipsia (Grossman *et al.* 1978; Stricker *et al.* 1978). Other evidence exists that there are projections from the lateral hypothalamus to the frontal and parietal cortex (Kievit and Kuypers 1975; Divac 1975) and to the substantia nigra (Arbuthnott *et al.* 1976; Swanson 1976; Nauta and Domesick 1978), through which the hypothalamus could influence the initiation of feeding responses. Also consistent with this possibility is the evidence on brain-stimulation reward and the hypothalamus, described next. Nevertheless, the hypothalamus is not essential for simple reflex acceptance of sweet solutions during hunger, and of rejection of these solutions during satiety. Rather, this can occur in decerebrate animals, in which the hypothalamus can no longer influence the brain stem (Grill and Norgen 1978).

The importance of the hypothalamus in feeding appears to be in its close relation to the forebrain, through which it must receive the highly coded food-related and learning-related visual inputs described previously (Rolls 1980). The fact that these inputs reach the hypothalamus in the primate helps us to emphasize the role and importance of visual stimuli and learning in the responses to and selection of foods in primates, including man.

RESPONSES TO FOOD REWARD AND TO BRAIN-STIMULATION REWARD IN THE LATERAL HYPOTHALAMUS

The experiments described above show that a population of lateral hypothalamic neurons responds when a food reward is given to an animal. The food is rewarding in that the monkey will work for it. Factors that determine whether the food or object is rewarding include factors that influence the responses of these hypothalamic neurons, such as which objects are associated during learning with food and whether the monkey is hungry. At this point we inquire into the effects of electrical *stimulation* of the hypothalamus. It is relevant that electrical stimulation of the lateral hypothalamus can be rewarding, in that the animal will work to obtain it. It is also important that the electrical stimulation is similar to food for a hungry animal, in that the animal will work to obtain stimulation in this region if he is hungry, but will work much less if he is satiated (Olds 1962, 1977; Hoebel and Teitelbaum 1962; Hoebel 1965, 1976; Rolls 1975, 1979, 1980; E.T. Rolls *et al.* 1980).

Food Reward and Brain Stimulation Reward Compared

It is interesting that (1) all the food-related lateral hypothalamic neurons described above were activated by brain-stimulation of a number of forebrain sites. (2) This activation was more likely to occur from self-stimulation than non-self-stimulation sites. (3) Self-stimulation through the recording electrode occurred when it was in the region of the neurons activated by food, and became less as the electrode was raised or lowered from this region (see Fig. 3.5). (4) Self-stimulation in the region of these neurons in the lateral hypothalamus was attenuated after the monkey was fed to satiety (i.e., until food was no longer rewarding in that the monkey would no longer work for or accept the food) (E.T. Rolls *et al.* 1980).

All this evidence is consistent with the hypothesis that the behavior of the animal is directed to obtain activation of these neurons, either by food reward or by brain-stimulation reward of some brain regions. This hypothesis would account for why animals will work to obtain stimulation of some brain-stimulation reward sites, and implies that activation of these hypothalamic neurons is something for which the animal will work. Insofar as this may be true, it implies that activation of these hypothalamic neurons, and the ways in which satiety and learning influence this, are important in the rewarding effects that different foods have, and whether they are selected. In fact, the evidence from brain stimulation reward studies provides one of the few ways in which evidence on whether activation of neurons or a brain region by food is related to whether the animal chooses to work for the food, or whether that activation merely reflects other processes produced by giving food to a hungry animal.

ROLE OF THE VENTROMEDIAL HYPOTHALAMUS IN FEEDING

Experimental Hyperphagia

It appears that the bilateral lesions of the ventromedial hypothalamus (VMH), which lead to hyperphagia and obesity, do so at least partly by altering endocrine mechanisms. The lesions lead to lipogenesis

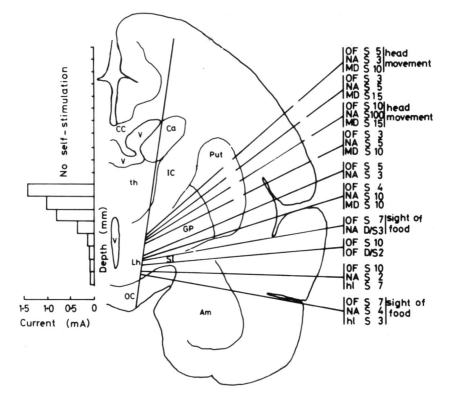

FIG 3.5A.   HYPOTHALAMIC UNITS ACTIVATED BY BOTH BRAIN-STIMULATION RE-
WARD AND BY NATURAL REWARD (THE SIGHT OF FOOD) WERE RECORDED AT THE
BASE OF THIS MICROELECTRODE TRACK

Self-stimulation through the recording microelectrode occurred in the region of these units as
shown in the histogram of the current threshold for self-stimulation through the recording
microelectrode. Both the response of the units to food and the self-stimulation in this region
were attenuated if the animal was not hungry. Above this region, in the globus pallidus, some
activation of units, particularly from reward sites in the orbitofrontal cortex and mediodorsal
nucleus of the thalamus, occurred, but the firing of these units occurred in relation to head
movements, and self-stimulation of this region was poor (it probably occurred because of
current spread to the hypothalamus below). The activation of the units was transsynaptic (S) or
direct (D) from self-stimulation sites in the orbitofrontal cortex (OF), nucleus accumbens (NA),
mediodorsal nucleus of the thalamus (MD) or lateral hypothalamus (hl) with the latencies
shown in ms. Abbreviations: Am, amygdala; Ca, caudate nucleus; CC, corpus callosum; GP,
globus pallidus, IC, internal capsule; Lh, lateral hypothalamus; OX, optic chiasm; Put, putamen; SI, substantia innominata; th, thalamus; V, ventricle.

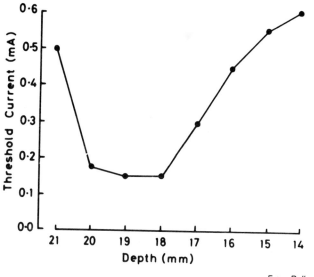

From Rolls et al. (1980)

FIG. 3.5B. THE MEAN OF THE SELF-STIMULATION THRESHOLD CURRENT (mA) AS A FUNCTION OF THE DEPTH (mm) OF THE MICROELECTRODE IN THE BRAIN FOR EIGHT SEPARATE EXPERIMENTS IN THE SQUIRREL MONKEYS
The lowest thresholds in the eight experiments were found at 18–20 mm below the dura, that is, at the level of the lateral hypothalamus and substantia innominata. The stimulation (0.1-msec pulses at 100 Hz lasting for 0.3 sec) was applied through the recording microelectrode after recording had finished as the microelectrode was repeatedly raised and lowered to different depths.

throughout the day as well as the night, and this is associated with hyperinsulinemia (Le Magnen et al. 1973). If the hyperinsulinemia is abolished by destruction of the β cells of the pancreas with streptozo-tocin, the hyperphagia and obesity are abolished (York and Bray 1972). However, these results may be misleading because the hypoinsulinemia impairs normal metabolism. Although Inoue et al. (1977) did not find that transplanation of a functional (but, of course, denervated) pancreas into experimentally diabetic rats allowed VMH obesity to develop, Vilberg and Beatty (1975) were able to demonstrate that VMH lesions still led to obesity in diabetic animals whose insulin levels were main-tained by exogenous insulin injections. Further, although there are reports that subdiaphragmatic vagotomy (which would prevent neu-rally mediated release of insulin by the pancreas, produced, for exam-ple, by food given to the hungry animal) can prevent VMH hyperphagia (Powley and Opsahl 1974; Inoue and Bray 1977), Wampler and Snowdon (1979) did obtain obesity in vagotomized VMH lesioned rats. They suggested that earlier failures might be due to surgically produced damage to the esophagus during vagotomy. Thus the hyperinsulinemia produced by VMH lesions may not fully account for the overeating and obesity produced, and there may be some other effect of the lesions that tends to produce obesity (see further Panksepp, et al. 1979).

Nevertheless, the neurally mediated elevation in the secretion of insulin produced by giving food to a hungry animal (one of the cephalic phase alimentary reflexes) could lead to more intense eating, and may be enhanced by ventromedial hypothalamic lesions (Powley 1977). In fact, the evidence described above that stimulation produced by food reaches the hypothalamus is consistent with Powley's hypothesis that VMH lesions can influence autonomic and endocrine responses to food. These lesion effects may be related to damage to the ventral noradrenergic bundle, which projects to the paraventricular nucleus, which in turn sends axons to the dorsal motor nucleus of the vagus (Leibowitz 1980).

THE NEURAL CONTROL OF EATING IN MAN

Clinical Studies

Although the studies described above on the neural control of feeding have been on animals, many were on nonhuman primates, and therefore are as relevant as possible to the factors that control feeding and body weight in man. The direct evidence that is available for man is consistent with the evidence from animal studies (although, of course, precise localization in the brain is usually not possible in the human material).

Obesity. Reeves and Plum (1969) described a patient with a ventromedial hypothalamic tumor who ate 8000 to 10,000 calories per day, and in one 2-month period of hospitalization gained 24 kg. Bray and Gallagher (1975) described eight cases of obesity associated with hypothalamic damage, and found in detailed metabolic studies of four of the hyperphagic patients that fasting insulin concentration was higher than in control obese patients. This is consistent with the possibility that hyperinsulinemia produced by the hypothalamic damage at least contributed to the obesity in these patients. Of course, these findings do not imply that in most obese humans there is hypothalamic damage.

Anorexia

Mecklenberg et al. (1974) have provided indirect evidence for hypothalamic damage (impaired thermoregulation and partial diabetes insipidus) in patients with anorexia, and White and Hain (1959) and Kamalian, *et al.* (1975) have provided direct evidence for brain damage, which included the lateral hypothalamus. Quaade (1974) and Quaade *et al.* (1974) electrically stimulated the lateral hypothalamus in (obese) humans and reported in three of five patients "convincing hunger responses." These verbal responses included, "I am so hungry that I could eat a whole fried chicken with chips," and "I am so hungry that my entire belly feels as a vacuum." In two patients, unilateral hypothalamic lesions produced a transient suppression of feeding, but no significant weight reduction.

Surgical Lesions to Control Feeding?

Although these observations are consistent with our understanding of the neurology of feeding in animals, clearly our present understanding of this in animals argues against direct therapeutic intervention in obesity. First, our understanding of the neurology of feeding in animals is limited. Second, it is clear that anatomically the hypothalamus is a heterogeneous region, with many fiber systems coursing through or near it, so that there is no one "center" that can be separated from other systems. It is not even clear yet to what degree damage to the different cell and fiber systems in and near the hypothalamus contributes to the effects of lesions on eating. Third, it is clear from the neurophysiological studies that only a small proportion (13.4% in one sample of 764 neurons) of the hypothalamic neurons recorded are feeding-related, and that these are widely distributed from the anterior commissure anteriorly to the lateral hypothalamus posteriorly, and laterally out into the substantia innominata (see, e.g., Rolls *et al.* 1979A). These neurons are intermingled with neurons having other functions (see Rolls, 1980), so that again no one center that can be isolated from other systems can be identified and damaged by lesions. For these reasons, it is inappropriate to conceive of feeding centers in man and to attempt to selectively disrupt them.

THE ROLE OF CATECHOLAMINE PATHWAYS IN FEEDING

Damage to the dopaminergic nigrostriatal bundle leads to a complex sensorimotor deficit, which includes an inability to orient to environmental stimuli and to initiate behavior, and aphagia and adipsia, which are probably secondary to these changes (Ungerstedt 1971; Marshall *et al.* 1974). When recordings are made in the caudate nucleus and putamen—that is, in the structures to which the nigrostriatal bundle projects—a partially topographical organization of neurons is found. These neurons respond to visual stimuli (in the tail of the caudate nucleus, which receives neural projections from visual inferotemporal cortex); to environmental stimuli, which the animal uses as cues for the initiation of behavior, including feeding responses (in the head of the caudate nucleus); and in relation to movements (for example, in the putamen). Taken together with the evidence on the effects of nigrostriatal bundle damage, these and other neurophysiological findings suggest that the striatum is involved in the initiation of behavioral responses to environmental stimuli (Rolls *et al.* 1979B; Rolls 1981), and that this function is modulated by the dopaminergic input (see Fig. 3.6). It is likely that

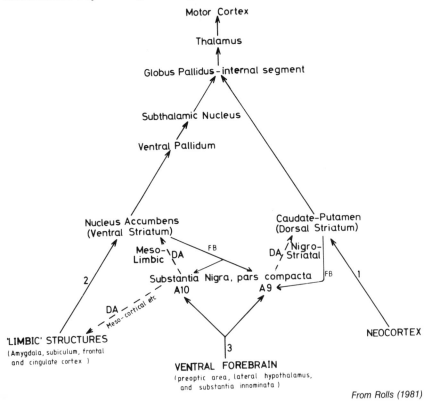

From Rolls (1981)

FIG. 3.6. THE ANATOMICAL SITUATION OF DOPAMINE (DA) PATHWAYS
The nigrostriatal dopaminergic system is in a position to influence transmission through the caudate and putamen, which receives inputs from the neocortex (1) and projects to motor structures, primarily via the globus pallidus. The mesolimbic and mesocortical dopaminergic systems are in a position to influence transmission through the ventral striatum (nucleus accumbens), which receives inputs from "limbic" areas such as the frontal and cingulate cortex, and the amygdala, and projects to motor structures, as shown. Dopaminergic activity itself is under feedback control as shown (FB), and is influenced by other inputs, from, for example, ventral forebrain systems (3) including the lateral hypothalamus and preoptic area.

the aphagia and adipsia produced by nigrostriatal bundle lesions result from disruption of the normal function of these neurons in the initiation of behavioral responses, rather than by disruption of a system concerned primarily or specifically with feeding. In line with this, we have not found visual responses to food or motivation-dependent responses to food in the caudate nucleus or putamen.

THE ROLE OF THE AMYGDALA IN FEEDING AND FOOD SELECTION

Food Selection Deficits Following Amygdala Damage

It is known that large bilateral lesions of the temporal lobe (which includes the amygdala) in monkeys lead to a syndrome in which nonfood as well as food objects are picked up and placed in the mouth, and in which the monkeys become tame (Klüver and Bucy 1939). For example, these monkeys may repeatedly pick up and place nuts and bolts as well as food in the mouth. These symptoms of the Klüver–Bucy syndrome are probably produced by damage to the amygdala, for bilateral amygdala lesions also produce these changes (Weiskrantz 1956). If monkeys with bilateral amygdala lesions are shown a "food board" in which each well contains a food or nonfood item, they reach out, retrieve, and place in the mouth both the food and the nonfood items, whereas normal monkeys select only the food items (J. Aggleton and R. Passingham, personal communication 1979). Thus, there is an impairment of the selection of food versus nonfood items following damage to the amygdala. Reasons for this impairment in food selection are considered next.

Inability to Learn About Foods

Jones and Mishkin (1972) showed that monkeys with damage to the temporal lobe and amygdala were poor at learning a visual discrimination to obtain food. They suggested that this was due to a failure to associate visual stimuli with reinforcement. This implies that when the animals learn to recognize foods, and select foods on the basis of their prior experience with the food, the amygdala is involved in this type of learning. Evidence consistent with this comes from a study by Rolls and Rolls (1973) who found that rats with amygdala lesions failed to learn to avoid the ingestion of a fluid which made them mildly ill (see Fig. 3.7). Nachman and Ashe (1974) were also able to obtain this deficit in learned aversion in rats with amygdala lesions.

These studies thus show that when a rat must learn not to select (that is to avoid) the ingestion of a particular fluid because of the conse-

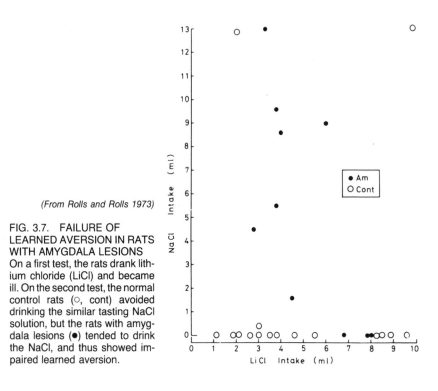

(From Rolls and Rolls 1973)

FIG. 3.7. FAILURE OF
LEARNED AVERSION IN RATS
WITH AMYGDALA LESIONS
On a first test, the rats drank lithium chloride (LiCl) and became
ill. On the second test, the normal
control rats (○, cont) avoided
drinking the similar tasting NaCl
solution, but the rats with amygdala lesions (●) tended to drink
the NaCl, and thus showed impaired learned aversion.

quences of its ingestion, this type of learning is dependent on the
amygdala. Comparable studies on "learned preference" (preference resulting from the ingestion of a flavor associated with the administration
of calories to a hungry rat, or from the relief of malnutrition), or conditioned satiety (a small intake of a flavor associated previously with the
ingestion of a high calorie food) have not been performed, but might be
very interesting.

Amygdala Lesions Affect Food Neophobias

Rolls and Rolls (1973) found that in a 10 min food preference test,
animals with amygdala lesions selected and ate much more of the foods
with which the rats were not familiar (e.g., cauliflower and sultanas)
than of the laboratory chow with which the animals were familiar. In
contrast, the control, nonlesioned, rats ate much more of the standard
chow (Fig. 3.8). However, the basic preferences of the control and lesioned rats were not very different, for with repeated testing the preferences of the control rats approached those of the amygdala-lesioned rats.
Thus, the difference between the groups was that the normal control

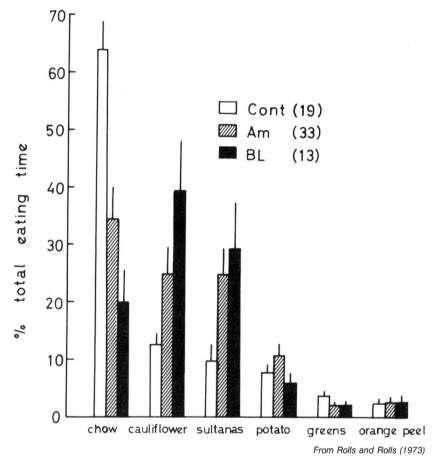

From Rolls and Rolls (1973)

FIG. 3.8. FOOD SELECTION OF AMYGDALA-LESIONED RATS (Am and BL) AND CONTROL RATS
The BL group had symmetrical lesions in the basolateral region of the amygdala, and was a subgroup of the Am group. The number of rats in each group is indicated in parentheses. Preferences are indicated by the mean percentage of the total times that the rats ate each food. The variability measure is the SE.

rats showed an innate food neophobia, only with repeated testing slowly coming to accept the new foods. The rats with amygdala lesions did not show neophobia for the new foods, and ate them in the first test.

This hypothesis received support from a further experiment in which four new foods replaced four of the foods with which the rats had by now become familiar. This produced a replication of the finding noted previously, in that the normal control rats now ate a relatively high proportion of the familiar chow and relatively little of the new foods, whereas the rats with amygdala lesions ate relatively much of the new foods—

that is, were not neophobic. These experiments thus also indicate that amygdala lesions affect the selection of foods because of a disorder of learning. In this case the defect is that instead of reacting to new foods with neophobia, and gradually coming to accept them through repeated experience, the animals with amygdala lesions do not display this learning, but instead select the new foods rapidly.

The amygdala is well placed anatomically for a learning mechanism that would influence, on the basis of previous experience, which foods are selected. It receives projections from cortical areas such as the visual inferior temporal cortex (Herzog and van Hoesen 1976) and projects to the hypothalamus (Nauta 1961). Further, it has been possible to demonstrate visual responses of neurons in the amygdala. Although in some neurons there was a tendency for the responses to occur to food-related visual stimuli, this type of association did not uniquely determine the responses of these neurons (Sanghera et al. 1979). Thus, the amygdala could be at an early stage in the learning process by which stimuli are associated with reinforcement. Further processing must come later, before the responses of hypothalamic neurons, which occur much more selectively to visual stimuli that the animal has learned are foods.

THE ROLE OF THE ORBITOFRONTAL CORTEX IN FEEDING AND FOOD SELECTION

The orbitofrontal cortex of the monkey receives an input from the inferior temporal visual cortex (Chavis and Pandya 1976) and sends efferents to and through the hypothalamus (Nauta 1964). It also has connections with the amygdala.

Lesions of Orbitofrontal Cortex

The orbitofrontal cortex is implicated in feeding and in feeding-related learning tasks by the following effects of lesions of the orbitofrontal cortex. (1) Monkeys with lesions of the orbitofrontal cortex show altered feeding behavior. Although their food preferences (in terms of the order in which foods are chosen) are normal, indicating that the monkeys can distinguish between foods, they select (i.e., pick up and mouth) the nonfood objects as well as the food objects (Butter et al. 1969). (2) The monkeys continue to respond during extinction to a previously rewarded stimulus (Butter 1969). (3) The monkeys are impaired on the reversal of a visual discrimination, in that they continue to respond to the previously rewarded stimulus when it is no longer rewarded (Butter 1969; Jones and Mishkin 1972). (4) The monkeys make errors in "Go−NoGo" tasks, in that they respond on the NoGo trials when they should inhibit responding (Iversen and Mishkin 1970). The impairments in the learning tasks appear to share in common the inability of the lesioned monkeys to prevent responses made to previously rewarded (or punished) stimuli. The food selection deficit may be related to these impairments, in that inhibition of responses to rewarded/unrewarded objects is inappropriate.

Unit Recordings of Orbitofrontal Cortex

In these studies, there is some evidence that lesions of different parts of the orbitofrontal cortex affect these tasks differentially, and it is not clear from the lesion studies exactly what kind of processing is occurring in the orbitofrontal cortex. To investigate this, recordings were made from single neurons in the orbitofrontal cortex during feeding, visual discrimination performance, its reversal, and extinction. Neurons with visual responses and with gustatory responses, sometimes occurring selectively to one type of food, were found (Thorpe *et al.* 1979).

Interestingly, some other neurons responded specifically during the reversal of a visual discrimination. These neurons showed clear increases in firing rate following the first incorrect trial in a reversal, i.e., when the monkey saw the previously rewarded stimulus, and licked, but obtained aversive hypertonic saline. In some of these neurons, this neuronal response was maintained for several seconds until the monkey had reversed his behavior (see Fig. 3.9). Responses were also found in some neurons during the extinction of licking previously rewarded by the delivery of fruit juice, as well as to frustrating events such as the removal of food. Responses of this kind in overlapping subsets of neurons suggest the existence of a neuronal mechanism involved in monitoring the consequences of behavior and altering behavior if appropriate. Also, the projections from the temporal lobe cortex may be important in introducing the information needed for this function into the orbitofrontal cortex. The absence of these neurons might be expected to result in the effects actually produced by lesions of the orbitofrontal cortex.

These findings suggest that when selection of a particular food is no longer appropriate, learning to inhibit the selection of that food depends on the orbitofrontal cortex. Although this may be part of a more general function of the orbitofrontal cortex, nevertheless it does suggest that the suppression of responses to particular foods is a function in which the orbitofrontal cortex is involved, and that in this way it can influence food selection.

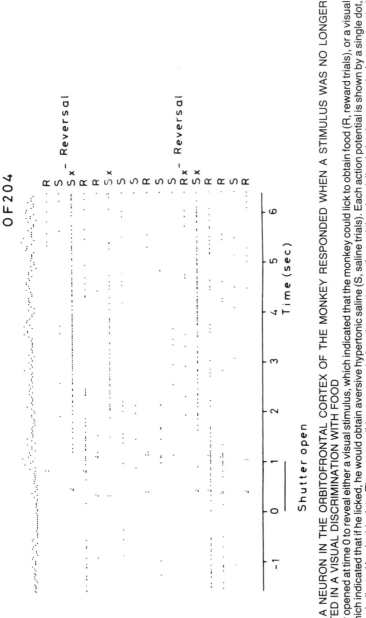

OF204

Reversal

Reversal

Shutter open

Time (sec)

FIG. 3.9. A NEURON IN THE ORBITOFRONTAL CORTEX OF THE MONKEY RESPONDED WHEN A STIMULUS WAS NO LONGER ASSOCIATED IN A VISUAL DISCRIMINATION WITH FOOD

The shutter opened at time 0 to reveal either a visual stimulus, which indicated that the monkey could lick to obtain food (R, reward trials), or a visual stimulus which indicated that if he licked, he would obtain aversive hypertonic saline (S, saline trials). Each action potential is shown by a single dot, and licks are indicated by double dots. The neuron did not respond when the monkey performed the visual discrimination correctly, but responded vigorously after the significance of the visual stimuli was reversed by the experimenter (reversal), when the monkey licked expecting food but received saline. The neuron did not respond when the monkey simply tasted saline from a syringe from which he was always fed saline, so that its responses were not associated just with taste, but rather occurred in a situation in which the monkey had to learn to inhibit responses to a stimulus previously paired with food. Other comparable neurons responded in the visual discrimination during extinction, that is when the monkey had to learn that food delivery was no longer associated with responses he made to a previously rewarded visual stimulus.

CONCLUSIONS

Although lesions of the lateral hypothalamus effectively reduce or abolish feeding, it is not possible to conclude from this evidence that the lateral hypothalamus contains a system for controlling feeding. This is so because damage to fiber pathways coursing in or near the lateral hypothalamus at least contributes to the reduction in feeding by producing a sensorimotor deficit. Direct evidence, obtained by recording the activity of neurons in the lateral hypothalamus during feeding, is therefore particularly relevant. It shows that a population of lateral hypothalamic neurons responds to the sight and/or taste of food, that this response only occurs if the monkey is hungry, and that the neuronal response to the sight of food precedes and predicts the responses of the hungry monkey to food. This suggests that this part of the brain is involved in the responses of the hungry monkey to food. These responses include autonomic and endocrine responses, such as the release of insulin, and also the initiation of feeding behavior. Interestingly, the responses of these lateral hypothalamic neurons to the sight of a particular food decreased when the monkey was fed to satiety with that food, yet the neuronal responses still occurred to other foods. This indication that appetite reduction could be relatively selective for particular foods led to studies that showed that ratings by humans of how pleasant a food tasted could be selectively reduced by eating that food, and to other studies that showed that this effect led to increased intake if a variety of foods was available. This is clearly one important factor that influences food selection.

Another important factor in food selection is learning, and the responses of these lateral hypothalamic neurons become associated with the sight of food during learning. This learning may involve temporal lobe mechanisms in the amygdala, which project into the lateral hypothalamus, for lesions to this system result in the selection of nonfood as well as food items. This is probably due at least in part to a deficit in this type of learning. When the selection of a particular food should be suppressed as a result of pervious experience, then this type of "unlearning" or inhibition of responses is impaired by damage to the orbitofrontal cortex. Neurons in this region are active during such suppression of choices. Thus, there is evidence that particular regions of the brain are involved in the effects that the sight of food produce during hunger, in the reduction in the selection of a particular food when that food is fed to satiety, and in the processes by which an animal learns to select, or to reject, particular foods.

ACKNOWLEDGMENTS

The collaboration of M.J. Burton, S. Maddison, F., Mora, D. Perrett, A. Roper-Hall, M.K. Sanghera, and S.J. Thorpe in some of the experiments described here is sincerely acknowledged.

REFERENCES

ANAND, B.K., and BROBECK, J.R. 1951. Hypothalamic control of food intake in rats and cats. Yale J. Biol. Med. 24, 123–140.

ARBUTHNOTT, G.W., MITCHELL, M.J., TULLOCH, I.F., and WRIGHT, A.K. 1976. Efferent pathways from lateral hypothalamic neurones. J. Physiol. 263, 131–132P.

BOOTH, D.A. 1977. Satiety and appetite are conditioned reactions. Psychosomat. Med. 39, 76–81.

BRAY, G.A., and GALLAGHER, T.F. 1975. Manifestation of hypothalamic obesity in man. Medicine 54, 301–330.

BURTON, M.J., ROLLS, E.T., and MORA, F. 1976. Effects of hunger on the responses of neurons in the lateral hypothalamus to the sight and taste of food. Exp. Neurol. 51, 668–677.

BUTTER, C.M. 1969. Perseveration in extinction and in discrimination reversal tasks following selective frontal ablations in Macaca mulatta. Physiol. Behav. 4, 163–171.

BUTTER, C.M., MCDONALD, J.A., and SNYDER, D.R. 1969. Orality, preference behavior, and reinforcement value of non-food objects in monkeys with orbital frontal lesions. Science 164, 1306–1307.

CHAVIS, D.A., and PANDYA, D.N. 1976. Further observations on corticofrontal connections in the rhesus monkey. Brain Res. 117, 369–386.

DIVAC, I. 1975. Magnocellular nuclei of the basal forebrain project to neocortex, brain stem, and olfactory bulb: Review of some functional correlates. Brain Res. 93, 385–398.

GRILL, H.J., and NORGEN, R. 1978. Chronically decerebrate rats demonstrate satiation but not bait shyness. Science 201, 267–269.

GROSSMAN, S.P. 1967. A Textbook of Physiological Psychology. Wiley, New York.

GROSSMAN, S.P. 1973. Essentials of Physiological Psychology. Wiley, New York.

GROSSMAN, S.P., DACEY, O., HALARIS, A.E., COLLIER, T., and ROUTTENBERG, A. 1978. Aphagia and adipsia after preferential destruction of nerve cell bodies in hypothalamus. Science 202, 537–539.

HAMBURG, M.D. 1971. Hypothalamic unit activity and eating behavior. Am. J. Physiol. 220, 980–985.

HERZOG, A.G., and VAN HOESEN, G.W. 1976. Temporal neocortical afferent connections to the amygdala in the rhesus monkey. Brain Res. *115*, 57–69.

HOEBEL, B.G. 1965. Hypothalamic lesions by electrocauterization: Disinhibition of feeding and self-stimulation. Science *149*, 452–453.

HOEBEL, B.G. 1976. Brain-stimulation reward and aversion in relation to behavior. *In* Brain-Stimulation Reward. A. Wauquier and E.T. Rolls (Editors). North-Holland Publ. Co., Amsterdam.

HOEBEL, B.G., and TEITELBAUM, P. 1962. Hypothalamic control of feeding and self-stimulation. Science *135*, 375–377.

INOUE, S., and BRAY, G.A. 1977. The effects of subdiaphragmatic vagotomy in rats with ventromedial hypothalamic obesity. Endocrinology *100*, 108–114.

INOUE, S., BRAY, G.A., and MULLEN, Y.S. 1977. Effect of transplantation of pancreas on development of hypothalamic obesity. Nature *266*, 742–744.

IVERSEN, S.D., and MISHKIN, M. 1970. Perseverative interference in monkeys following selective lesions of the inferior prefrontal convexity. Exp. Brain Res. *11*, 376–386.

JONES, B., and MISHKIN, M. 1972. Limbic lesions and the problem of stimulus-reinforcement associations. Exp. Neurol. *36*, 362–377.

JONES, E.G., BURTON, H., SAPER, C.B., and SWANSON, L.W. 1976. Midbrain, diencephalic and cortical relationships of the basal nucleus of Meynert and associated structures in primates. J. Comp. Neurol. *167*, 385–419.

KAMALIAN, N., KEESEY, R.E., and ZU RHEIN, G.M. 1975. Lateral hypothalamic demyelination and cachexia in a case of "malignant" multiple sclerosis. Neurology *25*, 25–30.

KIEVIT, J., and KUYPERS, H.G.J.M. 1975. Subcortical afferents to the frontal lobe in the rhesus monkey studied by means of retrograde horseradish peroxidase transport. Brain Res. *85*, 261–266.

KLÜVER, H., and BUCY, P.C. 1939. Preliminary analysis of functions of the temporal lobes in monkeys. Arch. Neurol. Psychiat. *42*, 979–1000.

LEIBOWITZ, S.F. 1980. Neurochemical systems of the hypothalamus. *In* Handbook of the Hypothalamus. P.J. Morgane and J. Panksepp (Editors), pp. 299–437. Marcel Dekker, New York.

LE MAGNEN, J. 1967. Habits and food intake. *In* Handbook of Physiology, Section 6, Volume 1. American Physiological Society, Washington, DC.

LE MAGNEN, J., DEVOS, M., GUADILLIÈRE, J.P., LOUIS-SYLVESTRE, J., and TALLON, S. 1973. Role of a lipostatic mechanism in regulation by feeding of energy balance in rats. J. Comp. Physiol. Psychol. *84*, 1–13.

MARSHALL, J.F., RICHARDSON, J.S., and TEITELBAUM, P. 1974. Nigrostriatal bundle damage and the lateral hypothalamic syndrome. J. Comp. Physiol. Psychol. 87, 808–830.

MECKLENBERG, R.S., LORCAUX, P.L., THOMPSON, R.H., ANDERSON, A.T., and LIPSETT, M.B. 1974. Hypothalamic dysfunction in patients with anorexia nervosa. Medicine 53, 147–159.

MORA, F., ROLLS, E.T., and BURTON, M.J. 1976. Modulation during learning of the responses of neurones in the lateral hypothalamus to the sight of food. Exp. Neurol. 53, 508–519.

MORGANE, P.J. 1961A. Electrophysiological studies of feeding and satiety centers in the rat. Am. J. Physiol. 201, 838–844.

MORGANE, P.J. 1961B. Evidence of a "hunger motivational" system in the lateral hypothalamus of the rat. Nature 191, 672–674.

MORGANE, P.J. 1961C. Medial forebrain bundle and "feeding centers" of the hypothalamus. J. Comp. Neurol. 117, 1–26.

NACHMAN, M., and ASHE, J.H. 1974. Effects of basolateral amygdala lesions on neophobia, learned taste aversions, and sodium appetite in rats. J. Comp. Physiol. Psychol. 87, 622–643.

NAUTA, W.J.H. 1961. Fiber degeneration following lesions of the amygdaloid complex in the monkey. J. Anat. 95, 515–531.

NAUTA, W.J.H. 1964. Some efferent connections of the prefrontal cortex in the monkey. In The Frontal Granular Cortex and Behavior. J.M. Warren and K. Akert (Editors). McGraw Hill, New York.

NAUTA, W.J.H., and DOMESICK, V.B. 1978. Crossroads of limbic and striatal circuitry: Hypothalamonigral connections. In Limbic Mechanisms. K.E. Livingston and O. Hornykiewicz (Editors). Plenum Press, New York.

NORGREN, R. 1970. Gustatory responses in the hypothalamus. Brain Res. 21, 63–77.

OLDS, J. 1962. Hypothalamic substrates of reward. Physiol. Rev. 42, 554–604.

OLDS, J. 1977. Drives and Reinforcement: Behavioral Studies of Hypothalamic Function. Raven Press, New York.

OLDS, J., MINK, W.D., and BEST, P.J. 1969. Single unit patterns during anticipatory behavior. Electroencephalogr. Clin. Neurophysiol. 26, 144–158.

OOMURA, Y. 1973. Central mechanism of feeding. Adv. Biophys. 5, 65–136.

OOMURA, Y., OOYAMA, H., NAKA, F., YAMAMOTO, T., ONO, T., and KOBAYASHI, N. 1969. Some stochastic patterns of single unit discharges in the cat hypothalamus under chronic conditions. Ann. N.Y. Acad. Sci. 157, 666–689.

PANKSEPP, J., BISHOP, P., and ROSSI III, J. 1979. Neurohumoral and endocrine control of feeding. Psychoneuroendocrinology (Oxford) 4, 89–106.

POWLEY, T.L. 1977. The ventromedial hypothalamic syndrome: Satiety and a cephalic phase hypothesis. Psychol. Rev. *84*, 89–126.

POWLEY, T.L., and OPSHAL, C.A. 1974. Ventromedial hypothalamic obesity abolished by subdiaphragmatic vagotomy. Am. J. Physiol. *226*, 25–33.

QUAADE, F. 1974. Stereotaxy for obesity. Lancet *i*, 267.

QUAADE, F., VAERNET, K., and LARSSON, S. 1974. Stereotaxic stimulation and electrocoagulation of the lateral hypothalamus in obese humans. Acta Neurochir. *30*, 111–117.

REEVES, A.G., and PLUM, F. 1969. Hyperphagia, rage, and dementia accompanying a ventromedial hypothalamic neoplasm. Arch. Neurol. *20*, 616–624.

ROLLS, B.J. 1979. How variety and palatability can stimulate appetite. Nutr. Bull. *5*, 78–86.

ROLLS, B.J., and ROLLS, E.T. 1973. Effects of lesions in the basolateral amygdala on fluid intake in the rat. J. Comp. Physiol. Psychol. *83*, 240–247.

ROLLS, B.J., ROWE, E.A., and ROLLS, E.T. 1980. Appetite and obesity: Influences of sensory stimuli and external cues. *In* Nutrition and Lifestyles. M.R. Turner (Editor), pp. 11–20. Applied Science Publishers, London.

ROLLS, E.T. 1975. The Brain and Reward. Pergamon Press, Oxford, England.

ROLLS, E.T. 1979. Effects of electrical stimulation of the brain on behaviour. *In* Psychology Surveys. K. Connolly (Editor), Vol. 2, pp. 151–169. George Allen and Unwin, Hemel Hempstead, England.

ROLLS, E.T. 1980. Activity of hypothalamic and related neurons in the alert animal. *In* Handbook of the Hypothalamus. P.J. Morgane and J. Panksepp (Editors), pp. 439–466. Marcel Dekker, New York.

ROLLS, E.T. 1981. Processing beyond the inferior temporal visual cortex related to feeding, memory, and striatal function. *In* Brain Mechanisms of Sensation. Y. Katsuki, M. Sato, and R. Norgren (Editors), Chapter 16, pp. 241–269. Academic Press, New York.

ROLLS, E.T., and ROLLS, B.J. 1977. Activity of neurones in sensory, hypothalamic and motor areas during feeding in the monkey. *In* Food Intake and Chemical Senses. Y. Katsuki, M. Sato, S. Takagi, and Y. Oomura (Editors), pp. 525–549. University of Tokyo Press, Tokyo, Japan.

ROLLS, E.T., BURTON, M.J., and MORA, F. 1976. Hypothalamic neuronal responses associated with the sight of food. Brain Res. *111*, 53–66.

ROLLS, E.T., SANGHERA, M.K., and ROPER-HALL, A. 1979A. The latency of activation of neurons in the lateral hypothalamus and substantia innominata during feeding in the monkey. Brain Res. *164*, 121–135.

ROLLS, E.T., THORPE, S.J., MADDISON, S., ROPER-HALL, A., PUERTO, A., and PERRETT, D. 1979B. Activity of neurones in the neostriatum and related structures in the alert animal. *In* The Neostriatum. I. Divac and R.G.E. Oberg (Editors), pp. 163–182. Pergamon Press, Oxford, England.

ROLLS, E.T., BURTON, M.J., and MORA, F. 1980. Neurophysiological analysis of brain-stimulation reward in the monkey. Brain Res. *194*, 339–357.

SANGHERA, M.K., ROLLS, E.T., and ROPER-HALL, A. 1979. Visual responses of neurons in the dorsolateral amygdala of the alert monkey. Exp. Neurol. *63*, 610–626.

SAPER, C.B., LOEWY, A.D., SWANSON, L.W., and COWAN, W.M. 1979A. Direct hypothalamo-autonomic connections. Brain Res. *117*, 305–312.

SAPER, C.B., SWANSON, L.W., and COWAN, W.M. 1979B. An autoradiographic study of the efferent connections of the lateral hypothalamic area in the rat. J. Comp. Neurol. *183*, 689–706.

STELLAR, E., HYMAN, R. and SOMET, S. 1954. Gastric factors controlling water intake and salt solution drinking. J. Comp. Physiol. Psychol. *47*, 220–226.

STRICKER, E.M., and ZIGMOND, M.J. 1976. Recovery of function following damage to central catecholamine-containing neurons: A neurochemical model for the lateral hypothalamic syndrome. Progr. Psychobiol. Physiol. Psychol. *6*, 121–188.

STRICKER, E.M., SWERDLOFF, A.E., and ZIGMOND, M.J. 1978. Intra-hypothalamic injections of kainic acid produce feeding and drinking deficits in rats. Brain Res. *158*, 470–473.

SWANSON, L.W. 1976. An autoradiographic study of the efferent connections of the preoptic region in the rat. J. Comp. Neurol. *167*, 227–250.

TANABE, T., YARITA, H., LINO, M., OOSLIIMA, Y., AND TAKAGI, S.F. 1975. An olfactory projection area in orbitofrontal cortex of the monkey. J. Neurophysiol. *38*, 1269–1283.

THORPE, S.J., MADDISON, S., and ROLLS, E.T. 1979. Single unit activity in the orbitofrontal cortex of the behaving monkey. Neurosci. Lett., S3, S77.

UNGERSTEDT, U. 1971. Adipsia and aphagia after 6-hydroxy-dopamine induced degeneration of the nigrostriatal dopamine system. Acta Physiol. Scand. *81*, Suppl. 367, 95–122.

VILBERG, T.R., and BEATTY, W.W. 1975. Behavioral changes following VHM lesions in rats with controlled insulin levels. Pharm. Biochem. Behav. *3*, 377–384.

WEISKRANTZ, L. 1956. Behavioral changes associated with ablation of the amygdaloid complex in monkeys. J. Comp. Physiol. Psychol. *49*, 381–391.

WHITE, I.E., and HAIN, R.F. 1959. Anorexia in association with a destructive lesion of the hypothalamus. Arch. Pathol. *68*, 275–281.

WAMPLER, R.S., and SNOWDON, C.T. 1979. Development of VMH obesity in vagotomized rats. Physiol. Behav. *22*, 85–93.

YORK, D.A., and BRAY, G.A. 1972. Dependence of hypothalamic obesity on insulin, the pituitary and the adrenal gland. Endocrinology *90*, 885–894.

Part II

Psychological Determinants of Food Choices

Over a period of hundreds of millions of years, evolutionary processes have produced humans and other organisms which are born with the ability to sense food. Taste buds on the tongue and olfactory receptors within the nasal cavities connect the brain with the environment by way of nerve fibers. Nutrients in the environment are detected by these sensors and the brain differentiates the edible from all other possible ingestants. These orosensory signals, in conjunction with nerve messages for the gut and vascular system, enter into feedback relationships within the brain to regulate amount as well as kind of food ingested. In this way each individual's energy needs are met and life is sustained.

Humans relate to their foods in much more complex ways than the above paragraph implies, however. In the first place, most humans do not select their own foods during the first few years of their lives. Infants and small children do, of course, taste and smell and exhibit preferences for what you are trying to feed them! But in large measure parents and "culture" guide the food selections of children. These early experiences and continuing interactions with foods determine the preferences we exhibit as adults.

In Part II we will examine some of the ways in which we humans interact with, learn about, and remember foods during the course of our lives. What is intriguing about this process is the subtle interplay that exists between our innate preferences and physiologically determined needs, on the one hand, and the acquired preferences accruing from parents, economic conditions, personal health, food availability, and geography—to name but a few sources of experience—on the other.

We begin this section with two chapters by psychologists who offer models, respectively, for how we learn about and how we remember the foods we eat. Chapter 4 by David Booth ("How Nutritional Effects of Foods Can Influence People's Dietary Choices") looks at the concept of "nutritional wisdom" within the framework of contemporary learning theory. Booth argues that flavors of foods, size of portions, the time of day we eat, and related ingestional behaviors become conditioned to the positive or aversive after-effects of meal ingestion. He calls this process "hedonic conditioning." Booth proposes that these learned factors outweigh any inherent "body wisdom" concerning food selection and urges educational messages and training programs to facilitate healthy eating that "hedonistic conditioning" will often assure.

Little is known about how we acquire our food memories. A human information processing model is proposed in Chapter 5, "Building Memories for Foods" by Lewis Barker. The similarities and differences of food memory formation are compared with audiovisual and word memory formation. Such factors as amount, duration, and flavor quality are identified as determinants of the strength of subsequent flavor memories.

Each of us has experienced how even the tastiest of foods change as one becomes full. This phenomenon, called here "sensory specific satiety," is examined in Chapter 6 by Barbara Rolls, Edmond T. Rolls, and Edward A. Rowe ("Influence of Variety on Human Food Selection and Intake"). External factors such as the sight, smell, taste, and texture of a particular food, combined with internal satiety signals, provide a degree of specificity to satiety. One does not merely get full, one "gets full" of a particular foodstuff. Both beneficial and deleterious aspects of this phenomenon are identified. On the positive side, satiating on a specific food early in a meal leads the eater to switch to another, thereby increasing the likelihood of a good balance of nutrients. However, overeating due to the presence of a variety of foods may result from the same behavior pattern.

Mixing foods and flavors can lead to some interesting, albeit unexpected, results. A laboratory analysis of one such mixing phenomenon is presented in Chapter 7 by James C. Smith, David F. Foster, and Linda M. Bartoshuk ("Synergistic Properties of Pairs of Sweeteners"). Both laboratory rats and humans treat sweet mixtures (such as glucose and saccharin solutions mixed together) in nonadditive ways. That is, when these two sweeteners are combined, their perceived sweetness is greater than expected from their individual properties. Insight into intense flavor craving and the resulting control over feeding behavior can be gleaned from Smith's laboratory rats.

All of us who have selected from myriad foods at the supermarket recognize the role that price and flavor have on what we choose to buy. Madla Krondl and D. Lau have studied these variables and the social factors of prestige and convenience of foods ("Social Determinants in Human Food Selection"). In their chapter we are reminded of the tremendous complexities involved in understanding even the simplest of food choices. The problems inherent in accomplishing this type of sociological research are evident.

These five chapters do not exhaust the current psychological conceptions of why we select particular foods to the exclusion of others. Indeed, none are exclusively "psychological." Rather, each theoretical position incorporates biological variables (such as postingestional regulation). One clear psychological factor emerges from all chapters in both Part I and Part II. *Flavor* is an overriding variable in our interactions with foods—in how we learn and remember and choose between them.

4

How Nutritional Effects of Foods Can Influence People's Dietary Choices

D.A. Booth

It is the thesis of this chapter that in large measure our appetite is determined by what we have learned from prior feeding and drinking experiences. More specifically, nutritional benefits increase our appetites and nutritional detriments decrease our appetites through a conditioning process. Palatability is in considerable part a nutrient-conditioned preference while hungry; palatability can be conceptualized from memory while in any bodily state. Satisfaction from food or water, moreover, is partly a conditioned aversion or lack of preference dependent on bodily cues of incipient repletion.

Nutritional Hedonic Conditioning: An Introduction

Such conditioning of the acceptance and rejection of particular foods and drinks in specific circumstances is the only mechanism (apart from scientifically sound instruction) by which habitat and physiology adapt to each other nutritionally in our species—indeed, in most other vertebrates as well—so far as has been formulated and evidenced to date. These learned components of appetite, which I will refer to as "nutritional hedonic conditioning," account for the calibration of "oral metering" of intake, and for the conditioned satiation cues that come from the gastrointestinal tract ahead of tissue repletion (Booth 1977A,B; Stunkard 1975). They account for the modicum of "nutritional wisdom" that can be shown in the face of frequently arbitrary relations between sensory cues and nutritional consequences (Booth et al. 1972, 1974). Some contribution to palatability and food selection from unlearned behaviors is also apparent (see Beidler, this volume, Chapter 1). However, nutritional hedonic conditioning appears to dominate the process by which the nutritional functions of a food are related to its sensory characteristics—indeed, to its conceptual identity. It dominates the reflection of nutrition into the bodily aftereffects of eating that influence intake. This kind of learning underpins culturally derived attitudes that benefit nutrition, both unaware, as in ecologically adapted cuisine, and deliberately, in responses to educational messages about diet and eating patterns.

Much of the evidence justifying this theme is from animals, but some crucial results have been obtained in human adults. Here I shall no more than allude to animal data, but will be giving the evidence for human nutritional conditioning and its cognitive elaborations.

UNDERSTANDING THE PROCESS OF FOOD SELECTION: ANALYSIS AND SYNTHESIS

Facilitatory and Inhibitory Influences

Dietary choice can be described in various ways, such as the daily intake of food and drink items or of nutrients by an individual, or annual national purchasing of the food commodities. Dietary choice will be explained, however, only if we consider all aspects of an individual's intake—the choice when to eat or drink (starting), the selection among items of food and drink (selecting), and the choice of how much to consume (stopping). I believe that meal sizes, meal times, food palatabilities in any static sense, are all epiphenomena of the immediately controlling processes. Dietary choice will ultimately be explained by consideration of the momentary mix of facilitatory and inhibitory influences on an individual's ingestion, and the way in which that mix changes during meals, snacks and drinks and between such bouts. These influences can be analyzed experimentally and observationally. Maybe they can be measured in a sufficiently strong sense of that term to permit one day a "cognitive algebra" of intake (Booth 1979A,B; 1980B).

Biological, Psychological, and Social Determinants

An analysis of the immediate determinants of actual food intake should include the influences of sensory inputs and somatic physiology as well as social, economic and cultural processes. Furthermore, conceptual division between external environment and internal environment factors is difficult, as are clean distinctions between sensory, physiological or social categories of influence. What is available to the mouth, moreover, is constrained by choices made during the preparation, purchase, production, and trade of food. Yet those choices are themselves strongly influenced by cooks', purchasers' and commercial suppliers' expectations of the eater's reactions at the meal table.

Summary of Analysis. The foregoing analysis is a start at lifting the unidisciplinary blinders that weaken or sometimes vitiate our investigations of appetite. The science of intake needs evidence from anthropology, history, economics and marketing, from sensory science, cognitive psychology and animal behavior processes, and from physiology, biochemistry and food technology. The present volume is a commendable and distinctive addition to recent attempts to generate a realistic cross-disciplinary approach to the phenomena of preference, appetite, and intake (Silverstone 1976; Solms and Hall 1981; Rodin *et al.* 1980).

An Example of Synthesis: Predicting Meal Patterns

The foregoing analysis is of little help unless there is prospect of synthesis. So first consider a result from a highly simplified synthesis of the moment-to-moment variations in the facilitation and inhibition of intake.

Booth and Mather (1978) calculated the influence of the momentary supply of energy-yielding substrates to the body's tissues on the desire to eat. A computer simulation was run for a particular set of physiological characteristics, and for specific diet and activity patterns. Table 4.1 gives the predicted meal pattern for a normal-weight adult male, simulated to be working at a desk from 9 to 5 and to wind down during the evening in front of the TV.

TABLE 4.1. CALCULATED MEAL PATTERN FOR A SEDENTARY WORKER[1]

Prior activities	Meal start	Meal end	Meal size (kcal)
Sleep from 23.30 to 07.30 Increasing activity Start work at 09.00	08.20	08.40	950
(1.4 kcal/min) Finish work at 17.00	13.17	13.40	1093
Decreasing activity	19.04	19.24	925

[1]Results from Booth and Mather (1978).

Three Meals per Day? We had expected that the presupposed strong influence of physiology would give results that were widely at variance with the social constraints of living in the real world. So we were initially very surprised when the simulation predicted breakfast, lunch and supper without our adding further specifications (see Table 4.1). However, on second thought, we did not take the result as an argument against the social determinants of when to eat and even how much to eat. Rather, we felt that the results expose the mutual adaptation of culture and biology. The pattern of three meals a day is, according to this calculation, well-adapted motivationally and nutritionally to the average physiology of an adult with a sedentary lifestyle. If a culture is rich and leisured enough (and perhaps living in or creating a temperate climate?), conventions of "breakfast," "lunch" and "supper" may be an overall easier and healthier compromise than one or two meals or even four or six meals daily, food intake held constant.

HEDONIC CONDITIONING BY EFFECTS OF NUTRIENT INGESTION

Conditioned Appetites and Satieties

Considerable evidence for nutritional wisdom in birds (Dove 1935), rats (Richter 1941), and human infants (Davis 1928) offered natural foods was found prior to the 1940s. Satisfactory experimental analysis of the immediate determinants of the influence of nutrients on dietary choice seems to have begun with Harris et al. (1933) but not to have been pursued until the late 1950s by Le Magnen (1956A,B; 1957).

Taste Cues Deficient Diet. Harris et al. (1933) showed that selection of thiamin in rats made deficient of that vitamin was a conditioned response to arbitrary tastes associated with the thiamin-deficient diets. This learned response was later (Rozin and Kalat 1971) shown to be similar in principle to the finding of Garcia et al. (1955) of radiation-induced conditioned aversion to saccharin flavored water. From the 1960s Garcia and many others used taste aversion conditioning to extend greatly our understanding of the processes of classical conditioning in animals (Barker et al. 1977; Milgram et al. 1977). In particular, it was shown that bodily effects could condition reactions to flavors with many minutes or even hours occurring between flavor and aftereffect. It had been established that postingestional effects of nutritious materials would reward instrumental behavior in hungry animals (Miller and Kessen 1952) and that effects of food or water deprivation could serve as good learned cues (Bailey 1955). Furthermore, there was evidence that food or water would condition incentive to act (Holman 1968) and relative preference (Revusky 1967, 1968) in deprived rats.

Diet Influences Flavor Preference. We found in rats that carbohydrate in a diet conditions preferences for particular levels of sweetness, other tastes, and odors—even when the sweetness of sugars was disguised or absent (Booth *et al.* 1972, 1974; Booth and Davis 1973; Booth 1977A,B, 1980A). Dietary protein (Booth 1974) or balanced amino acid mixture tubed to the stomach (Booth and Simson 1971; Simson and Booth 1973A,B) also conditioned preferences to odors and tastes arbitrarily associated with the amino acid repletion in mildly deprived rats.

Conditioned Satiation. Substantial amounts of concentrated starch were found also to condition the satiating effect of eating (Booth 1972C, 1977A,B, 1980A; Booth and Davis 1973). This conditioned satiation is sensory-specific, like the aversions conditioned by toxins, but is also apparently specific to nutritionally relevant bodily cues. That is, the aversion is conditioned to both flavor and the state generated, presumably in gut and/or tissues, by the eating of most of a meal. Such postingestional changes tend to reduce the appetite for all foods, but that response might have been conditioned by long experience and in any case has been conditioned by the carbohydrate in combination with the experimental flavor. Thus, the evidence is that the motivational structure of the whole dietary choice situation is at least in part acquired by past experience of the nutritional consequences of eating in similar states of the internal and external environment.

Human Conditioning

Conditioning of absolute preferences has yet to be formally demonstrated in man as it has been in rat, but hunger-contingent relative conditioned preferences have been observed in pleasantness ratings (Mather 1977; Booth 1981B). Conditioning of satiation has been demonstrated in both intake (Booth *et al.* 1976; Mather 1977; Booth 1981A) and in symbolic responses to foods (Mather 1977; Fuller 1980; Booth 1981B). Figure 4.1 illustrates the conditioning of intake to food flavor by augmenting starch ingestion early enough in the meal to produce effects close to the end of eating. When the starch difference comes in the dessert, its effects are too delayed to condition intake reliably under these conditions; however, symbolically expressed satiation—the fall in pleasantness ratings from start to finish of the main sandwich course— is sensitive enough to show a conditioning effect (see Fig. 4.2). The starch is sufficiently well disguised, and its satiating aftereffect is sufficiently modest, for people to be unable to guess reliably which of the two soups is higher in calories, even when the soup is taken as a snack by itself (Fuller 1980). Thus, although the intakes and the ratings show that the brain is monitoring the effects of starch, the effects that produce

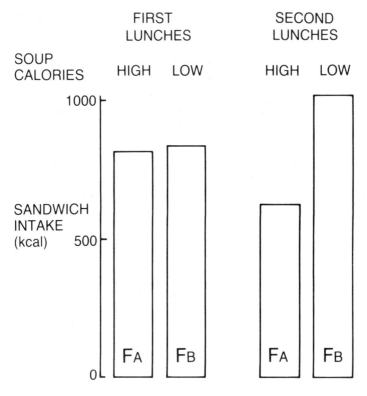

From Booth (1981A)

FIG. 4.1. INTAKES OF SANDWICHES (THE ONLY COURSE *ad libitum*)
Lunches in which each participant had one set of flavors (F_A) associated with starch-augmented soup (high calories) and another set of flavors (F_B) associated with low-calorie soup.
The postingestional satiating effect of the soup was not prompt enough to affect intake in the
first pair of lunches. Yet in the second pair of lunches, flavors cued a differentiation of lunch
intake in anticipation of that after-effect.

the conditioning may not enter the forefront of attention and the dietary
choices are not necessarily deliberate responses in the light of conscious
memories.

Starch, Fat and Protein as Conditioning Agents

The nutrient that produces these conditioning aftereffects of ingestion in the human experiments, as with the rats, is starch. Starch is
readily disguised, for example, in soups, desserts, and shakes, especially
in the partly predigested and highly soluble form of low-glucose malto-
dextrin. It can be matched for texture by a nonnutritive bulking agent
such as food-grade carboxymethylcellulose and for taste by a small

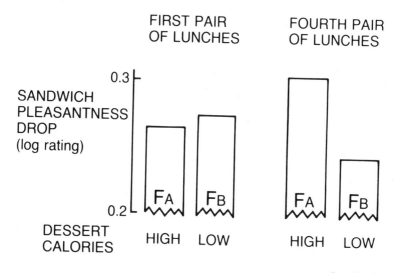

FIRST PAIR
OF LUNCHES

FOURTH PAIR
OF LUNCHES

SANDWICH
PLEASANTNESS
DROP
(log rating)

0.3

0.2

DESSERT
CALORIES

HIGH   LOW   HIGH   LOW

F_A F_B F_A F_B

From Booth (1981A)

FIG. 4.2. DECREASES IN PLEASANTNESSES OF SANDWICHES *(ad libitum)*
From the start to the finish of that course, before and after three pairings of flavors F_A with starch-augmented dessert and F_B with low-calorie dessert. Balancing flavor–calorie pairings across the group of eight participants.

amount of nonnutritive sweetener or of sucrose. In concentrated form, starch creates a powerful but transient satiating effect after a delay following ingestion that is sufficient to allow absorption of the glucose from digestion to get well under way (Booth 1979A; also compare Booth et al. 1970A; Wooley et al. 1972A,B) The time course is consistent with the hypothesis that metabolism of the glucose for energy creates the satiety, as is more directly evidenced in the rat (Booth 1972A,B; Booth and Jarman 1976). Intravenous infusions of glucose that produce this satiating effect are also capable of conditioning food odor preferences in rats (Mather et al. 1978).

Protein. In rats that are using much of their dietary protein for energy, protein disguised in the diet, or balanced amino acid mixtures tubed to the stomach, rapidly condition odor and taste preferences in similarly hungry states (Simson and Booth 1973A,B; Booth 1974; Booth et al. 1974). Satiation has not been conditioned by protein. This may simply be because protein has been delivered in smaller amounts than starch, or it may be that protein carbon is oxidized and satiates after a longer delay (Booth et al. 1970B; Geliebter 1979) and so conditions less effectively.

Fats. More striking is the failure to obtain conditioning of either preferences (Booth *et al.* 1974) or satiation (Booth 1972C) by dietary fat effects. This again could be because of relative slow oxidation of dietary triglyceride circulating in chylomicra, whether or not its absorption is normally as much delayed as is widely supposed. The satiating effect of fat is late (Geliebter 1979). This relative lack of direct and conditioned satiating effects from dietary fat may be particularly unfortunate for the obese because the sensory characteristics of fat are thought to contribute as much as those of sugar to the high palatability of affluent diets (Cantor and Cantor 1977). The high energy per weight of fat slips in the calories unnoticed (especially as hidden fat), and perhaps for these and other reasons a high-fat diet may be prejudicial to overweight and to cardiovascular and other disease. All in all, at present we should look to dietary starch and the less sweet sugars (e.g., lactose in yogurt, etc.) to teach people about the effects of food on energy metabolism.

Nutritional Perceptiveness in Thoughts and Actions on Diet

Changes in hedonic reaction, perceptions or attitudes are likely once the conditioned appetite and/or satisfaction to a particular food or drink has been sufficiently well established. Attitudes might be reflected in abstract verbalization, referring to the food in its absence and in the absence of the bodily state of depletion or repletion on which the preference or aversion might be dependent. A food that had had depletion-dependent relative preference conditioned to it might be perceived as more palatable, more appetizing, or suited to the start of meals. Such conceptualizations would then formulate expectations of a food that could affect selection of it and decisions as to the amount of it to eat. Indeed, such expectations might be so clearly formulated and indeed based on so much past experience that they might overwhelm other indications (e.g., from the body) that they are inappropriate on a particular occasion (Table 4.2). Even when food items are unfamiliar, visual appearances create conceptions (and often misconceptions) of how filling, fattening, or pleasant to eat they are when hungry. Repeated experience of eating and evaluating the food items corrects these misconceptions only to a limited extent (Table 4.3) (Fuller 1980). This is one argument for a readily comprehended form of nutritional labeling, especially as some people are less capable of improving their perception of energy in the face of strong misleading cues. These readily distracted individuals are liable to gain weight on shifting into an environment with abundant snacks and meals (Rodin and Slochower 1976; Rodin 1980). There is a tendency to eat what is put in front of one, which Siegel and Pilgrim (1958) referred to as the "completion compulsion."

TABLE 4.2. EFFECTS ON RATED SATIETY OF GUESSING WHICH SOUP WAS HIGHER IN CALORIES AND OF A 200-kcal DIFFERENCE IN STARCH CONTENT BETWEEN TWO SOUPS

	"High calorie"	"Low calorie"	N	P
Guessed calorie difference	7.0 ± 9.9	1.6 ± 8.3	28	<0.02
Actual calorie difference	6.9 ± 9.7	2.4 ± 8.6	32	<0.04

Source: Booth et al. 1982.

TABLE 4.3. IMPROVEMENTS IN THE REFLECTION OF FOOD ENERGY CONTENT IN CONCEPTS CONCERNING THE FOOD (SIX SNACK FOODS)

	Summed deviations of conceptual from actual	
	Before experience of the food items	After three occasions of eating each item
Estimated calorie content	23.5 ± 9.5	21.3 ± 8.9
Ranked how filling	9.9 ± 2.5	8.5 ± 2.5*
Ranked how fattening	11.9 ± 2.8	10.1 ± 3.0**
Ranked how nice to eat when hungry	11.0 ± 2.9	10.2 ± 3.0

Source: Fuller, 1980; cf. Booth, 1980B.
*P <0.05, **P <0.01 for difference between inaccuracy scores.

Increased intake with larger portions in the short term has been seen by Fuller (1980) and others (Shaw 1973; Becker and Cotta 1976).

Energy Labeling. In the absence of energy labels, people are capable of perceiving and learning something about the energy content of a food, as expressed worst in judgment of calories, better in judgments of filling effect, and possibly best of all in intake and in the conditioned satiation effect seen in pleasantness ratings at the time of eating (Booth 1980A; Fuller 1980). Even when packaging and item shape are not potentially misleading, current technology creates notorious hazards for energy perception: the fat content of French fries and or potato chips (crisps) is not well evident to sight or mouthfeel; the energy contents of yogurts vary widely, unrelated to flavor or texture. One advantage of mass production, for example in fast foods or domestic convenience foods, is that both sizing and nutrient composition are often much less variable than in the traditional analogues. Thus, even without labeling, there is more opportunity for direct experience to teach dietary choices better attuned to energy effect.

Portion Sizes. The realization that ingestional and postingestional satieties can be finely tuned by learning and the observation of large effects of differences in portion size indicates that we should pay more attention to this variable, as Scala (1978) acknowledged. Choice of portion size should be increased as much as possible, and that within modest fractions (70% or even 80%, not just 50% or 200%).

OTHER SOURCES OF APPETITE AND SATIATION

There are of course many other facilitatory and inhibitory influences on intake beside the nutrient-conditioned appetites and satieties. Sometimes they improve the nutritional wisdom of dietary choice. Sometimes they apparently have irrelevant nutritional influences. In certain circumstances an influence can be harmful. Maladaptive behavior and its persistence is not a puzzle for the determinist in biological evolution or cultural survival. A behavior may be important to survival of genes or traditions in one way while remaining detrimental in other circumstances, for example (Desor et al. 1973).

Postingestional Influences

The changes in bodily state that contribute to loss of interest in food seem to occur more rapidly than the bodily changes contributing to the return of that interest. Therefore, physiological study has proved more productive in recent years in "satiation signals" than in "appetite signals." For example, in the study of human food intake, it is easier to disguise the composition of the diet and hence the postingestional effects of its nutrient contents than it is to disguise the time since the last meal and hence the rise of bodily appetizing factors (Wooley 1976). Thus, for reasons that may be more technical than conceptual, this discussion will be couched in terms of postingestionally generated satiety.

Wisdom and Foolishness in Postingestional Satiation

Although the idea of activation of all behaviors by bodily need states is quite insufficient to explain motivation and learning, deprivation-induced activation (Nisbett 1972) and its instigation of eating compared with other activations (Robbins and Fray 1980) remain widely recognized phenomena. They are difficult to study, in animals or people, for arousal is a notoriously inchoate concept. Discriminative and instigational properties of activation have to be distinguished (Fray and Robbins 1980) and the (learned) drive cue concept invoked in my account of state-dependent conditioned preferences may sit uneasily with that distinction.

Ingestion-Specific Deactivation. Workers on satiating agents often assume that their deactivating effect should be specific to ingestion (specificity to ingestate comes next). Yet, as common experience of the aftereffects of heavy meals will testify, sedation is part of the observed behavioral sequence of normal satiation (Antin et al. 1975). EEG sleep results from the same changes in energy metabolism that are fundamental to satiation for food (Danguir and Nicolaidis 1980). Furthermore, discomfort and even nausea may accompany at least occasional meals in the healthy individual, whether the gorging results from relief of famine, emotional distress, or sheer gluttony. Any satiety signal at high enough levels is liable to cause coma, pain, emesis or expectoration. Such consequences of ingestion may condition the aversions to combinations of bodily and dietary cues that precede them.

Distension of the stomach and upper intestine does not in itself indicate the chemical composition of the ingestate. Thus, gastric satiation may make little distinction between food and water (Fitzsimons 1972). The sensation of fullness, to the extent that it reflects gastrointestinal distension (Booth 1981B), may not be very discriminating. Nutritional wisdom lies in integrating the volume information with chemospecific information, from the diet, from the intestine and tissues, and even perhaps from the stomach itself (Deutsch 1978). Additional information to discriminate water from other macronutrients comes from the time course of gastric emptying, as that is controlled by the energy yield of a normal diet (Hunt and Stubbs 1975), barring complications with dietary salts.

Unlearned Postingestional Control of Meal Size?   I have already explained how state-dependent hedonic conditioning can account for adjustment of meal size toward energy content. An additional possibility in principle, apparently widely assumed to operate, is that chemospecific actions on the duodenum send neural or hormonal signals to the brain before the end of a meal. A suitable range of chemospecific neural pathways or hormone releases has yet to be demonstrated in my opinion. In any case, an early sample of digestion and absorption can reach the tissues within a few minutes of ingestion (Pilcher et al. 1974). The problem remains of calibrating the signal of gastrointestinal or absorptive chemical composition to reflect amount ingested rather than concentrations resulting from early digestion. Thus unlearned postingestional effects are unlikely to contribute refined wisdom to the choice of amount to eat.

Psychologists advising on weight control seem to assume that postingestional satiation develops with a fixed time course and therefore advise their clients to eat more slowly in the hope that satiety will catch up before they have eaten too much. Chewing will indeed give the stomach less to do before the duodenum is provided with a representative sample of the meal composition (Malagelada 1976). However, gastric distension and duodenal and postintestinal satiation signals will depend on a dynamic interaction between rate of eating, gastric emptying pattern, and digestion, quite apart from variations in nutrient density. Thus, it is by no means clear that eating more slowly will give satiety "time to catch up" and reduce meal size (Booth and Mather 1978; Booth 1978). Slow enough eating could delay satiation indefinitely!

INTEGRATION AND CONFLICT BETWEEN BIOLOGY AND CULTURE

Many of the particularities of human food preferences and eating or drinking patterns are culturally specified. However, as I have already argued and as other participants in this symposium also illustrate, the cultural specification is subject to biological influences more subtle than the absolute constraints of our animal nature.

I suggest that this susceptibility to biological influence depends largely on nutritional hedonic conditioning. Traditions of eating practice would not be transmitted without the conditioning of contextual appetites and satieties. Familiarization and social modeling by themselves are insufficient to establish strong personal preference (Duncker 1938), although social-affective reward may condition food preference (Birch et al. 1980). If a child finds a food item sufficiently palatable and acceptable in amount, then the liking for and satisfaction from that item in the future will be established as long as the nutritional conditioning effects are appropriate. The traditional cuisine will determine the particularities of preparation and serving as long as it operates within a framework of dietary compositions that often enough generate adequate nutrition on the parameters we are built to monitor and be conditioned by. If a trick of preparation creates a nutritional advantage, the conditioning mechanism provides the means by which a new tradition may become established for transmission from the discoverers, however untutored in nutrition they or their successors may be. Neither miraculously versatile sensory and brain mechanisms nor unaccountably veridical pre-scientific food theories are necessary to account for the similarity of the "general balance of rationing" (Mursell 1925) across the cultures or the nutritional wisdom of human infants whose "appetite could function freely and beneficially as in animals and primitive people" (Davis 1928, 1935).

It is essential to note that this is a theory of how culture is attuned to the broadest of nutritional requirements, not an explanation of all phenomena of dietary choice. Whether or not we regard all human thinking and learning as an elaboration of elemental conditioning processes (Booth 1977B), many other associates besides nutrition can condition human eating and drinking. Some of these preference- or aversion-conditioning mechanisms may prove to be the basic nutritional conditioning carried beyond their original purview in typically human fashion by powerful culturally mediated conceptual structures: that remains to be proved or disproved. Thus, for example, one can wonder whether the disgust reaction so neatly elucidated by Rozin (this volume, Chapter 11) differs fundamentally from strong conditioned aversion or perhaps conditioned nausea (emetic rather than spitting reactions), overlaid with the indispensable attributional structure. "Perceived" contamination is serving as the associate, rather than a neurally monitored bodily toxin or excess. The actual contamination is negligible, even to the untutored rationality of the disgusted individual. Yet the conceptual structure of secular dirt or religious uncleanness focuses attention on sufficiently similar information to activate the same conditioning mechanism.

Disgust (Rozin and Fallon 1980) and food taboo (Simoons, this volume, Chapter 12) are not nutritionally necessary. They may be uneconomical. The theoretically important point is that they do not generally prejudice adequate nutrition. Occasionally, the conceptual structures and the circumstances may combine to the detriment of the individual's nutrition: people can choose to starve, even to death. Any conditioning mechanism is no more than influence that may conflict with or support any other influence. Whether nutritional hedonic conditioning wins or loses against a conflicting hedonic conditioning or any other influence will depend on details of conditioning processes. Animal psychology has only recently begun to study these processes. Furthermore, cognitive processing about diet is a research area hardly yet recognized to exist, despite longstanding interest in consumer behavior, dietary attitudes, and sensory evaluation of food.

The immediate sources of hedonic conditioning of food preferences are at the table and in the kitchen, canteen and restaurant, and among family and peers more than from commerce, school, media and health professionals. Eating experiences should be organized to encourage the individual's attention to his or her own nutrition. That may be a relatively simple matter of "eating sensibly"—freeing the appetites and satieties to operate in selection and amount, without any persistent large contrasts in palatability or context, and with due attention to bodily changes during and between meals (Booth 1981C). If nutritional advice really should be more complicated, medical science is a long way from showing us why and how.

Thus, we have the faith of our biological and cultural inheritances, the hope of scientific education, and our automatically acquired love of a particular cuisine and eating pattern—these three. Yet the greatest of these is the love of food acquired from its nutritional effects.

REFERENCES

ANTIN, J., *et al.* 1975. Cholecystokinin elicits the complete behavioral sequence of satiety in rats. J. Comp. Physiol Psychol. *89*, 784–790.

BAILEY, C.J. 1955. The effectiveness of drives as cues. J. Comp. Physiol. Psychol. *48*, 183–187.

BARKER, L.M., BEST, M., and DOMJAN, M. (Editors). 1977. Learning Mechanisms in Food Selection. Baylor University Press, Waco, Texas.

BECKER, E.E., and COTTA, R.F. 1976. Effects of portion size on intake. Presented at Eastern Psychological Association, April 1976.

BIRCH, L.L., ZIMMERMAN, S.I., and HIND, H. 1980. The influence of social-affective context on children's food preferences. Child Dev. *51*, 856–861.

BOOTH, D.A. 1972A. Satiety and behavioral caloric compensation following intragastric glucose loads in the rat. J. Comp. Physiol. Psychol. *78*, 412–432.

BOOTH, D.A. 1972B. Post-absorptively induced suppression of appetite and the energostatic control of feeding. Physiol. Behav. *9*, 199–202.

BOOTH, D.A. 1972C. Conditioned satiety in the rat. J. Comp. Physiol. Pyschol. *81*, 457–471.

BOOTH, D.A. 1974. Acquired sensory preferences for protein in diabetic and normal rats. Physiol. Psychol. *2*, 344–348.

BOOTH, D.A. 1977A. Appetite and satiety as metabolic expectancies. *In* Food Intake and Chemical Senses. Y. Katsuki, M. Sato, S.F. Takagi, and Y. Oomura (Editors). University of Tokyo Press, Tokyo, Japan.

BOOTH, D.A. 1977B. Language acquisition as the addition of verbal routines. *In* Recent Advances in the Psychology of Language: Formal and Experimental Approaches. Plenum Press, New York.

BOOTH, D.A. 1978. First steps towards an integrated quantitative approach to human feeding and obesity, with some implications for research into treatment. *In* Recent Advances in Obesity Research, Vol. II. G.A. Bray (Editor). Newman, London.

BOOTH, D.A. 1979A. Metabolism and the control of feeding in man and animals. *In* Chemical Influences on Behavior. K. Brown and S.J. Cooper (Editors). Academic Press, New York.

BOOTH, D.A. 1979B. Preference as a motive. *In* Preference Behavior and Chemoreception. J.H.A. Kroeze (Editor). Information Retrieval, London.

BOOTH, D.A. 1980A. Acquired behavior controlling energy intake and output. *In* Obesity. A.J. Stunkard (Editor). Saunders, Philadelphia, Pennsylvania.

BOOTH, D.A. 1980B. Conditioned reactions in motivation. *In* Analysis of Motivational Processes. F.M. Toates and T.R. Halliday (Editors). Academic Press, New York.

BOOTH, D.A. 1981A. Hunger and satiety as conditioned reflexes. *In*

Brain, Behavior, and Bodily Diseases. H. Weiner, M.A. Hofer, and A.J. Stunkard (Editors). Raven Press, New York.

BOOTH, D.A. 1981B. How should questions about satiation be asked? Appetite 2, 237–244.

BOOTH, D.A. 1981C. Momentary acceptance of particular foods and processes that change it. In Criteria of Food Acceptance: How Man Chooses What He Eats. J. Solms and R.L. Hall (Editors). Forster, Zurich.

BOOTH, D.A., and DAVIS, J.D. 1973. Gastrointestinal factors in the acquisition of oral sensory control of satiation. Physiol. Behav. 11, 23–29.

BOOTH, D.A., and JARMAN, S.P. 1976. Inhibition of food intake in the rat following complete absorption of glucose delivered into the stomach, intestine, or liver. J. Physiol. 259, 501–522.

BOOTH, D.A., and MATHER, P. 1978. Prototype model of human feeding, growth and obesity. In Hunger Models. D.A. Booth (Editor). Academic Press, New York.

BOOTH, D.A. and SIMSON, P.C. 1971. Food preferences acquired by variation in amino acid nutrition. Q. J. Exp. Psychol. 23, 135–145.

BOOTH, D.A., CAMPBELL, A.T., and CHASE, A. 1970A. Temporal bounds of post-ingestive glucose induced satiety in man. Nature 228, 1104–1105.

BOOTH, D.A., CHASE, A., and CAMPBELL, A.T. 1970B. Relative effectiveness of protein in the late stages of appetite suppression in man. Physiol. Behav. 5, 1299–1302.

BOOTH, D.A., LOVETT, D., and MC SHERRY, G.M. 1972. Post-ingestive modulation of the sweetness preference gradient. J. Comp. Physiol. Psychol. 78, 485–512.

BOOTH, D.A., STOLOFF, R., and NICHOLLS, J. 1974. Dietary flavor acceptance in infant rats established by association with effects of nutrient composition. Physiol. Psychol. 2, 313–319.

BOOTH, D.A., LEE, M., and MC ALEAVEY, C. 1976. Acquired sensory control of satiation in man. Br. J. Psychol. 67, 137–147.

BOOTH, D.A., MATHER, P., and FULLER, J. 1982. Starch content of ordinary foods associatively conditions human appetite and satiation, indexed by intake and eating pleasantness of starch-paired flavours. Appetite 3, 163–184.

CANTOR, S.M., and CANTOR, M.B. 1977. Socioeconomic factors in fat and sugar consumption. In Chemical Senses and Nutrition. M.R. Kare and O. Maller (Editors). Academic Press, New York.

DANGUIR, J., and NICOLAIDIS, S. 1980. Intravenous infusions of nutrients and sleep in the rat: An ischymetric sleep regulation hypothesis. Am. J. Physiol. 238, E307–E312.

DAVIS, C.M. 1928. Self-selection of diets by newly weaned infants: An experimental study. Am. J. Dis. Child. 36, 651–689.

DAVIS, C.M. 1935. Self-selection of food by children. Am. J. Nurs. 35, 402–410.

DESOR, J.A., MALLER, O., and TURNER, R.E. 1973. Taste in acceptance of sugars by human infants. J. Comp. Physiol. Psychol. *84*, 496–501.

DEUTSCH, J.A. 1978. The stomach in food satiation and the regulation of appetite. Prog. Neurobiol. *10*, 135–153.

DOVE, W.F. 1935. A study of individuality in the nutritive instincts and of the causes and effects of variations in the selection of food. Am. Nat. *69*, 469–544.

DUNCKER, K. 1938. Experimental modification of children's preferences through social suggestion. J. Abnorm. Soc. Psychol. *33*, 489–507.

FITZSIMONS, J.T. 1972. Thirst. Physiol. Rev. *52*, 468–561.

FRAY, P.J., and ROBBINS, T.W. 1980. Stress-induced eating: Rejoinder. Appetite *1*, 349–354.

FULLER, J. 1980. Human appetite and body size control. Ph.D. Dissertation, University of Birmingham, Birmingham, England.

GARCIA, J., KIMELDORF, D.J., and KOELLING, R.A. 1955. A conditioned aversion towards saccharin resulting from exposure to gamma radiation. Science *122*, 157–158.

GELIEBTER, A.A. 1979. Effects of equicaloric loads of protein, fat, and carbohydrate on food intake in the rat and man. Physiol. Behav. *22*, 267–273.

HALPERN, B.P. and MEISELMAN, H.L. 1980. Taste pyschophysics based on a simulation of human drinking. Chem. Senses *5*, 279–296.

HARRIS, L.J., CLAY, J., HARGREAVES, F.J., and WARD, A. 1933. Appetite and choice of diet. The ability of the vitamin B deficient rat to discriminate between diets and lacking the vitamin. Proc. R. Soc., London Ser. B *113*, 161–190.

HOLMAN, G.L. 1968. Intragastric reinforcement effect. J. Comp. Physiol. Psychol. *69*, 432–441.

HUNT, J.N., and STUBBS, D.F. 1975. The volume and content of meals as determinants of gastric emptying. J. Physiol. *245*, 209–225.

LE MAGNEN, J. 1956A. The effects of postprandial administrations of insulin on alimentary uptake in the white rat, and the caloric appetite mechanism. J. Physiol. (Paris) *48*, 789–802. (French).

LE MAGNEN, J. 1956B. Hyperphagia induced in the white rat by alteration of the peripheral satiety mechanism. C. R. Soc. Biol. *150*, 32–35. (French).

LE MAGNEN, J. 1957. The mechanism of the establishment of differential appetite for diets of varying caloric density. J. Physiol. (Paris) *49*, 1105–1107. (French)

LE MAGNEN, J. 1967. Habits and food intake. *In* Handbook of Physiology, Section 6, Vol. 1. American Physiological Society, Washington, DC.

MALAGELADA, J.R. 1976. Quantification of gastric solid-liquid discrimination during digestion of ordinary meals. Gastroenterology *72*, 1264–1267.

MATHER, P., NICOLAIDIS, S., and BOOTH, D.A. 1978. Compensatory and conditioned feeding responses to scheduled glucose infusions in the rat. Nature *273*, 461–463.

MILGRAM, N.W., KRAMES, L., and ALLOWAY, T.M. (Editors). 1977. Food Aversion Learning. Plenum Press, New York.

MILLER, N.E., and KESSEN, M.L. 1952. Reward effects of food via stomach fistula compared with those of food via mouth. J. Comp. Physiol. Psychol. *45*, 555–564.

NISBETT, R.E. 1972. Hunger, obesity, and the ventromedial hypothalmus. Psychol. Rev. *79*, 433–453.

PILCHER, C.W.T, JARMAN, S.P., and BOOTH, D.A. 1974. The route of glucose to the brain from food in the mouth of the rat. J. Comp. Physiol. Psychol. *87*, 56–61.

REVUSKY, S.H. 1967. Hunger level during food consumption: Effects on subsequent preference. Psychonom. Sci. *7*, 109–110.

REVUSKY, S.H. 1968. Effects of thirst level during consumption of flavored water on subsequent preference. J. Comp. Physiol. Psychol. *66*, 777–779.

RICHTER, C.P. 1941. Total self-regulatory functions in animals and human beings. Harvey Lec. Ser. *38*, 63–103.

ROBBINS, T.W., and FRAY, P.J. 1980. Stress-induced eating: Fact, fiction or misunderstanding? Appetite *1*, 103–133.

RODIN, J. 1980. The externality theory today. *In* Obesity. A.J. Stunkard (Editor). W.B. Saunders, Philadelphia, Pennsylvania.

RODIN, J., and SLOCHOWER, J. 1976. Externality in the obese: The effects of environmental responsiveness on weight. J. Pers. Soc. Psychol. *29*, 557–565.

RODIN, J., MOGENSON, G.J., and BOOTH, D.A. 1980. Editorial. Appetite *1*, 1.

ROZIN, P., and FALLON, A. 1980. The psychological categorization of foods and non-foods: A preliminary taxonomy of food rejections. Appetite *1*, 193–201.

ROZIN, P., and KALAT, J.W. 1971. Specific hungers and poison avoidance as adaptive specializations of learning. Psychol. Rev. *78*, 459–486.

SCALA, J. 1978. Weight control and the food industry. *In* Recent Advances in Obesity Research, Vol. II. G.A. Bray (Editor). Newman, London.

SHAW, J. 1973. The influence of type of food and method of presentation on human eating behavior. Ph.D. dissertation, Department of Psychology, University of Pennsylvania, Philadelphia.

SIEGEL, P.A., and PILGRIM, F.J. 1958. The effect of monotony on the acceptance of food. Am. J. Psychol. *71*, 756–759.

SILVERSTONE, T. 1976. Introduction. *In* Dahlem Workshop on Appetite and Food Intake. Dahlem Konferenzen, Berlin, Germany.

SIMSON, P.C., and BOOTH, D.A. 1973A. Olfactory conditioning by association with histidine-free or balanced amino acid loads. Q. J. Exp. Psychol. *25*, 354–359.

SIMSON, P.C., and BOOTH, D.A. 1973B. Effect of CS-US interval on the conditioning of odour preferences by amino acid loads. Physiol. Behav. *11*, 801–808.

SOLMS, J. and HALL, R.L. (Editors). 1980. Criteria of Food Acceptance: How Man Chooses What He Eats. Forster, Zurich, Switzerland.

STUNKARD, A.J. 1975. Satiety is a conditioned reflex. Psychosom. Med. *37*, 383–387.

WOOLEY, O.W., WOOLEY, S.C., and DUNHAM, R.B. 1972A. Calories and sweet taste: Effects on sucrose preference in the obese and non-obese. Physiol. Behav. *9*, 765–768.

WOOLEY, O.W., WOOLEY, S.C., and DUNHAM, R.B. 1972B. Can calories be perceived and do they affect hunger in obese and non-obese humans? J. Comp. Physiol. Psychol. *80*, 250–258.

WOOLEY, S.C. 1976. Psychological aspects of feeding. *In* Dahlem Workshop on Appetite and Food Intake. T. Silverstone (Editor). Dahlem Konferenzen, Berlin, Germany.

Building Memories for Foods

Lewis M. Barker

I tasted Mom's apple pie recently, and it was as good as I've always remembered it. I've eaten lots of apple pie during the 20 plus years that I've been away from home—yet, as I told her, hers really is the best. She remarked that, indeed, her apple pie was good, that her mother had taught her how to make it, and that *her* mother made the best apple pie that *she* had ever eaten.

Within this personal vignette there are a number of themes that comprise the various topics of the contributors to this volume. These themes include, among others, the transmission of established food habits across generations from parent to child. Other sociocultural factors are evident, including the kinds of foods eaten at family reunions, and the fact that much of our dinner table conversation centers on foods and on previous feeding experiences as a family. The hedonic pleasures of eating, including palatability, are major factors in the food we select, and Mom's apple pie certainly rates highly in this regard.

The aspect of the "Mom's apple pie is best!" phenomenon that I will restrict my discussion to is the quite remarkable feat of memory that is involved. I am intrigued with how that apple pie got into my memory in the first place, and how it persists as such an accurate representation of the chemical, textural, and visual properties of the pie the memory represents, even after 20 years. There is very little scientific literature on "building memories for foods." That which follows is an often speculative, personal view of this process, supported by such empirical evidence as can be garnered.

Ebbinghaus and "Memory for Words"

The scientific study of how humans form memories is in its infancy. About 100 years ago Hermann Ebbinghaus published a book entitled "Memory." For his research he devised the "nonsense syllable" and helped focus the attention of future researchers on the processes of memorization and forgetting of lists of words, symbols, and other written materials (Ebbinghaus 1964). There was an applied emphasis of these early investigations concerning memory. This was due, perhaps, to the educational methods used in the elementary and secondary school systems, namely, a heavy reliance upon rote memorization.

Indeed, learning and remembering words remains essential for successful performance in the modern classroom and most other civilized activities. Learning to read and write places heavy demands on our visual and auditory memory systems. These two memory systems are studied together and appear to be most intimately connected.[1] For the above reasons the study of "memory" has become synonymous with inquiry into the memory formation of the visual and auditory aspects of language. Before we look at "food memories," therefore, we need to look at the conceptually rich models of visual and auditory memory.

INFORMATION PROCESSING MODELS OF MEMORY

The emphasis on visual and auditory memory for words led to the development of a theoretical orientation in the early 1950s, which blended cognitive psychology, traditional perception, and computer analogies. This approach to human memory is known as human information processing. Over the past 25–30 years human information processing experiments have helped us to better understand memory formation, in part by providing a model of memory which incorporates various features, or operating characteristics, of the human nervous system. One such model is displayed as Fig. 5.1. In this diagram the flow of information from outside the human, through various sensory systems, ending eventually in some type of permanent memorial form, is indicated.

---

[1] If while reading you recognize a word, the assumption is made that the word exists in some form as a visual memory. Moreover, since it is typically impossible to "see" the word without saying it—albeit silently—the word must simultaneously exist in auditory memory as well. Vocalization of the word, or writing the word, would further involve the memory systems of, respectively, complicated motor systems involved in vocalization (including the tongue and larynx) and memory systems controlling the fingers at a typewriter or holding a pen.

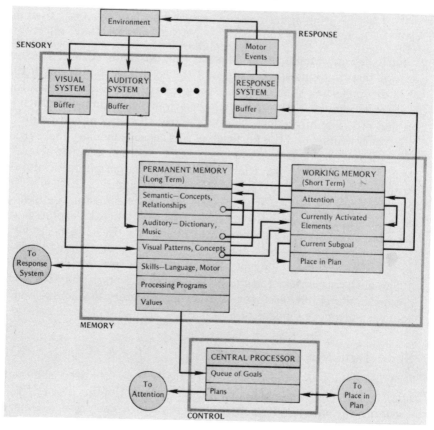

From Dodd & White (1980)

FIG. 5.1. A MODEL OF THE HUMAN INFORMATION PROCESSING SYSTEM

Sensory Memory

We know the most about the initial stages of the information processing scheme presented in Fig. 5.1. The box labeled "sensory" (upper left) is comprised of our knowledge of sensory receptor functioning. Sensory physiologists and sensory psychologists have adequately described, for example, the transduction of photic energy by the rods and cones of the retina, and we can follow the continued processing of this transformed energy through the visual nervous system, many synapses into the brain. The same can be done for hearing, the skin senses, and the chemical senses of taste and olfaction. That indicated in Fig. 5.1 as "sensory" accounts for our observations that environmental events initiate bioelectrical activity which persists for a brief time after the termination of the physical stimulus. In vision these sensory memories of 1–2 sec duration are commonly experienced "afterimages"; in audition these early sensory memories constitute an "echo-box" effect.

Early Sensory Memories for Flavor. The onset and offset characteristics of taste and smell stimuli are sufficiently diffuse that the analogue of afterimages and echo boxes is unclear. In audition, vision, and the skin sense of touch, a stimulus can be briefly presented (abruptly turned on and off). The aftereffect of brief sensory stimulation can be quite easily determined and the duration of this sensory memory measured. (This measure of memory, namely, the brief persistance of neural activity and conscious representation in the absence of a peripheral stimulus, is seldom noticed outside the laboratory.) The chemical senses of olfaction and taste, however, are less discrete. In these "contact senses" a physical stimulus remains in contact with the peripheral receptors (e.g., taste buds and olfactory nerves in the olfactory mucosa, respectively). For as long as these peripheral nerves continue to be stimulated there is sensory nerve activity but not sensory "memory" per se.

The early responses of the taste and smell receptors and attendant nerves, however, do not appear sufficiently different to warrant major deviations from the model in Fig. 5.1.

Short-Term Memory

The second stage of processing is typically conceptualized as a transient, relatively fragile memory of the physical stimulus event. While there are various specifications of the operating characteristics of short-term memory, for present purposes we can liken this aspect of memory to our "span of attention"—the time during which we are aware or are conscious of various aspects of the stimuli that have impinged on our receptors (cf. "working memory," Fig. 5.1). Again, as indicated in the model, most of the experimental work in this area has been concerned with the visual and auditory processing of words, numbers, etc. A commonly cited example that illustrates some of the temporal properties of this stage of memory is the experience of looking up a telephone number and rehearsing it several times by repeating it to yourself as you are dialing the number. If, for whatever reason, you are distracted (i.e., the number temporarily leaves your consciousness), or if you fail to reach your party and try to re-dial in a few minutes, you typically must look up the number again. Various experiments suggest that this short-term store for words and numbers lasts less than a minute. As we will see later, there is some evidence that the working memory for chemical and olfactory stimuli may last longer than for auditory and visual stimuli.

Long-Term Memory

The permanent representation of processed information (labeled "long-term memory" in the figure) is the common sense, dictionary definition of what we ordinarily mean by the term "memory." Various theories address the operating characteristics of long-term memory, including experimentally testable constructs such as forgetting, interference or inhibition during memory retrieval, transfer, generalization, and so forth. Again, the bulk of the experimental work with humans is concerned with semantic memory, the memory for words.

As indicated in Fig. 5.1, humans are "active" information processors. That is, we are not passive organisms upon which stimuli impinge, and due to which a reflexive, automatic memory sequence is initiated. Rather, past memories interact with and influence that which we are presently seeing and hearing and tasting. Expectancy and anticipation and prior memories influence that which is selected for inclusion in working memory. In some unspecified manner we actively select certain features of the environment for further processing, and this selection process draws on our long-term memories.

MEMORIES FOR FLAVORS

The question at hand is whether the foregoing human information processing approach to memory formation can be extended to account for my memory of Mom's apple pie. That is, can a model that was principally formulated to account for the findings of experiments concerned with words, sights and sounds, typically of brief duration, help us understand the formation of memories for foods? There are no clear answers to this question. A statement in a recent textbook in cognitive psychology is representative of the predominance of research interest in visual and auditory aspects of information processing, to the exclusion of research interest in food memory formation.

(In addition to vision and audition) . . . long-term memory also apparently contains codes that correspond to taste and olfaction . . . . We must have these, for how else could we recognize the taste of an orange or the smell of fresh roasted coffee? . . . Clearly visual information ranks somewhere near the top of the list. The prevalence and variety of visual images have made imagery a topic that has captured the attention of cognitive psychologists around the world. Images can be visual, tactual, auditory, gustatory, or olfactory. Thus, if we imagine the appearance of a bag of popcorn, how it feels when we pick up a handful, how it sounds when we munch it in the movies, how it tastes in our mouth, how it smells, we are experiencing a variety of images in the absence of an actual box of popcorn. For the most part psychologists have confined themselves to visual images (Bourne *et al.* 1979).

In the remainder of this chapter, I would like to propose a model for how flavors can get into our various memory systems. This model will be supported with appropriate experimental evidence from studies with laboratory animals. Lastly, and perhaps most importantly, I will attempt to delineate some questions and research strategies concerning the development of flavor memories.

A Model of Taste Memory

Let us begin by accepting in general form the scheme proposed for word memory formation (Fig. 5.1), although there is no *a priori* reason that flavor memory must resemble word memory. Modifications to this basic model include, first, the assertion that humans are born with some flavor memories already present. Presumably, this has no analogue in the word memory system. Second, there is evidence that some flavor memories may be laid down more easily at earlier ages than at adult stages of development. Finally, there are at least four factors that appear to govern the entry of flavor into permanent storage from working memory—factors that are not predicted from existing studies of auditory and visual memory formation.

Inherited Memory for Flavors?

Humans are born with a built-in flavor recognition system which is modified during each individual's lifetime. The existence of innate sensing mechanisms (in the form of the human newborn's relative acceptance of sweet and salty solutions and relative rejection of bitter and sour tastes) can be interpreted as inherited memory for these tastes. Likewise, newborns display appropriate facial expressions to food-related odors, prior to any feeding experiences (Steiner 1977). Referring back to Fig. 5.1 (bottom portion) we can characterize the human, therefore, as being born with certain flavor "expectations" or goals that yield pertinence to the incoming sensory information. Certain flavors predict goal fulfillment, such as satisfying hunger, thereby capturing and directing the infant's attention.[2]

---

[2] It could be alternatively argued that humans inherit various "survival reflexes" (such as the patellar and pupillary reflexes), including sweet-elicited head turning and sucking movements, and bitter elicited oral rejection responses, rather than inherited "memo-

It seems apparent also that these unlearned "flavor expectations" are probably not well developed or differentiated. Indeed, it is these expectations that become modified through experience, and it is to the aspect of memory modification that the present model is directed. Given a basic predisposition to prefer or reject various flavors, how does experience mold our flavor memories?

Stages of Flavor Memory Development

Humans may better remember flavored foods to which they were exposed at particular times of their lives. For example, there is evidence that learned taste aversions to specific flavors develop more readily between the ages of 6 and 12 than at any other comparable time period (Garb and Stunkard 1974). Likewise, studies with laboratory animals indicate that exposure to specific flavors early in development (but not postadolescence) will influence the selection and preference of that flavor during the animal's adult life (Capretta 1977; for an overview of this area see Weiffenbach 1977).

It is not known why a flavor memory system would be time-biased in this manner. At an intuitive level this early developmental memory factor appears to be very important in understanding the "Mom's apple pie is best" phenomenon. There do exist societal constraints on the types of flavor memories that accrue during the first few months through the first few years of our lives. Adults select infant's foods and in large part initially restrict these selections to relatively bland, safe, digestible foods (for which adults have little memory!). Although there is considerable cultural variability, typically humans have 5–10 years experience with culturally defined, parent-selected, safe foods before they are entrusted to make their food selections more or less independently. We may expect, therefore, different demands on our developing flavor memory systems at different stages of development. The previously noted learning of food aversions between 6 and 12 years of age may reflect "foraging errors" of young humans learning to select independently and

ries." Such a view preserves the tabula rasa approach to human development and effectively restricts the definition of memory to "that which is acquired through experience." The posited innate flavor memories differ from traditional reflexes in several ways. First, the feeding reflex is both more complex in expression and imminently more modifiable by experience than are the simpler reflexes. Second, the neonate behaves as if he or she had prior experience with the flavors in question. The neonate appears to do more than "sense" that she is being stimulated; indeed, the recognition response and appropriate behavior adjustment can be taken as evidence that the neonate "perceives" the various flavors to which it is exposed. Finally, unlike the simpler reflexes, changes in responsivity to sour or bitter flavors during the course of a lifetime, for example, are evidence that these inherited flavor memories are modifiable, unlike other survival reflexes.

to ingest appropriate foods. Perhaps it is the increased attention to foods (and flavors) that self-selecting children bring to feeding situations that makes the foods—and the consequences of their ingestion—more memorable. We become aware of apple pie between the ages of 6 and 12?

Working Memory for Flavors

Flavor information enters into our awareness, our consciousness during feeding experiences. The extent to which this flavor information can get from working, or short-term memory, into secondary, or permanent memory, is in part a function of the following four factors.

Intrinsic flavor quality. The intrinsic flavor quality of particular foods in part determines which ones will be remembered. Distinctive flavors are remembered better than bland flavors.

Duration of contact. The duration of contact of these foods with the receptors, and thereby the duration of the representation of the flavor in working memory in part determines what flavors will be represented in permanent memory.

Post-ingestive consequences. The post-ingestive consequences of ingestion of the flavored food is an important factor in memory formation. For example, getting sick after eating fresh pineapple will facilitate memory for the flavor of pineapple.

Flavor rehearsal. There is a cumulative effect of flavors repeatedly experienced on successive meals entering permanent memory. These cumulative trials, or rehearsal-like events, constitute a fourth identifiable factor in building memorial representations of flavors.

The remainder of this paper will present empirical evidence in support of the foregoing considerations.

LABORATORY STUDIES OF FLAVOR MEMORY

Taste Aversion Conditioning Experiments

There are several hundreds of taste aversion conditioning experiments using many species, including humans. Most work has been done on the laboratory rat and these experiments provide us with information concerning the operating characteristics of working or short-term memory. We are here concerned with how this initial processing stage leads to the development of permanent memories (see Best and Barker 1977; Barker, *et al.* 1977, for an overview).

The basic methodology is quite simple. Laboratory rats are first exposed to a target flavor—usually a novel distinctive taste such as saccharin—which initiates a memory trace. This novel flavor is then followed by administration of a sickness-inducing drug. The animal is allowed to recover and is subsequently retested with the target flavor. Typically the rat avoids or rejects the flavor it preferred before the conditioning treatment. It has a new memory of the original flavor.

Flavor Duration Effects of Memory Formation

What kinds of operating characterisitcs of short-term or working memory for flavors can be learned from this experiment? First, we can ask whether the amount or duration of the initial flavor exposure is important in how much flavor aversion is learned. The following experiment provides a preliminary answer to this question.

Independent groups of laboratory rats were allowed to taste and ingest either 0.1 (a "taste") or 1.0 ml (several mouthfuls) of a dilute saccharin solution from a petri dish placed on the floor of their home cage. They were then injected with a solution of sickness-inducing lithium chloride either 0.5, 2 or 21 hr later. The 21-hr groups were the control groups in which the taste experience was separated 21 hr in time from the illness event. Two days later, after all rats had recovered from the effects of the lithium treatment, they were allowed to express their preference for or aversion to the dilute saccharin solution by choosing to drink from either a water-filled bottle or a saccharin-filled bottle attached to their cages. As Fig. 5.2 indicates, those rats *not* having experienced sickness after tasting the saccharin solution preferred the saccharin to water, while those rats which became sick either 0.5 or 2 hr after the brief taste demonstrated an aversion to the saccharin flavor. (The dots represent individual preference scores).

Two findings are of interest in those groups of rats avoiding saccharin. First, those rats drinking the larger amount of saccharin, even though it was only 1.0 ml (in rats that could consume 15 ml within a 10-min drinking period) formed stronger aversions to the saccharin flavor than did the groups which merely tasted 0.1 ml. Second, less aversion was learned when the sickness event followed the saccharin taste by 2.0 hr than by 0.5 hr.

"Longer Tastes" Are Better Remembered.   What do these data tell us about short-term memory? One interpretation is that "longer tastes," or greater amounts tasted, initiate memory traces that last longer and are stronger. Therefore, these tastes are better associated with the sickness event when the animal is poisoned some time later. This interpretation is also a common sense one. Other things being equal, I am going to remember Mom's apple pie better if I eat a whole piece of it than I will if I eat only a bit of it.

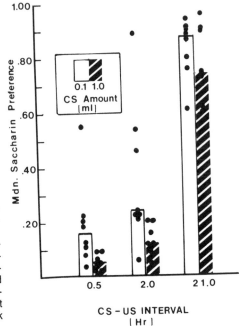

FIG. 5.2. SACCHARIN PREFER-
ENCE FOLLOWING AVERSIVE CON-
DITIONING
The 21-hr groups are controls and prefer saccharin because they failed to associate saccharin ingestion with an illness episode 21 hr later. The 0.5- and
2.0-hr groups avoid the saccharin, especially if they drank the larger amount
(1.0 ml) during conditioning. The black
dots are individual scores.

Flavors Associated with Illness Are Better Remembered. Before
leaving this example, it is important to note that even though these
minute amounts of saccharin that the rats tasted are nonnutritive and
by themselves have little post-ingestive consequence, the sickness induced by the lithium chloride injection most certainly provided a
powerful aversive consequence. Presumably, that is why such a strong
persistent memory for saccharin was evident during the subsequent
preference test in which the saccharin was avoided. Other evidence
leads us to believe that the memory initiated by tasting 0.1 ml of
dilute saccharin in the absence of a sickness experience would not be
so eventful and would not lead to the formation of such a strong memory
trace. We will return to this later.

Flavor Quality Effects on Memory Formation

A second example of the kind of information relevant to a memory
model which can be gained from the taste aversion conditioning methodology is illustrated in Fig. 5.3. This experiment was conducted in a
manner similar to the previous one. Different groups of rats were allowed to drink for 10 min from bottles containing either a sugar solution, a dilute saccharin solution, or cold coffee. Other rats were allowed

to eat as much cheese as they could in the 10-min period of time. All rats were then made sick either 45 min, or 2, 4, 8 or 24 hr later by an injection of lithium chloride. The figure shows the relative preference of each group for their target flavor during preference testing conducted 2 days later.

Strong Aversions to Cheese and Coffee.   Follow first the group which was conditioned to avoid the sugar solution. Note that relative to the 24 hr sugar control group, those rats made sick 45 min or 2 hr after drinking the sugar solution formed quite strong aversions to the sugar. When, however, sickness followed the sucrose drinking by 4 or 8 hr, little to no aversion was learned. Compare these results with the rats drinking coffee. All rats up to and including the 8-hr trace group learned some aversion relative to the 24-hr control group. The cheese groups were even more pronounced in the amount of aversion they learned, while the saccharin groups were intermediate.

Working Memory for Flavors Several Hours Long.   What these data tell us about primary, or short-term, memory is that the quality of flavor is of critical importance in the extent to which the memory for that flavor persists. Some flavors apparently initiate memory traces that are

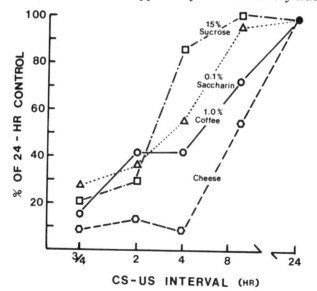

FIG. 5.3.   RELATIVE TO CONTROLS THAT WERE NOT CONDITIONED, PREFERENCE FOR SUCROSE, SACCHARIN, COFFEE, AND CHEESE IS SYSTEMATICALLY REDUCED AS THE FLAVOR-TO-ILLNESS INTERVAL DECREASES
Note that some flavors (e.g., sucrose) do not bridge the flavor-to-illness interval as well as others (e.g., saccharin and coffee). The cheese flavor in this study was the most easily conditioned (most memorable?) of the four flavors.

relatively transient, whereas other flavors persist for several hours. It is not possible to see this from the data presented in Fig. 5.3, but even the coffee and cheese flavor memory traces are transient. Little conditioning can be accomplished with flavor-to-illness intervals extending beyond 8–12 hr—no matter what flavor is used.

Flavor Memory Formation Compared with Word Memory. The data depicted in Fig. 5.2 and 5.3 point up one aspect of short-term memory for flavors that clearly makes flavor memory formation different from word memory formation, namely, the observation that conditioning can be accomplished over intervals of hours rather than minutes for most audiovisual stimuli. This aspect of flavor aversion conditioning has captured the attention of psychologists interested in learning and memory (Barker *et al.* 1977). Note, moreover, that the information processing model depicted in Fig. 5.1 includes no reference to how long an item can be or need be in short-term, or working, memory. We merely need to extend the time duration parameter of working memory to accommodate the above data on flavor memory formation.

Attending to Flavor Enhances Memory. This experiment also allows some conjecture concerning the differences in memory for different flavors. In point of fact, I do not especially remember Mom's mashed potatoes, cooked carrots, or oatmeal. I do remember her potato salad and meat loaf, as well as the apple pie. Some foods and flavors *are* more memorable than others. And, in part, this long-term memory appears to be related to particular flavor characteristics, perhaps because of their attention-getting properties while in short-term memory. These distinctive flavors may be processed longer—attended to and re-attended to for longer periods of time—thereby facilitating entry into long-term representation.

Latent Inhibition and Long-Term Memory

The foregoing taste aversion conditioning experiments are important in indicating some of the factors relevant to short-term memory processing. A second methodology called "latent inhibition," provides information concerning the long-term, relatively more permanent, stage of memory. The basic methodology is quite simple. Subjects are exposed to a target flavor, following which time is allowed to pass. Subjects are then re-exposed to the same target flavor in a conditional pairing with an aversive stimulus. What this procedure accomplishes is to see what effect, if any, the memory formed to the first flavor exposure has on the subsequent aversive conditioning to that flavor. Less conditioning to target flavors which have been previously experienced by subjects is known as "latent inhibition." Conditioning an aversion to the second presentation of the target flavor is apparently interfered with to the degree that the subject *remembers* the first flavor exposure. In this instance, "remembering" has to do with the expectations about the flavor stored in permanent memory following the initial exposure. These expectations influence the primary memory processing during the second flavor exposure (that is, when the conditioning trial occurs).

A Test of Long-Term Flavor Memory. White laboratory rats were allowed to taste and ingest a concentrated sugar solution (20% sucrose in water) for a 1-week period at one of several developmental stages of life. One group drank the sugar solution for 7 days on days 23–30 of their life. Since they were weaned to this sugar solution, they were designated Group Weaning. Other groups had one week's exposure to the sugar solution on days 56–63 (Group Young Adult), and days 115–122 (Group Adult). A sucrose control group had access on all these days, thereby having the most total input into their flavor memory system. A water control group had no prior exposure to the sugar solution and presumably no flavor memory for sucrose. Finally, one group nursed from dams who drank concentrated sugar solutions, thereby sweetening their milk.

"Remembering" Sucrose Makes It Less Aversive. These 1-week periods constituted the first exposure to a sucrose target flavor. The second exposure occurred on day 123 for all groups and was followed immediately by an aversive conditioning treatment. This should normally result in making sucrose taste bad to all rats. The results of a posttreatment preference test for sucrose conducted two days later are displayed in Fig. 5.4. Note first that the water control group which had no exposure to the sucrose solution prior to the conditioning trial shows a strong aversion to the sucrose. Compare that value with the group labeled "Adult," which had previously experienced the sucrose solution for 1 week only a few days before the conditioning treatment. They display markedly less aversion, the classical latent inhibition effect. Presumably, the Adult group remembered their recent sucrose experience and had expectations concerning the solution that caused them to process the flavor differently during the flavor-illness conditioning trial.

The remaining groups are no less interesting. The groups tasting the sucrose initially during the weaning period showed less conditioning than the water control group and more than the Young Adult, Adult, and Sucrose Control groups. This is interpreted as evidence of forgetting, or at least not remembering quite as well, the previous 1-week exposure to the sucrose solution.

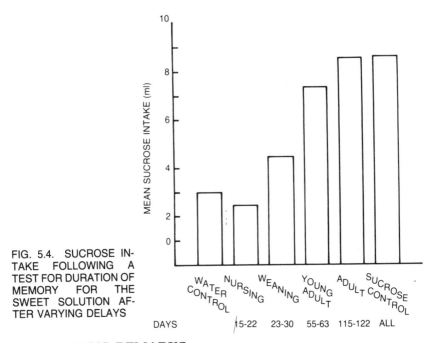

FIG. 5.4. SUCROSE IN-
TAKE FOLLOWING A
TEST FOR DURATION OF
MEMORY FOR THE
SWEET SOLUTION AF-
TER VARYING DELAYS

CONCLUDING REMARKS

The foregoing taste aversion conditioning and latent inhibition experiments do not exhaust the kinds of laboratory-generated information
relevant to the question of how our memories for foods come about. They
are presented as supportive evidence for a human information processing model of flavor memory acquisition. I must admit that I am im-
pressed by how applicable to flavor memory formation the model in Fig.
5.1 seems to be. Recall that this model was initially proposed to account
for how we learn and remember the visual-auditory components of
words. Note also that laboratory rat conditioning experiments provided
supporting evidence for this model.

There are a number of experiments on humans that are suggested by
this information-processing model, including the gathering of basic
psychophysical information on flavor detection. One line of experimen-
tation suggested by Eliot Stellar (see Preface to this volume) would be to
measure the duration of a flavor memory to a brief flavor stimulus by
first presenting the target flavor (or odor), waiting a period of time
(weeks? months?) and asking the subject to identify the target from a
group of similar detractor stimuli. Using this methodology the hypothesis that some flavors are better remembered than others could be tested,
as could hypotheses concerning flavor memory formation in children vs.
adults.

When all is said and done, I am not entirely convinced that I better understand my memory for Mom's apple pie. There is a vividness, an experiential component, of this memory that is entirely lacking in these attempts at laboratory reconstruction and demonstration of the phenomenon. At the same time, the analysis of this memory formation into the various components of flavor duration, vividness, trials, and age of formation may not be totally irrelevant. The suggestion that flavors may be processed in short-term memory longer than words are processed may have some meaningful neurophysiological and neuroanatomical concommitants. Other considerations aside, such an analysis does not in any way detract from the private pleasures of my present memories for certain foods.

REFERENCES

BARKER, L.M., BEST, M.R., and DOMJAN, M. (Editors). 1977. Learning Mechanisms in Food Selection. Baylor University Press, Waco, Texas.

BEST, M.R., and BARKER, L.M. 1977. The nature of "learned safety" and its role in the delay of reinforcement gradient. In Learning Mechanisms in Food Selection. L.M. Barker, M.R. Best, and M. Domjan (Editors). Baylor University Press, Waco, Texas.

BOURNE, L.E., DOMINOWSKI, R.L., and LOFTUS, E.F. 1979. Cognitive Processes. Prentice Hall, Englewood Cliffs, New Jersey.

CAPRETTA, P. 1977. Establishment of food preferences by exposure to ingestive stimuli early in life. In Learning Mechanisms in Food Selection. L.M. Barker, M.R. Best, and M. Domjan (Editors). Baylor University Press, Waco, Texas.

DODD, D.H., and WHITE, R.M. 1980. Cognition: Mental Structures and Processes. Allyn and Bacon, Boston, Massachusetts.

EBBINGHAUS, H. 1964. Memory. H.A. Ruger and C.E. Bussenius (Translators). (Reprint.) Translation of 1885 original first published in 1913 by Teachers College, New York. Dover, New York.

GARB, J.L., and STUNKARD, A.J. 1974. Taste aversions in man. Am. J. Psychiat. 131, 1204–1207.

STEINER, J.E. 1977. Facial expressions of the neonate infant indicating the hedonics of food-related chemical stimuli. In Taste and Development: The Genesis of Sweet Preference. J.M. Weiffenbach (Editor). Publ. No. NIH 77-1068 U.S. Department of Health, Education and Welfare, Bethesda, Maryland.

WEIFFENBACH, J.M. (Editor). 1977. Taste and Development: The Genesis of Sweet Preference. Publ. No. NIH 77-1068 U.S. Department of Health, Education, and Welfare, Bethesda, Maryland.

6

The Influence of Variety on Human Food Selection and Intake

Barbara J. Rolls, Edmund T. Rolls and Edward A. Rowe

In the Western World most people, including those with little nutritional knowledge, select an appropriate balance of nutrients to maintain healthy body functions. Thus, when food is abundant the major nutritional problem is not one of deficiency, but rather that a high proportion of people eat more than is needed to meet energy losses and consequently become obese. In this chapter, we consider the effect that the availability of a wide variety of foods may have on the selection of a balanced diet and on the maintenance of body weight.

Where food is abundant one of the surest ways of ensuring that essential nutrients are consumed is to eat a very varied selection of foods. In doing this we may take in more of some essential nutrients such as amino acids, vitamins, minerals, etc., than we need, but this normally does not matter providing we do not get too fat. An interesting question that arises is whether, in a situation where food is abundant, a variety of foods is selected; or is only the favorite palatable food consumed?

SENSORY SPECIFIC SATIETY AND DIETARY SELECTION

Cafeteria Studies. In her now classic studies of dietary self-selection by newly weaned infants, Davis (1928) found that a nutritionally adequate diet was ingested and normal growth was maintained over a 6–12 month period. The infants who were given a free choice of a variety of foods at every meal had no preconceived ideas about the available foods, since this was their first experience of solids. They often preferred and ate large quantities of foods that would be aversive to many adults, such as raw beef and bone marrow. Generally within any one meal they consumed several solid foods and a drink. Thus, in these infants, the normal strategy was to select a varied and balanced diet, rather than eating the most preferred foods exclusively. It should be added, however, that all the foods were high in nutritional value; there were no highly palatable foods such as cookies, cakes, pastries, etc.

Preference Reversals.   There have been controlled laboratory studies on the selection of foods where one is more preferred than another. It was found in rats that after an initially preferred food (sugar) had been consumed freely just before preference testing, the initial preference was reversed and the rats selected wheat (Young 1940). A similar finding has been reported for fluids. Prior drinking of a distinctively flavored fluid lowers the subsequent palatability of that flavor. For example, in a two-bottle choice situation, preference will shift away from the flavor previously tasted (Morrison 1974).

For some wild predators even highly attractive and abundant prey will rarely become the sole constituent of the diet as long as other food is encountered. It has been suggested that a special "switch" mechanism reduces responsiveness of a predator to a given prey that begins to form too large a part of the menu. Several mammals and birds, when presented exclusively with one palatable food item for a long time, will initially avoid that item when additional, normally less palatable food is also provided (De Ruiter 1967).

Thus, it appears from observations of infants in a cafeteria situation and from studies of wild and laboratory animals that the palatability of foods and consequently the preference for them may change after the foods have been eaten freely. Such shifts in preference would aid the selection of a varied diet. Let us move on, then, to consider the relevance of these findings to food selection in adult man.

Preference Reversals and "Alliesthesia" in Man

In his paper "Physiological role of pleasure," Cabanac (1971) suggested that a stimulus can feel pleasant or unpleasant depending on its usefulness as determined by internal signals. In relation to feeding he found that sweet solutions of sucrose and a food-related smell (orange) were rated as pleasant when subjects were hungry, but after they had been given a load of glucose or sucrose either orally or directly into the stomach, the previously pleasant taste and smell became relatively unpleasant. He called this changing sensation "alliesthesia." In a subsequent extension of the original report it was found that food-related smells became relatively unpleasant after a meal but that nonfood-related smells were unchanged (Duclaux *et al.* 1973). A more recent study has confirmed that many subjects do show this shift in pleasantness of food-related odors after a meal, but some subjects show no change. It is possible that some of the people who did not show a change did not recognize the smells as food related. A most interesting finding was that after the meal there was no change in any subjects in the perceived intensity of the smells, indicating that changes in pleasantness may not simply be due to sensory adaptation or habituation (Mower *et al.* 1977).

What Becomes Unpleasant? Looking at effects of hunger and satiety on the perceived pleasantness of odors tells us a limited amount about a real feeding situation. It appears that the pleasantness of food-related odors changes with feeding, but does this mean that if the odors were actually coming from food, those foods would not be eaten? If there is a change in the perceived pleasantness of odors or foods after eating, how specific is the change? Do only those odors or foods similar to those just eaten become less pleasant or do all food-related odors and foods become relatively unpleasant? We decided to try to answer these questions by testing subjects with real foods (Rolls *et al.* 1981B).

Does Eating a Food Make It Less Palatable During a Meal?

Twenty-four "naive" undergraduates were asked to come to the laboratory for lunch and to do some tasting experiments. They were alone in cubicles and were tested as set out in Fig. 6.1. They were given a plate of eight foods (listed in Fig. 6.2) and were asked to taste them without swallowing and rate how much they liked the taste and how much they

N	First Course (eat as much as like)	Unexpected second course (eat as much as like)
8	Sausage	Sausage
8	Cheese on cracker	Cheese on cracker
4	Sausage	Cheese on cracker
4	Cheese on cracker	Sausage

do ratings   do ratings
2 min after meal

Δ rating

FIG. 6.1. SUBJECTS WERE GIVEN A FIRST COURSE FOLLOWED BY A SECOND COURSE OF EITHER THE SAME OR A DIFFERENT FOOD
Subjects rated the food they were given in the first course and seven other foods for how much they liked the taste and how much they would like to eat before and 2 min after the first course. They were unaware that they would receive the second course until the second rating was complete.

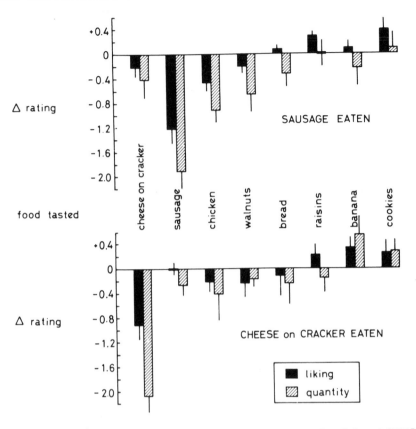

From Rolls et al. (1981B)

FIG. 6.2. THE MEAN CHANGE IN RATINGS (+SEM) OF LIKING OF THE TASTE AND THE QUANTITY SUBJECTS WANTED TO EAT FROM BEFORE THE FIRST COURSE TO 2 MIN AFTER THE FIRST COURSE, FOR THE FOOD EATEN IN THE FIRST COURSE AND SEVEN OTHER FOODS
The results are shown separately for sausage (top) and cheese on cracker (bottom) in the first course.

wanted to eat, on scales ranging from +2 to −2. (For ratings of liking of the taste the scale ranged from +2 = very strong liking to −2 = very strong dislike in 0.5 unit increments. For ratings of the amount of a particular food a subject would like to eat the scale was +2 = very large amount to −2 = none at all). Subjects were then given a plate of food and told that that was their lunch and to eat as much as they wanted. The meal consisted of either sausages or cheese on crackers. These foods were used because they were found in a preliminary study to be eaten in similar amounts, and to be of similar energy densities. Two minutes after they finished the meal subjects were asked to rate the eight foods tasted previously. The changes in rating after the meal are shown in Fig. 6.2. The liking for the food eaten went down significantly more than for the foods not eaten, as did the amount they wanted to eat (both $p < 0.01$.). The changes appeared to be relatively specific to the food which had been eaten. There was little change in the foods not eaten, except that after eating sausages the subjects' liking for the chicken and the quantity they wanted to eat did decrease a little. Interestingly, the fruits (raisins and bananas) and the cookies were liked slightly more after both sausages and cheese on crackers. This could be because people are accustomed to eating these foods as a last course after the main meal or because there was a bigger contrast between these foods and the foods eaten. We conclude that after a meal there is a decrease in the pleasantness or liking of the food eaten, with other foods remaining relatively unchanged. We have shown this effect previously with a different selection of foods (Rolls et al. 1980A).

Are Previously Eaten Foods Consumed In Lesser Quantities?

After the report of our previous experiment we were asked whether this change in liking bears any relation to the amount of a food that would be eaten subsequently. To test this we offered our subjects in the present study an unexpected second course which was either the same food eaten in the first course, or the food not eaten (see Fig. 6.1). The total energy intakes in the two courses are shown in Fig. 6.3. There were no significant differences in the intakes in the first course, but during the second course, subjects ate significantly more if given a different food than if given the same food. In Fig. 6.4 the food intake in the second course is expressed as a percentage of that eaten in the first course. Although the subjects had been told to eat as much as they wanted in the first course and they did not know they were getting more, if they were given a different food in the second course they ate virtually the same amount (i.e., 98%) as they had eaten in the first course. Surprisingly, those subjects given the same food again also ate significant quantities (40% of the amount in the first course). This could have been because they thought they were expected to eat (although the instructions did not imply this), or because giving them a new plate of food, even though it was the same, stimulated them to eat, or that while doing the ratings they regained their appetites. The results for the question of whether the change in liking of a food predicts how much of it will be eaten, are summarized in Fig. 6.4. There is a significant correlation between the change in liking and the energy intake in the second course as a percentage of that in the first course. Thus, when the liking for a particular

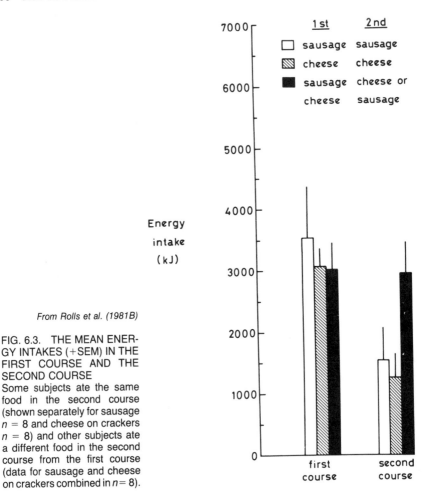

From Rolls et al. (1981B)

FIG. 6.3.   THE MEAN ENER-
GY INTAKES (+SEM) IN THE
FIRST COURSE AND THE
SECOND COURSE
Some subjects ate the same
food in the second course
(shown separately for sausage
n = 8 and cheese on crackers
n = 8) and other subjects ate
a different food in the second
course from the first course
(data for sausage and cheese
on crackers combined in *n* = 8).

food is decreased because it is eaten in a first course, this decrease in
liking is associated with a lower intake of that particular food in a
second course. If a food was not eaten in the first course, the liking for it
was only a little, if at all, decreased, and this was associated with a
relatively large quantity of it eaten in the second course. Similar effects
were found for the rating of the quantity of food the subjects wanted to
eat; this was decreased for the food just eaten and the degree of this
change was correlated with the amount subsequently eaten in the
second course.

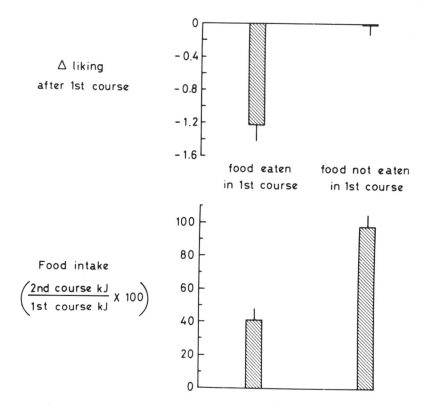

From Rolls et al. (1981B)

FIG. 6.4. (TOP): THE CHANGE IN THE SUBJECTIVE LIKING AFTER THE FIRST COURSE FOR THE FOOD EATEN (SAUSAGE OR CHEESE ON CRACKERS) AND FOR THE FOOD NOT EATEN (CHEESE ON CRACKERS OR SAUSAGE) AFTER THE FIRST COURSE. (BOTTOM): THE CORRESPONDING FOOD INTAKES IN THE SECOND COURSE EXPRESSED AS A PERCENTAGE OF THE FIRST COURSE FOR THE SUBJECTS GIVEN THE SAME FOOD IN THE SECOND COURSE AS IN THE FIRST, OR THE DIFFERENT FOOD IN THE SECOND COURSE
There is strong correlation between the change in liking for a food and the amount that will be eaten ($r = 0.66$, df-22, $p< 0.001$).

Possible Factors in Sensory Specific Satiety

Although we have not yet specifically studied the mechanism through which specific satieties act, it is worthwhile to consider briefly some possibilities. Cabanac (1971) suggested that the changing sensation he observed was due to changes in the internal state or need for particular nutrients. The decrease in pleasantness was found only if the substance ingested was similar to that tasted, i.e., glucose affected sucrose but not salt. This decrease in the pleasantness of sucrose solutions developed slowly after a glucose load, and maximal changes were seen about 45 min after the load. If a sucrose load was swilled in the mouth, but expectorated rather than swallowed, there was no change in the pleasantness of sweet solutions. He was able to observe the changes when the glucose was tubed directly into the stomach or the duodenum (Cabanac and Fantino 1977). Thus, his results favor the postingestive consequences of a load as being necessary for the changing sensation.

Other studies, however, favor the hypothesis that the sensory qualities of the load or meal at least contribute to the decrease in pleasantness. The nonnutritive sweetener, cyclamate, has been found to be nearly as effective in reducing the pleasantness of sucrose solutions as is glucose (Wooley *et al.* 1972). Also, our studies, while not discounting the possibility that postabsorptive factors are involved, indicate that either sensory or cognitive factors must be important in that the change in rating was measured just 2 min after the end of the meal to minimize the opportunity for absorption. In another study, when we measured the change in rating again after 20 min there was no significant further reduction in pleasantness. Another point is that the change in pleasantness tends to be specific to the food eaten. We find, for example, that if a food high in fat is eaten, other high fat foods can remain relatively unchanged. Because this phenomenon can be at least partly specific for the sensory qualities of the food eaten, and is not solely dependent on metabolic feedback, we call the phenomenon "sensory-specific satiety" (Le Magnen 1967).

Adaptation or Habituation?   If the phenomenon we are studying is sensory, is it simply due to sensory adaptation or habituation? We cannot discount this possibility, but there was no indication that when subjects were doing the ratings that they could not taste the food they had been eating. Also, it should be recalled that when Mower *et al.* (1977) studied the effect of a meal on olfactory stimuli, although they observed some decreases in pleasantness, there were no changes in the perceived intensity of the stimuli. There is no way at present of knowing how important cognitive factors are for the change in sensation. It is possible that since people appear to learn how much of a particular food they can eat (see Booth, this volume, Chapter 4), when this limit is exceeded, the food becomes unpleasant. Clearly there is a need for more experiments to determine what factors are involved in specific satieties.

Summary.   Our experiments show that after a meal we prefer less the taste of a food we have been eating, and this change in liking is relatively specific to the food eaten. This change in liking is correlated with how much more of that food we will eat. Thus, if we are offered more of the same food, which has decreased in preference, we will eat less of it. But if we are offered another food, which has not decreased, intake will remain relatively high. Presumably at some stage we become so full that no more food of any kind will be eaten, but more work is needed to understand the relation between internal satiety signals and sensory or environmental influences on feeding. The implications of this finding for the selection of an adequate diet are that if satiety is specific to a food that has been eaten, and if as we eat a food our preference for it changes, we are likely to eat a varied diet, and thus take in essential nutrients. Thus, during a meal which is served in distinctive courses, we may, for example, find that we have had all that we want of the main course, but still have an appetite for the dessert.

THE INFLUENCE OF VARIETY ON FEEDING

Providing a wide variety of foods may be a good way of ensuring that a good balance of nutrients is consumed, but if satiety is specific to a food that has been eaten, it follows that overeating may occur if a wide variety of foods is readily available. Although it might be intuitively supposed that more food will be eaten when the selection is varied, little experimental work has been done in this area.

Laboratory Animal Experiments

The first experiments on the effect of variety on food intake were conducted on the laboratory rat. Le Magnen (1956) found that in a 2-hr period rats that were offered laboratory chow labeled with four different odors in succession ate 72% more than when the chow with just one odor was given. We tried to replicate this experiment, but had some difficulties. We could induce rats to drink more water if a variety of different odors in solution were presented in succession, but to our rats, chow appeared to be just chow no matter how it smelled. However, when we (B.J.R. and E.A.R.) performed a similar experiment using real foods (potato chips, cheese crackers, chocolate covered wafers, and shortbread), we found that in a 2-hr test variety enhanced intake by 50% (Rolls 1979). Cats have also been found to eat more when offered variety. Cats fed three times a day for 3 days ate on average 47% more in 1 day if fed three different diets than when fed one diet (Mugford 1977).

Human Experiments

Data on the effects of variety on human feeding are very scanty. In an unpublished thesis, Shaw (1973) reported that if subjects were allowed to ingest their normal meal intake 15 min prior to a meal they ate significantly more if the preload and meal were different than if they were the same (metrecal and sandwiches were the foods used). Thus, from this experiment it appears that variety stimulates extra intake in a meal. To understand the significance of the variety effect, this experiment needs to be extended in a number of ways. The foods used were very different, e.g., a liquid and a solid. Does the effect occur with foods of the same type, e.g., solids, and if so, how similar can the foods be and still produce an enhancement of appetite? In the study by Shaw, the subjects were not allowed to eat freely in the preload condition. What happens to intake when subjects are allowed to eat as much as they like in a succession of courses? In the study by Shaw the preload preceded the meal by 15 min. What happens when courses follow rapidly in succession as is often the case in a normal meal? Another possibility in studies of variety which must be considered is that the effect is due to the presentation of the preferred food in the variety condition, but not always in the nonvariety tests. We have been conducting a series of experiments designed to examine the enhancement of feeding in a meal by variety.

Effect of Variety of Sandwiches on Amount Eaten

In the first study (Rolls *et al.* 1981B), the subjects were a group of 36 student nurses from the Radcliffe Infirmary, Oxford. All were females aged between 18 and 25. They were told to treat the meal as lunch and to eat as much as they wanted. They thought the object of the study was to assess the saltiness and pleasantness of sandwiches, and did not realize that the number they ate was being counted. Each subject was tested twice: once with sandwiches that all had the same filling, and once with sandwiches with four different fillings (egg, tomato, ham, cheese) presented successively. They were tested alone in cubicles, and did not know which test condition to expect. Each test lasted 32 min and consisted of four 8-min periods. At the start of each period each subject was given a fresh plate of sandwiches and was asked to rate the sensation of hunger on a visual analogue scale. Each whole sandwich had been cut into eight pieces.

The results are shown in Fig. 6.5. During the first 8-min period the subjects ate the same amount in both conditions. However, when the variety was introduced in the subsequent three periods, the subjects ate significantly more. Total intake in the variety condition was increased by 33% ($p < 0.001$), or one whole sandwich. The eating apparently depended on the sensory qualities of the food and not on hunger since there was no relationship between the hunger rating and the amount eaten.

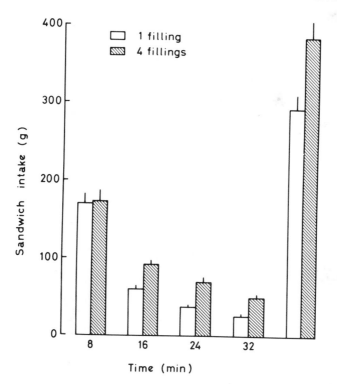

From Rolls et al. (1981A)

FIG. 6.5. THE INTAKE OF PIECES OF SANDWICHES (+SEM) IN FOUR SUCCESSIVE 8-MIN PERIODS WHEN SUBJECTS WERE GIVEN EITHER THE SAME FILLING THROUGHOUT THE TEST (1 FILLING) OR WERE GIVEN FOUR DIFFERENT FILLINGS IN SUCCESSION (4 FILLINGS), ONE IN EACH OF THE TIME PERIODS
The total intakes for subjects eating one filling or the four fillings over the test are shown.

After the first time period, hunger ratings were consistently lower when subjects were eating the variety of sandwiches. It is possible that this enhanced intake was because subjects had a greater chance of receiving a preferred food than in the plain condition. However, this did not have an important influence on the results because the enhancement of intake in the variety condition in those subjects having their most preferred food in the plain condition was not different from that in subjects who had their least preferred food in the plain condition (Rolls et al. 1981A).

Effect of Variety of Yogurt on Amount Eaten

For our next studies we used yogurt because the different flavors are of similar energy densities and the amount eaten was easy to measure.

Subjects were tested four times: with each of three flavors (hazelnut, blackcurrant, orange) presented in succession in a test and with each of the three flavors alone. By testing with each flavor alone we could determine whether consumption of the favorite flavor was comparable to or exceeded the variety condition. A group of 24 students (12 male, 12 female) was studied. Each test lasted 30 min and consisted of three 10-min periods. The results are shown in Fig. 6.6. There was no difference in intake for any of the conditions in the first period. When variety

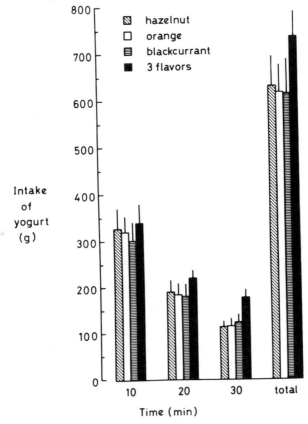

From Rolls et al. (1981A)

FIG. 6.6.   THE AMOUNT OF YOGURT EATEN (+SEM) IN THREE SUCCESSIVE 10-MIN PERIODS WHEN SUBJECTS WERE GIVEN EITHER ONE OF HAZELNUT, ORANGE, OR BLACKCURRANT FLAVOR IN EACH OF THE TIME PERIODS, OR THE THREE FLAVORS SUCCESSIVELY, ONE IN EACH OF THE TIME PERIODS IN COUNTERBALANCED ORDER
The total intakes during the test for subjects eating each of the single flavors or the three successive flavors are shown.

was introduced in the subsequent two periods, intake was lower if the same flavor was given than if a different flavor was introduced. Total intake over the 30-min test was increased by 19.5% in the variety condition ($p<0.001$, matched pairs t test). If the intake of the subject's favorite flavor was compared to that in the variety condition, total intake with the succession of different flavors was still significantly elevated (656.5 ± 74.4 g of favorite; 739.2 ± 54.7 of variety, $p <0.001$) Rolls $et\ al.$ 1981A).

Effects of Color and Texture

In our first yogurt study the flavors used differed not only in taste, but also in color (light brown, pink, and light orange) and texture (small pieces of nut, whole blackcurrants, or small pieces of orange). Since we were interested in how similar foods could be and still produce an enhancement of intake we reduced some of the differences between flavors. Three pink flavors were chosen—cherry, raspberry and straw-berry—thus eliminating any large color difference. The shades of pink varied only slightly, and we also removed any pieces of fruit to eliminate differences in texture. The tastes were distinctive and subjects could tell what flavors they were eating. The procedure was the same as in the previous yogurt study. Twenty-four female student nurses were tested on four different days at lunch time. The results are shown in Fig. 6.7. There was clearly no enhancement of intake in the variety condition. Thus it appears that having a difference in just the flavor of yogurt is not enough to produce an enhancement of intake.

Effects of Three Kinds of Chocolates

To obtain further evidence on this, we looked again at the effect of altering just flavor. For this study we chose three distinctively flavored chocolates (coffee, mint and orange) called Matchmakers (Rowntree Mackintosh). They are all chocolate shaped like small logs with tiny bits of chewy candy dispersed throughout and thus are very similar in appearance and texture. We tested 24 schoolgirls (7–11 years old from the Crescent School, Oxford). The procedure was the same as in the yogurt studies except rather than the test being a meal it was the last course of lunch. Subjects were tested with each individual flavor and in the variety condition. The experiment consisted of three successive time blocks of 6 min each. The results are shown in Fig. 6.8. Again, although the flavors were distinctive, there was no enhancement of intake when the variety was offered.

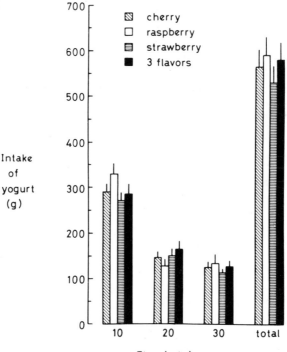

From Rolls et al. (1981A)

FIG. 6.7.   THE AMOUNT OF YOGURT EATEN (+SEM) IN THREE SUCCESSIVE 10-MIN PERIODS WHEN SUBJECTS WERE GIVEN EITHER ONE OF CHERRY, RASPBERRY, OR STRAWBERRY FLAVOR IN EACH OF THE TIME PERIODS, OR THE THREE FLAVORS SUCCESSIVELY, ONE IN EACH OF THE TIME PERIODS IN A COUNTERBALANCED ORDER
The total intakes for subjects eating each of the single flavors or the three successive flavors are shown.

Further Studies of the Effects of Color on Intake

Thus, in foods of the same basic type, changes in flavor alone did not enhance food intake. It is possible that appearance, texture or some other feature of foods might be important. One interesting property of foods to study experimentally is color and we used candy. Smarties (Rowntree Mackintosh) are small disks of chocolate covered with a thin colored sugar layer (they are very similar to M and M's in America). The Smarties we used did not differ in taste. We tested 24 13-year-old boys from St. Edward's School, Oxford. There were four 7-min time blocks

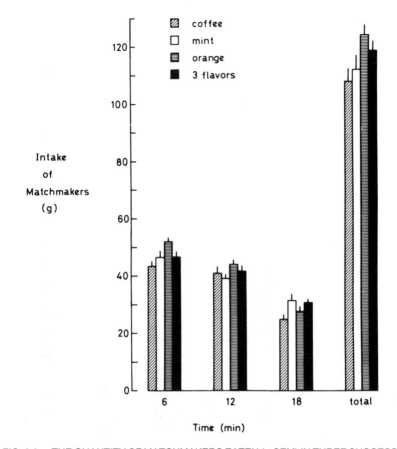

FIG. 6.8:   THE QUANTITY OF MATCHMAKERS EATEN (+SEM) IN THREE SUCCESSIVE
6-MIN PERIODS WHEN SUBJECTS WERE GIVEN EITHER ONE OF COFFEE, MINT, OR
ORANGE FLAVOR IN EACH OF THE TIME PERIODS, OR THE THREE FLAVORS SUC-
CESSIVELY, ONE IN EACH TIME PERIOD IN COUNTERBALANCED ORDER
The total intakes over the test are shown for each of the three flavors and for the three
flavors given successively.

since we were using four different colors (pink, yellow, green, violet).
The boys were tested three times under the following conditions: with
their favorite color presented in all four time blocks (if only one plain
condition is being run, it is essential that the food be the favorite to
control for the possibility that consumption of the favorite in the variety
condition may be responsible for any increased intake); with all four
colors presented in succession, one in each time block; with all four

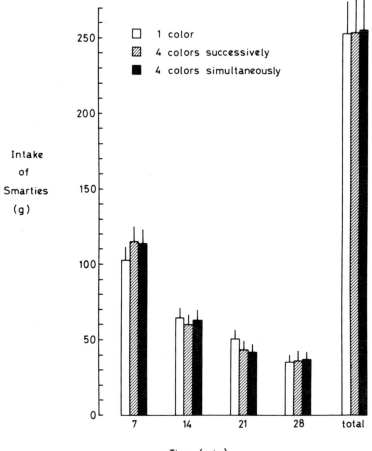

FIG. 6.9. THE QUANTITY OF SMARTIES EATEN (+SEM) IN FOUR SUCCESSIVE 7-MIN PERIODS WHEN SUBJECTS WERE GIVEN EITHER ONE OF FOUR COLORS (GREEN, PINK, YELLOW, VIOLET) IN EACH OF THE PERIODS, OR THE FOUR DIFFERENT COLORS SUCCESSIVELY, ONE IN EACH PERIOD IN COUNTERBALANCED ORDER, OR THE FOUR COLORS SIMULTANEOUSLY IN EACH OF THE FOUR PERIODS
The total intakes throughout the test for the different conditions are also shown.

colors presented simultaneously as a mixture in each time block (since part of the appeal of these sweets is the mixture of colors). The results are shown in Fig. 6.9. The variety of colors presented either in succession or simultaneously did not affect food intake. We have confirmed this result with an additional group of 6- to 11-year-old school girls. Thus, although the bright and varied colors of these sweets may be important in marketing, color has little effect on the amount consumed by an individual in the short term.

Summary of Present Studies

In summary, our experiments on variety indicate that if several foods are offered, which differ in taste, appearance, texture, etc., more will be consumed in a meal than if only one food is given, even if that food is the favorite. It appears that the more dissimilar the foods are, the more likely it is that the effect will appear. If foods of the same basic type (i.e., yogurt or candy) differ just in flavor or just in color there appears to be no enhancement of intake. It seems likely, however, that changing flavor alone could give an effect if the flavors were more distinctive. In our tests the foods, although different flavors, had strong background flavors coming from the yogurt or chocolate, and all were sweet. Cabanac (1971) found that sweet and salty tastes led to different responses when pleasantness was rated after loads of sugar. It seems likely that flavors which differ fundamentally, i.e., sweet, sour, bitter, salty, will produce an enhancement of intake if presented in succession (Rolls et al. 1982). Certainly the cuisines of various cultures consist of a composite of these fundamental flavors (see E. Rozin, this volume, Chapter 11).

Variety in Meals. In our experiments the usual procedure was to present the various foods in successive courses. Meals were also typically served as a buffet with many different foods available simultaneously. Intuitively it seems likely that variety would also act as an appetite stimulant in this situation. It has been found experimentally that the simultaneous presentation of sausage rolls, egg rolls, and pizzas led to a greater intake than did presentation of any of the foods served alone (Pliner et al. 1980). It is, however, particularly difficult in a situation where an assortment of food is presented together to know if the increased intake was simply due to the greater likelihood that the favorite food would be available.

VARIETY, MONOTONY AND OBESITY

We have only studied the enhancing effect of variety on appetite in short-term tests, but it might be interesting to speculate about the contribution that the very varied diet we encounter might make to the development of obesity. Jordan and Eyton (1979) give the following advice to readers of a well-known slimming magazine:

> Variety, in taste and texture of food, is certainly one of the greatest appetite stimulants. At least one medical expert we know, experi-

menting in the field of obesity control, is beginning to wonder whether the common practice of making diets as varied as possible is such a good thing. Certainly, every obesity expert knows that if food choice of any overweight person is restricted to just one or two foods, this will result in an inevitable reduction of calorie intake—even if those two foods are calorie-laden cream cakes and dough-nuts! Without variety, our appetites are greatly diminished.

They go on to recommend that a good aid to weight control is to keep the number of foods and courses in a meal to a minimum to provide the essential nutrients. It is clearly established that offering laboratory rats a variety of palatable energy dense foods leads to the development of obesity (Sclafani and Springer 1976; Rolls et al. 1980B). It has also been shown that over 3- to 6-day periods the provision of a plentiful and varied supply of palatable foods will lead to overeating and weight gain in both obese (Porikos et al. 1977) and normal weight subjects (Porikos et al. 1982). It is quite possible, however, that if the diet were offered longer, and if weight began to rise dramatically, cognitive or physiologi-cal controlling mechanisms might enable some individuals to resist the stimulating influence of variety on appetite. Clearly with the enormous problem that weight control now presents, it is important to initiate long-term studies of the influence of variety on weight gain.

Monotonous Diets

Although the long term effects of increased variety on body weight regulation have not yet been established in man, there have been controlled studies of the effect of monotony of the diet. These studies have been primarily concerned with the psychological effects of offering little change in daily menus, as might occur, for example, with soldiers in the field. Most people could probably list a number of foods that they could eat day after day without tiring of them. For example, most staple foods such as bread, milk, eggs, and cereals would be put in this catego-ry, as might sweets. Other foods, however, sometimes even those which are highly preferred (lobster perhaps), if eaten often, will decline in palatability. Studies in both the laboratory and in the field with army rations have confirmed these observations. If either two (with approxi-mately 15 foods) or four (with 41 foods) daily menus are repeatedly presented, the palatability of some of the food declines significantly (Schultz and Pilgrim 1958; Siegal and Pilgrim 1958). Staple foods and foods of high initial rating showed little decline in palatability over 18 days when two daily menus were alternated or over 37 days when four daily menus were used. Other foods which had a low initial rating and particular types of foods such as tinned meats declined significantly in pleasantness during the tests, and for these foods there was no recovery to initial pleasantness levels over the next 3–6 months.

Self-Selection of Monotonous Diets

Monotony in the diet, moreover, led to frequent complaints of gastrointestinal upsets and to decreased consumption of foods of low palatability in the above studies. Unfortunately, these studies cited did not report total food intakes or body weights, so we do not know if decreased acceptance of some foods was balanced by increased consumption of others. A further study has attempted to clarify some of the factors that contribute to food monotony (Kamen and Peryam 1961). They compared the effects over 24 days of offering a 3-day menu cycle (48 foods that were either preplanned by someone else or self-selected) or a 6-day cycle (80 foods preplanned by someone else). Smaller monotony effects were observed in this study than in the earlier ones, and there were no significant changes in body weight. The main finding was that self-selection of the items to be included in a repetitive diet reduces dissatisfaction with the diet. Overall satisfaction with the 3-day self-planned diet was at the same level as the 6-day preplanned diet. Both of these diets were superior to the 3-day preplanned diet.

Thus, all of the studies of monotony in the diet indicate that a number of factors may influence the decline in acceptability of a food as it is given repeatedly; for example, the basic food type is important, and its initial palatability rating and who selected the food for the menu are also significant. It appears that the sensory specific satiety that we observed within a single meal can extend beyond a meal to general acceptability of a food if some foods are presented too often. It is not known whether the decline in acceptability of some foods only occurs in societies where food is plentiful and varied. Studies of sensory specific satiety and of monotony have not been conducted in people used to subsisting on a repetitive diet.

Liquid Diets. The only studies of the effect of a monotonous diet on the maintenance of body weight have employed liquid diets. Both obese (Hashim and van Itallie 1965) and normal weight individuals (Cabanac and Rabe 1976) voluntarily restrict food intake and lose weight when consuming a complete liquid diet for 3 weeks. This decrease in intake may be a function of the relatively low palatability of the liquid diet compared to normal foods as well as to the lack of variety. These findings suggest that body weight maintenance at "normal" levels depends to some extent on the availability of a varied diet.

CONCLUSIONS

Having a variety of foods available aids the selection of a nutritionally balanced diet. We appear to have an inbuilt mechanism that helps to ensure that we consume a variety of foods. As a particular food is eaten its taste is liked less, but the taste of other foods and the desire to eat them remains relatively unchanged. Thus to keep palatability at a high level we will select a varied diet. The changes in liking for foods eaten and not eaten are highly correlated with the amount of those foods that will be eaten if an unexpected second course if offered. This implies that more will be eaten of a varied meal than one consisting of a single food. This has been shown to be the case if subjects are offered in succession a variety of sandwiches or yogurt with distinctive flavor, texture and appearance. It seems that the more dissimilar the foods are the more likely it is that the enhancing effect of variety will be seen. This stimulating effect of variety may extend beyond a single meal in man and may lead to excessive weight gain. On the other hand when some foods are presented frequently, they become relatively unpleasant and may no longer be consumed even some months after the last presentation. The long-term effects of a monotonous diet on weight maintenance have not yet been adequately assessed. Ingestion of just a monotonous (but also relatively unpalatable) liquid diet will lead to weight loss, but the effects of a more normal montonous diet have not yet been determined. Clearly, if we are to understand food selection during a meal and over a longer period of time, more studies are needed on the influence of variety on feeding.

ACKNOWLEDGMENT

Our research is supported by the Medical Research Council on Great Britain. We thank Rowntree Mackintosh Limited for supplying the Matchmakers and Smarties and Associated Milk Products Limited for supplying the yogurt. We are grateful to the nursing staff of the John Radcliffe Hospital and the staffs of the Crescent School and St. Edward's School for providing us with subjects for the studies. We also thank all of the subjects who so willingly took part in the experiments.

The following researchers' collaboration in some of the foregoing experiments is hereby acknowledged: K. Sweeney, B. Kingston, F. Bowen, R. Gunary, A. Megson, and G. Patterson.

REFERENCES

CABANAC, M. 1971. Physiological role of pleasure. Science *173*,1103–1107.

CABANAC, M. and FANTINO, M.   1977.   Origin of olfactory-gustatory alliesthesia: Intestinal sensitivity to carbohydrate concentration?   Physiol. Behav. *18*, 1039–1045.

CABANAC, M., and RABE, E.F.   1976.   Influence of a monotonous diet on body weight regulation in humans.   Physiol. Behav. *17*, 675–678.

DAVIS, C.M.   1928.   Self selection of diet by newly weaned infants.   Am. J. Dis. Child. *36*, 651–679.

DE RUITER, L.   1967.   Feeding behavior of vertebrates in the natural environment.   *In* Handbook of Physiology, Section 6, Vol. 1.   American Physiological Society, Washington, DC.

DUCLAUX, R., FEISTHAUER, J., and CABANAC, M.   1973.   Effects of eating a meal on the pleasantness of food and non-food odors in man.   Physiol. Behav. *10*, 1029–1033.

HASHIM, S.A. and VAN ITALLIE, T.B.   1965.   Studies in normal and obese subjects with a monitored food dispensing device.   Ann. N.Y. Acad. Sci. *131*, 654–661.

JORDAN, H., and EYTON, A.   1979.   Temptations.   Slimming Magazine *62*, 86.

KAMEN, J.M., and PERYAM, D.R.   1961.   Acceptability of repetitive diets.   Food Technol. *15*, 173–177.

LE MAGNEN, J.   1956.   Hyperphagia induced in the white rat by alteration of the peripheral satiety mechanism.   C. R. Soc. Biol. *150*, 32–35.   (French).

LE MAGNEN, J.   1967.   Habits and food intake.   *In* Handbook of Physiology, Section 6, Vol. 1.   American Physiological Society, Washington, DC.

MORRISON, G.R.   1974.   Alterations in palatability of nutrients for the rat as a result of prior tasting.   J. Comp. Physiol Psychol. *86*, 56–61.

MOWER, D.G., MAIR, R.G., and ENGEN, T.   1977.   Influence of internal factors on the perceived intensity and pleasantness of gustatory and olfactory stimuli.   *In* The Chemical Senses and Nutrition.   M.R. Kare and O. Maller (Editors).   Academic Press, New York.

MUGFORD, R.A.   1977.   External influences on the feeding of carnivores.   *In* The Chemical Senses and Nutrition.   M.R. Kare and O. Maller (Editors).   Academic Press, New York.

PLINER, P., POLIVY, J., HERMAN, C.P., and ZAKALUSNY, I.   1980.   Short-term intake of overweight individuals and normal weight dieters and non-dieters with and without choice among a variety of foods.   Appetite *1*, 203–213.

PORIKOS, K.P., BOOTH, G., and VAN ITALLIE, T.B.   1977.   Effect of covert nutritive dilution on the spontaneous food intake of obese individuals: A pilot study.   Am. J. Clin. Nutr. *30*, 1638–1644.

PORIKOS, K.P., HESSER, M., and VAN ITALLIE, T.B.   1982.   Calorie regulation in normal weight men maintained on a palatable diet of conventional foods.   Physiol. Behav. *29*, 293–300.

ROLLS, B.J. 1979. How variety and palatability can stimulate appetite. Nutr. Bull. *5*, 78–86.

ROLLS, B.J., ROWE, E.A., and ROLLS, E.T. 1980A. Appetite and obesity: Influences of sensory stimuli and external cues. *In* Nutrition and Lifestyles. M.R. Turner (Editor). Applied Science Publishers, London.

ROLLS, B.J., ROWE, E.A., and TURNER, R.C. 1980B. Persistent obesity following a period of consumption of a mixed, high energy diet. J. Physiol. *298*, 415–427.

ROLLS, B.J., ROWE, E.A., ROLLS, E.T., KINGSTON, B., MEGSON, A., and GUNARY, R. 1981A. Variety in a meal enhances food intake in man. Physiol. Behav. *26*, 215–221.

ROLLS, B.J., ROLLS, E.T., ROWE, E.A., and SWEENEY, K. 1981B. Sensory specific satiety in man. Physiol. Behav. *27*, 137–142.

ROLLS, B.J., ROWE, E.A., and ROLLS, E.T. 1982. How flavour and appearance affect human feeding. Proc. Nutr. Soc. *41*, 109–117.

SCHUTZ, H.E., and PILGRIM, F.J. 1958. A field study of monotony. Psychol. Rep. *4*, 559–565.

SCLAFANI, A., and SPRINGER, D. 1976. Dietary obesity in adult rats: Similarities to hypothalamic and human obesity syndromes. Physiol. Behav. *17*, 461–471.

SIEGEL, P. S., and PILGRIM, F.J. 1958. The effect of monotony on the acceptance of food. Am. J. Psychol. *71*, 756–759.

SHAW, J. 1973. The influence of the type of food and method of presentation in human eating behavior. Ph.D. Dissertation. University of Pennsylvania, Philadelphia, Pennsylvnia.

WOOLEY, O.W., WOOLEY S.C., and DUNHAM, R.B. 1972. Calories and sweet taste: Effects on sucrose preference in the obese and nonobese. Physiol. Behav. *9*, 765–768.

YOUNG, P.T. 1940. Reversal of food preferences of the white rat through controlled pre-feeding. J. Gen. Psychol. *22*, 33–66.

7

The Synergistic Properties of Pairs of Sweeteners

James C. Smith, David F. Foster, and Linda M. Bartoshuk

Humans and laboratory rats respond in characteristic ways to both nutritive and nonnutritive sweeteners. For reasons that are not well understood, the perceived sweetness of pairs of sweeteners mixed together is greater than would be predicted from tasting either alone. In this chapter we will focus on experiments with both humans and laboratory rats that shed light on how we perceive sweeteners.

POLYDIPSIA FOR A SACCHARIN/GLUCOSE MIXTURE IN THE LABORATORY RAT

The laboratory rat prefers sweetened solutions to water in almost any concentration of nutritive or nonnutritive sweeteners. However, the total amount of sweet fluid consumed varies considerably with the concentration of the solution. With the nutritious sweeteners, this variation depends not only on the inferred taste in the rat, but on caloric input and other postingestional factors. On the other hand, intake of the nonnutritive sweeteners such as sodium saccharin is not influenced by osmolarity or caloric intake and these intakes are thought to be regulated primarily by the taste of the solution.

Valenstein *et al.* (1967) experimented with laboratory rats and measured the daily consumption of a mixture of the nutritive and nonnutritive sweeteners, glucose and sodium saccharin. They reported a profound polydipsia (markedly enhanced fluid intake) and referred to a synergistic action of saccharin and glucose. In their initial experiments they presented saccharin and glucose mixtures in one bottle, with either

3% glucose, 0.25% saccharin or water in another bottle and in each case found a marked preference for the glucose + saccharin (G+S) mixture. (The mixture consisted of 30 g of dextrose, either 1.25 or 2.50 g of sodium saccharin, and a liter of water). They reported that average daily intake was nearly 200 ml and that some rats' total consumption exceeded its' own body weight. This extraordinary drinking behavior had not previously been reported with any other solutions and it seemed to be dependent on the appropriate mixture of the glucose and saccharin. Valenstein et al. (1967) concluded that the G+S mixture may be a very palatable solution to the rat, possibly because the small amount of glucose added to the mixture eliminated the bitter taste component of saccharin but was not concentrated enough to appreciably affect caloric intake and osmolarity.

The motivational properties in the laboratory rat of this "synergistic action" are truly remarkable and have been largely overlooked by investigators in regulation of fluid intake. We began several years ago to replicate the work of Valenstein and his co-workers and to extend their findings in order to more clearly understand the basis of this excessive drinking behavior. With the standard G+S mixture we have also observed extremely high average daily intakes of the sweetened solution. It is of interest to look at a particular male rat as an example. The rat in question consumed 440 ml of G+S in a 24-hr period. While normal daily H_2O consumption by this rat averaged about 35 ml, when G+S was presented the daily fluid intake increased by an order of magnitude. In this case the caloric intake from the G+S would be about 51 calories. And since the normal daily food intake would be about 22 g or 79 calories, it can be seen that the caloric input from the G+S is not trivial.

The behavior of this rat is markedly altered during a 24-hr period. Assuming that licking rate is stable (at 5–6 licks/sec) this rat would have had to lick the G+S spout over 58,000 times, spending over 3 hr in the process, compared to approximately 15 min., which would have normally been spent drinking H_2O. It seemed to us that if we were to understand why the G+S phenomenon occurred, an important component of this understanding could come from knowing how the rat drinks the solution. Indeed, is local lick rate important? Does the rat have more drinking bouts or merely larger drinking bouts? Is more fluid taken per lick?

Analysis of Drinking Patterns

A detailed analysis of G+S drinking in the rat has been reported (Smith et al. 1980) and here we will merely summarize the most important features.

Observations were made of *ad libitum* food and water drinking of six rats for 7 days followed by G+S drinking for 7 days and then a return to an *ad libitum* food and water period. The mean total fluid intake and mean number of licks increased significantly during the G+S phase. The mean fluid per lick and modal interlick interval (local lick rate) did not change, however, when the G+S was presented. The average frequency of drinking episodes or bouts increased by a small amount. The most significant change was the large increase in bout size and bout duration. In summary, the rats initiated drinking the G+S only a few more times but once started, the G+S bout lasted on the average four times longer than that of a water bout. A typical computer generated interlick interval frequency distribution for a water session and a G+S session can be seen in Fig. 7.1. Licking on the G+S tube exceeded water

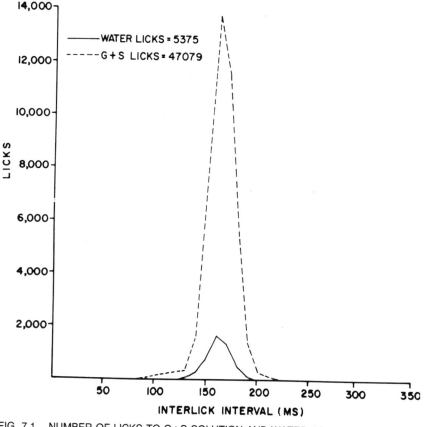

FIG. 7.1. NUMBER OF LICKS TO G+S SOLUTION AND WATER AS A FUNCTION OF INTERLICK INTERVAL FOR ONE RAT (NO. 5)
Modal interlick interval was 160 msec for both fluids. Bin resolution was 10 msec.

drinking by a factor of 9, but the local rate of licking for both solutions was about 6 licks/sec.

Analysis of Caloric Intake

Our next investigation attempted to determine the role, if any, played by caloric input from the G+S solution in the maintenance of these larger drinking bouts. Valenstein et al. (1967) noticed that food consumption was lowered by about 20% from normal when the rats were drinking the G+S solution. We replicated this finding and studied the proportions of total caloric intake which came from the G+S solution and from the laboratory chow. The assumption was made that if drinking G+S did indeed lower food intake, this alteration in diet could, in turn, possibly be involved in the excessive drinking of the G+S solutions.

During a baseline period of 1 week food and water intake were measured in six rats. The next week the rats received 24-hr preference tests between G+S and water. For the final week, the rats were returned to ad libitum food and water intake. During the G+S period, food intake dropped from an average of 20.6 g to 17.9 g, a difference that was statistically significant. The mean daily caloric intake measured during the G+S period was 94.4 calories, a significant increase over baseline levels of approximately 79 calories. About 32% of the calories came from the G+S solution, and this significant caloric input may, therefore, be important in the maintenance of the G+S drinking bouts.

It is also possible that the excessive drinking of G+S results from conflicting information the rat receives from the oral cavity and from caloric counting mechanisms. The G+S solution could result in a very strong sweet taste, but yield only a small caloric feedback from the weak 3% glucose concentration. The hypothesis would be that the failure for an early ending of a drinking bout results from an attempt on the rat's part to increase the caloric input to more nearly match the taste of the sweet solution. In order to test this hypothesis, we compared G+S drinking in one group of rats with glucose drinking in another for both solutions. With the concentration of glucose increasing, the caloric input would be greater resulting in less discrepancy between taste input and caloric input.

After a period of baseline food and water intake, twelve G+S rats and twelve glucose rats were subjected to week-long tests with 24%, 12%, 6% and 3% glucose concentrations. The order of presentation was counterbalanced within each group and was found to not have any effect. The concentration of saccharin in the G+S solutions remained constant at 1.25 g/liter throughout.

The average daily consumption over the weekly periods for each solution is presented in Fig. 7.2. The vertical dotted lines in the figure show that the difference in G+S and glucose drinking decreases significantly as the concentration of the glucose increases. At face value, it looks as if the discrepancy between taste and caloric feedback could play a significant role in the rat's excessive drinking of the 3% G+S solution. However, when one looks at total caloric intake in these testing situations a quite different picture emerges. In Fig. 7.3 the total calories—

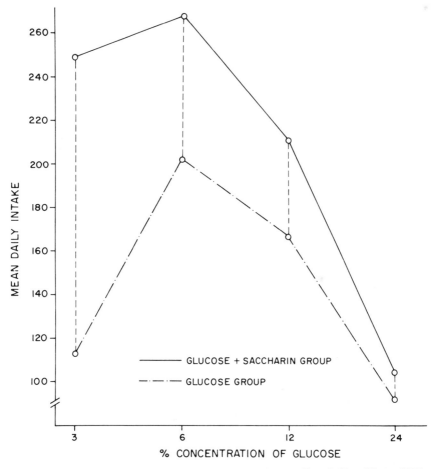

From Smith and Foster (1980)

FIG. 7.2.   MEAN DAILY INTAKE OF GLUCOSE AND GLUCOSE + SACCHARIN GROUPS IN TWO-BOTTLE 24-HR TESTS VS. WATER IS GIVEN AS A FUNCTION OF GLUCOSE CONCENTRATION
The difference in intake between the two groups for each concentration is represented by the vertical broken line. Water data were not plotted.

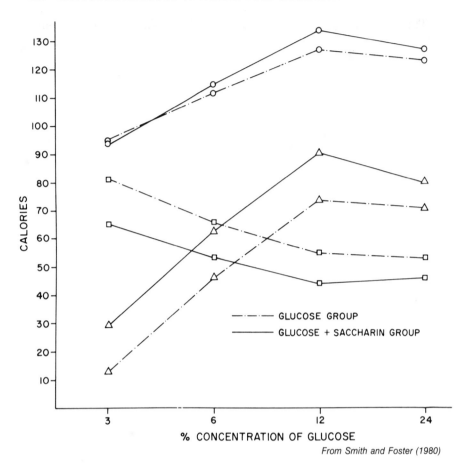

From Smith and Foster (1980)

FIG. 7.3.   CALORIES CONSUMED AT FOUR LEVELS OF GLUCOSE CONCENTRATION
FOR BOTH GLUCOSE AND GLUCOSE + SACCHARIN GROUPS IS SHOWN FOR CALO-
RIES TAKEN FROM THE FLUID (TRIANGLES), FROM LABORATORY CHOW (SQUARES),
AND FROM THE TWO SOURCES COMBINED (CIRCLES)

calories from the food and calories from the solutions—are plotted as a
function of each glucose concentration.

The difference between G+S and glucose solutions seen in Fig. 7.2 as
glucose concentration changes is not apparent in Fig. 7.3. The difference
in caloric intake between G+S and glucose rats remains constant at
about 15 calories for each concentration. Furthermore, the compensat-
ing difference in caloric intake from the food for these groups results in
an absence of differences in total caloric intake for the G+S and glucose
group at *any* concentration. These data make it likely that caloric input
plays little if any part in the large increase in drinking when G+S is
presented to the rat.

In fact, more and more evidence is available that indicates that this palatable solution is consumed largely on the basis of taste. If caloric input played any role, it seems likely that the preference for G+S would gradually build up over several hours or days. Valenstein *et al.* (1967) found that in the initial 30 min of contact with the G+S solution, nondeprived rats drank ten times more G+S than water. Even more dramatically, Smith *et al.* (1976) showed that even in the first 10 min of contact with the G+S solution, the rat drinks more G+S at a faster overall rate than a saccharin solution. While the local lick rate (about six per sec) does not differ for the G+S and the saccharin solutions during this 10-min test, the G+S drinking is more steady than saccharin drinking almost from the first minute of contact. On the average, the rat drinks about twice as much G+S as either glucose or saccharin in the first 10 min of contact with the solutions.

Analysis of Oral Factors

A second line of evidence that taste is the predominant determinant of G+S drinking comes from an experiment by Smith and Foster (1980). In this experiment various concentrations of G+S, glucose, or saccharin were tested against each other in 24-hr two-bottle tests. We wanted to know if the rat would treat the G+S mixture as a nutritive sweetener or as a nonnutritive sweetener. If the rat is first given the choice of one of three concentrations of a nonnutritive sweetener (sodium saccharin) or water, more of the middle range concentrations than of the higher or lower concentrations of saccharin solution is consumed. For example, the rat consistently takes more of 0.125% than of either 0.0125% or 1.25% saccharin. Moreover, if given a choice between 0.125% and 0.0125% saccharin or 0.125% and 1.25%, the rat prefers the 0.125% over the lower and higher concentrations, and there is a slight preference of 0.0125% over 1.25% saccharin. These preferences are presumably made from taste alone since there is no caloric feedback from the saccharin solutions.

Sugars, on the other hand, are handled differently. The laboratory rat drinks more of the middle than of the higher and lower concentrations of glucose when the glucose has been paired with water. For example, more 3% glucose is taken than is either of the 1% or 24% glucose solutions. When these solutions are paired with each other, i.e., 1% vs. 24%, 1% vs. 3%, and 3% vs. 24%, the rat always drinks more of the higher concentrations than of the lower ones. This drinking is presumably determined not only by the taste of the solution, but by caloric feedback during these 24-hr tests.

Now, if one pairs a low, middle, and high concentration of G+S with water, it can be seen that more of the middle concentration of solution is consumed. In Fig. 7.4 it can be seen that more 3% G+S is consumed than 1% G+S or 24% G+S. (The concentration of the glucose is varied in these solutions, but the concentration of saccharin remains constant at 0.125% for all three solutions.) If one now pairs these concentrations of G+S against each other, i.e., 1% G+S vs. 3% G+S, 1% G+S vs. 24% G+S, and 3% G+S vs. 24% G+S, the rat drinks more of the 3% G+S than of the 1% G+S or the 24% G+S and slightly more of the 1% G+S than of the 24% G+S. The rat treats G+S as if it is noncaloric—in the same manner as he treats sodium saccharin—in spite of the fact that it is the glucose concentration that is varied in these solutions. We take this as further evidence that the G+S phenomenon is the result primarily of oral inputs and not postingestional factors.

Another line of evidence implicating the predominance of oral factors in controlling the intake of G+S solution comes from experiments in which the glucose and saccharin are presented in separate bottles. First, we noted that when Valenstein *et al.* (1967) provided rats with 0.125% saccharin and 3% glucose in separate bottles, the total fluid consump-

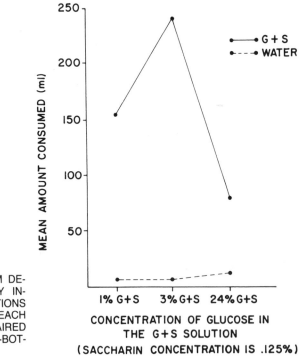

FIG. 7.4. HISTOGRAM DE-PICTING MEAN DAILY IN-TAKE OF G+S SOLUTIONS AND WATER WHEN EACH G+S SOLUTION IS PAIRED WITH WATER IN TWO-BOT-TLE 24-HR TESTS

CONCENTRATION OF GLUCOSE IN
THE G+S SOLUTION
(SACCHARIN CONCENTRATION IS .125%)

tion never exceeded 65 ml. Reasoning that *when mixed together*, these solutions yield a G+S mixture half as concentrated as the standard G+S solution, we offered the rat 0.25% saccharin vs. 6% glucose in separate bottles. The total consumption of these concentrations was *not* significantly different from the G+S consumption of the rats when offered the standard G+S solution paired with water. Even more interesting was the behavior of rats drinking from two bottles. Some of the rats drank the two solutions in rapid alternation as if they were mixing the standard G+S on their tongues (Smith *et al.* 1976). Examples of six such "mixers" are given in Fig. 7.5.

The above identified "mixers" are not significantly greater G+S drinkers than nonmixers. For mixers, average daily intake of G+S was 231.5 ml while for nonmixers this average was 216.1 ml. In the glucose vs. saccharin test, however, a difference between the two groups *was* apparent. Mixers generally consumed less of the 6% glucose solution (149.9 ml compared to 167.1 ml) and more of the saccharin solution (101.3 ml compared to 56.3 ml). The level of daily intake of saccharin solution seems to be the best predictor of whether a rat mixes glucose and saccharin. However, from these consumption data, that an animal mixes provides little or no information about the G+S polydipsia.

We found one further difference between mixers and nonmixers. Saccharin drinking episodes for mixers seem to follow glucose episodes more closely in time than vice versa. In other words, rats would switch faster from the glucose to the saccharin bottle than they would going back to the glucose bottle. From the dozens of records of mixers with variable patterns in our laboratory, that finding has been consistent under all conditions.

Analysis of Motivational Properties of G+S Drinking

In a final experiment, we tested the strength of the rats motivation to mix the saccharin and glucose solutions by placing a barrier between the two tubes. The length of the barrier was changed systematically from 0.5 in. to 6 in. (the maximum length for our cages which still allows the rats to switch sides) to hinder the mixing process.

The manipulation of the barrier length had two effects. The first of these, predictably so, was to decrease the number of alternations of all subjects. Three of the rats stopped mixing altogether when the barrier size was between 1.5 and 3.5 in. Two remaining rats never ceased mixing even with the 6 in. barrier. The second effect of increasing the barrier length was to increase the average G to S and S to G switching time with the latter measure affected to a greater degree. These results are given in Fig. 7.6 which shows the effect of systematically increasing the barrier length from the baseline of 0.5 in.

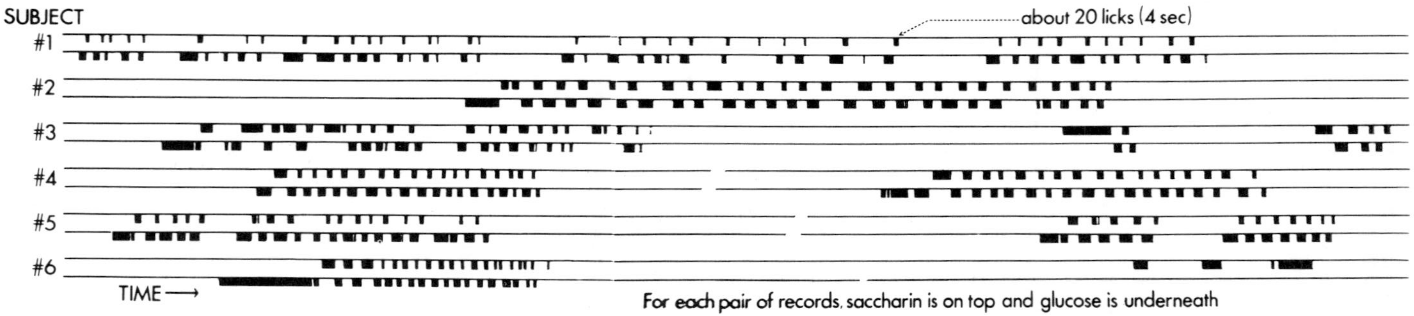

SUBJECT

#1

#2

#3

#4

#5

#6

TIME →

about 20 licks (4 sec)

For each pair of records. saccharin is on top and glucose is underneath

FIG. 7.5. THE INDIVIDUAL LICKS FOR EACH OF SIX SUBJECTS ARE PLOTTED ON A PAIR OF EVENT RECORDS, THE TOP RECORDING SACCHARIN LICKS, THE BOTTOM, GLUCOSE LICKS

Recording of licks for each rat begins at the left of the figure. the unbroken records (all but nos. 4 and 5) span a time period of approximately 18 min, while the broken ones are only slightly longer.

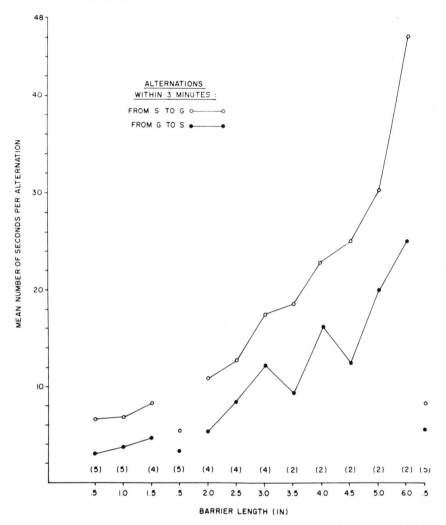

FIG. 7.6.   OPEN CIRCLES REPRESENT AN AVERAGE IN SECONDS OF ALL INTERVALS LESS THAN 3 MIN IN LENGTH AS A FUNCTION OF THE SIZE OF THE BARRIER AS THE RAT SWITCHES FROM THE SACCHARIN TO THE GLUCOSE BOTTLE
Filled circles are averages of the glucose-to-saccharin intervals. The values in parentheses above the abscissa give the number of subjects mixing for each barrier length, that is, the number of subjects whose data contribute to the new circles directly above.

This analysis of the temporal characteristics of glucose−saccharin mixing gives us two pieces of information. First that G to S and S to G switches are not equivalent to the rat, thereby suggesting that they serve separate purposes. And second, since the G to S times are less affected by the barrier, this is perhaps the temporal locus of the taste inputs.

Summary of Rat Data

While it is not clear how the mixing phenomenon contributes to our understanding of G+S drinking in general, similar nutritive and non-nutritive sweeteners are used and taste appears to be the dominant motivation in their relative ingestion. The fact that rats will engage in this unique behavior with its stereotyped patterning and consistent temporal characteristics is worthy of independent investigation. And any knowledge about the taste system gained from studying these mixers can only aid in our understanding of the polydipsia elicited by the sapid G+S solution.

THE HUMAN SUBJECT

The experiments described above suggest a sensory explanation for saccharin−glucose polydipsia: a particular glucose−saccharin mixture tastes better to the rat than either substance alone. Recent human psychophysical studies demonstrate taste phenomena that offer some hints about how this could happen.

How Sweeteners Add to Each Other

Sensory systems often do not show simple addition. For example, Fig. 7.7 shows three hypothetical functions of perceived taste intensity plotted versus concentration. In taste as well as other sensory modalities these psychophysical functions tend to be power functions with the form:

$$\psi = \phi^\beta$$

where ψ is the perceived intensity and ϕ the concentration. The exponent β varies systematically depending on the substance tasted as well as how the tasting is done.

Making taste mixtures really amounts to adding one substance to another. Consider the simplest kind of taste "mixture," adding a substance to itself. The functions in Fig. 7.7 show how to predict how such mixtures will taste. For example, consider function B in Fig. 7.7. The perceived intensity of concentration 1 of B is 1. If concentration 1 of B were to be added to concentration 1 of B, then the resulting mixture would be concentration 2 of B. The perceived intensity of that mixture would be 2 which is the simple sum of the perceived intensities of the components. However, the same operations performed on A and C will produce very different results. With A, the mixture (concentration 2) produces a perceived intensity of 1.4. Since this is less than the simple

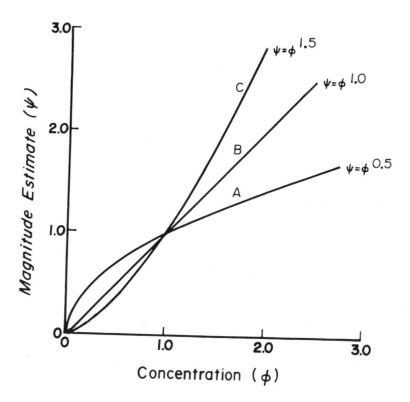

FIG. 7.7. THREE PSYCHOPHYSICAL FUNCTIONS FOR TASTE

From Bartoshuk (1975)

sum of the components, we say that this mixture shows suppression. With C, the mixture produces a perceived intensity of 2.8. Since this is greater than the simple sum of the components, we say that this mixture shows synergism. In summary, when dealing with a substance and tasting conditions that produce a psychophysical function like C in Fig. 7.7 (i.e., with an exponent greater than 1.0), mixtures of that substance with itself *must* produce a taste intensity greater than the simple sum of the perceived intensities of the components.

Glucose, tasted at room temperature by human subjects, produces a function like C in Fig. 7.7 (Bartoshuk and Cleveland 1977). If saccharin stimulates the same receptors as glucose, then adding saccharin to glucose would be like adding glucose to itself and the mixture would have to be sweeter than the sum of the sweetnesses of the glucose and the saccharin.

Unfortunately, the bitter taste of saccharin complicates the picture.

THE BITTERNESS OF SACCHARIN

When a bitter substance is mixed with a sweet one, mutual suppression often results. Interestingly enough, the bitter is often suppressed more than the sweet (the shapes of the psychophysical functions may play a role). Thus we could expect the addition of a sweet substance like glucose to reduce the bitter of saccharin. This supports the early suggestion by Valenstein et al. (1967) that saccharin–glucose polydipsia might be related to suppression of saccharin bitter. Saccharin's sweet and bitter tastes probably interact themselves. This would mean that we do not see the true sweet and bitter functions of saccharin but only what results after the interaction. This could be why the saccharin sweet function looks so different from that for gluose.

Human Variability in Tasting Bitter.   The bitterness of saccharin varies across human subjects. One of the sources of this variation is the genetic status of the individual for the ability to taste phenyl-thiocarbamide (PTC). Individuals who carry two recessive genes for this trait are relatively insensitive to PTC and are called nontasters. Individuals who carry one or both dominant genes taste PTC as bitter and are called tasters. Tasters of PTC tend to taste saccharin as more bitter than nontasters do (Bartoshuk 1979).

Richter and Clisby (1941) examined PTC thresholds in rats as well as in human subjects. Their data suggest the possibility that there may be taster and nontaster rats. If there are, and if saccharin bitter is related to PTC bitter in rats, then saccharin would taste more bitter to some rats than to others. To see what this might mean to saccharin–glucose polydipsia, we ran the following experiment.

Synergism in Saccharin–Glucose Mixtures

Eighteen human subjects (11 tasters, 7 nontasters) evaluated saccharin, glucose, and mixtures of the two with the method of magnitude estimation (Stevens 1969). The solutions were at room temperature (approximately 22°C), were sipped from small cups and then spit into a sink, and subjects rinsed with water before tasting each solution.

The results are shown in Fig. 7.8. Each subject tasted a series of glucose and saccharin concentrations. The concentrations marked with arrows produce polydipsia in rats when mixed. The bar graph on the right in Fig. 7.8 shows the sweetness and bitterness of the mixture of 0.18 M glucose and 0.0056 M saccharin and the simple sum of the two. Note that for nontasters the mixture is sweeter than the sum of the sweetnesses of the components (synergism). To get an index of the synergism we divide the mixture sweetness by the sum sweetness for

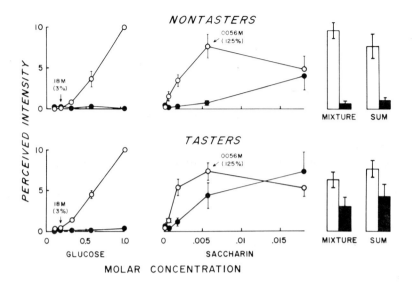

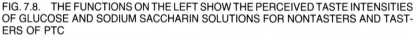

FIG. 7.8.   THE FUNCTIONS ON THE LEFT SHOW THE PERCEIVED TASTE INTENSITIES OF GLUCOSE AND SODIUM SACCHARIN SOLUTIONS FOR NONTASTERS AND TASTERS OF PTC

Sweetness is shown by open circles and bars. Bitterness is shown by filled circles and bars. The sweet and bitter tastes of a mixture of 0.18 m saccharin and 0.0056 m glucose (marked by arrows on the functions) are shown in the bar graph labeled "mixture." the simple sum of the sweetness and bitterness of the components in the mixture is shown in the bar graph labeled "sum."

each subject. The mean values for nontasters and tasters, respectively, are 1.45 and 0.94. These values are significantly different (two-tailed Mann-Whitney U; $p = 0.02$).

Subjects also tasted 0.0056 M saccharin plus 0.32 M glucose and plus 0.56 M glucose. The results were similar to those with 0.18 M glucose. The indexes of synergism for nontasters and tasters were significantly different for both 0.32 and 0.56 M glucose.

Interpretation.   We can explain these results by referring back to the phenomenon described previously (1) sweeteners often add "synergistically," (2) bitterness can be suppressed by the addition of a sweetener, and (3) nontasters of PTC perceive less bitterness in saccharin than tasters do. First look at the nontaster data in Fig. 7.8. The function for glucose accelerates upward like C in Fig. 7.7. However, we do not know what the "real" saccharin sweetness function looks like because the presence of bitterness suppresses sweetness. Now look at the taster data. The glucose function looks similar to the nontaster function: it accelerates upward like C in Fig. 7.7. The sweetness function for saccharin does not look like the nontaster function. The taster sweetness function for saccharin curves down more noticeably. In fact, it pulls down particularly where the bitterness rises. Suppose the "real" sweetness function for saccharin were really similar to that for glucose. We would expect synergistic addition of the sweet tastes, but the presence of bitter would be expected to suppress the sweetness of the mixture. Thus the mixture sweetness shows synergism for nontasters (where there is little bitterness in the saccharin to suppress the sweetness of the mixture). The mixture sweetness fails to synergize for the tasters (where the bitterness of saccharin is greater), but the bitterness of the saccharin tends to be suppressed (the reduction in bitter is not statistically significant in these data).

All of this suggests that saccharin–glucose mixtures may taste better than either the saccharin or glucose components to both tasters and nontasters but for different reasons. To the nontaster, the mixture is sweeter. To the taster, it may be less bitter.

REFERENCES

BARTOSHUK, L.M.   1975.   Taste Mixtures: Is mixture suppression related to compression?   Physiol. Behav. *14*, 643–649.

BARTOSHUK, L.M.   1979.   Bitter taste of saccharin: Related to the genetic ability to taste the bitter substance 6-*N*-propylthiouracil (PROP).   Science *205*, 934–935.

BARTOSHUK, L.M. and CLEVELAND, C.T.   1977.   Mixtures of substances with similar tastes: A test of a new model of taste mixture interactions. Sens. Process. *1*, 177–186.

RICHTER, C.P., and CLISBY, K.H.   1941.   Phenylthiocarbamide taste thresholds of rats and human beings.   Am. J. Physiol. *134*, 157–164.

SMITH, J.C., and FOSTER, D.F.   1980.   Some determinants of intake of glucose and saccharin solutions.   Physiol. Behav. *25*, 127–133.

SMITH, J.C., WILLIAMS, D.P., and JUE, S.S.   1976.   Rapid oral mixing of glucose and saccharin by rats.   Science *191*, 304–305.

SMITH, J.C., CASTONGUAY, T.W., FOSTER, D.F., and BLOOM, L.M.   1980. A detailed analysis of glucose and saccharin drinking in the rat.   Physiol. Behav. *24*, 173–176.

SNAPPER, A.G., and KODDEN, R.M.   1973.   Time sharing in a small computer through the use of a behavior notation system.   *In* Digital Computers in the Behavior Laboratory.   B. Weiss (Editor).   Appleton-Century-Crofts, New York.

STEVENS, S.S.   1969.   Sensory scales of taste intensity.   Percept. Psychophys. *6*, 302–308.

VALENSTEIN, E.S., COX, V.C., and KAKOLEWSKI, J.W.   1967.   Polydipsia elicited by the synergistic action of a saccharin and glucose solution. Science *157*, 552–554.

8

Social Determinants in Human Food Selection

M. Krondl and D. Lau

INTRODUCTION

The process of food selection is part of a complex behavior system shaped by many factors. This complex process has obvious implications with regard to the nutritional and health status of a population (Gifft *et al.* 1972). Through the ages, various environmental factors such as the discovery of fire, the change from a rural to an urban way of life, increased mobility of people and improved communication have influenced food use (see Todhunter 1973; Newman 1975). Food practices are continually being altered in response to ongoing environmental changes (Simoons, this volume, Chapter 12). Of the environmental factors that influence food use, our research has focused on social factors, specifically those affecting availability and accessibility of food, rather than those affecting agricultural food production.

In the modern world, the availability of food is dependent on marketing strategy and efficiency (Caliendo 1979). The accessibility of food is governed not only by the available food dollar but also by the time and skills of the consumer and the facilities that can be utilized for storage and food preparation. Social factors are superimposed on existing food-related values stemming from the individual's particular cultural heritage. Food advertising and nutrition education may be included along with the social factors; the former influences social status of a food and the latter leads to the imposition of specific health attributes on food. Besides the social and environmental influences, food choice has yet another component, namely acceptability. Acceptability encompasses such phenomena as the sensory qualities of foods, degree of familiarity with them, and their basic role in satisfying hunger.

Conceptual Approaches to Food Selection Research

A wealth of literature exists pertaining to various aspects of the factors influencing food choice. Reference is made especially to three researchers who have profoundly influenced the conceptualizing in the area. The approach of Newman (1975), looking at food habit research through time, provides an understanding of the increasing and intricate role of social factors on food behavior. Schachter (1967) offers insight into the external forces that become, for some people, regulators of their food and nutrition behavior. These individuals, through a process of altering the internal regulator or mechanism, are stimulated to eat by external cues rather than relying on internal cues. Finally, Jerome (1977) has identified the profound role of culture in making dietary choices resistant to change.

Cultural Anthropological Framework for Food Selection Study

The various research approaches reported in the literature, though valuable in recognizing specific determinants as factors responsible for food selection, are limited in helping us to better understand the complex mechanisms of the food selection process. Of the several factors shown to affect food use, there is little indication of their relative importance, possible interaction, or the strength and direction of effect of each on food use. We have sought to conceptualize food selection in such a way as to offer a more suitable structure for systematic study (Krondl and Boxen 1975). We proposed a structure incorporating the anthropological development model and Schachter's (1967) concept of the external and internal cues regulating feeding. This model was further refined (Krondl and Lau 1978) with recognition of the work of Fewster et al. (1973), relating to food meanings, and Schutz et al. (1975) classifying foods according to attitudinal values. The overall process of food selection was then visualized as a barrier between food availability and the decision to choose among foods. A set of food perceptions related to social, cultural, psychological, and physiological experiences were delineated as the barrier components. As shown in Fig. 8.1, the model also takes into account feedback mechanisms of ingested nutrients. It was within this framework that various studies of the social determinants of food selection were accomplished in which food perceptions were measured and related to frequency of food use.

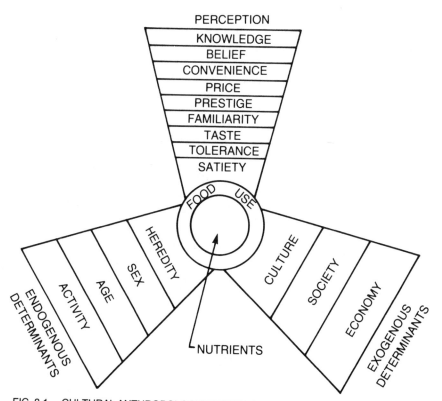

FIG. 8.1.   CULTURAL ANTHROPOLOGY FRAMEWORK FOR FOOD SELECTION STUDY

RELATIONSHIP OF PRICE, CONVENIENCE, AND PRESTIGE TO FOOD USE

The first testing of the model was directed toward the relationship of perceived food price, convenience, and prestige to food use. These are essentially cross-sectional studies: both endogenous and exogenous determinants such as age, sex, culture, and economic status have been controlled in each study.

Food Price and Frequency of Food Usage

The societal definition of price is the quantity of one thing that is exchanged and demanded in sale for another. The perception of the price of food is rather different; it is the cost of food in relation to personal wants and needs. Fewster et al. (1973) measured this as "high or low food value" for the "dollar value." Reaburn et al. (1979) used a five-point scale with wording indicating price, ranging from "very cheap" to "very expensive." The perception of price relates to a number of influences other than dollar value for unit quantity. Reaburn *et al.* (1979) identified such factors as quantities of food needed to satisfy family appetite and rejection or waste of food such as broccoli by children as affecting the perception of price of that particular food. In addition, the form in which the food is purchased and the cost of other ingredients used in combination with the food before serving also relate to the perception of price.

Price Alone Not a Significant Factor? In considering the effect of price perception on food use, it had generally been assumed that frequency of use of a specific food would fluctuate with its market cost. It was therefore postulated that if a food is perceived as being low-priced, it would be associated with higher consumption; conversely, if an item is perceived to be high-priced, it would be associated with low consumption. The data collected from a number of studies in which analyses of price perceptions of specific foods and their association with food use were determined, indicate a more complicated situation. In a study of adult female homemakers, Reaburn *et al.* (1979) found that the frequency of usage of only *one* (pork/chicken liver) out of 52 foods studied showed a significant negative correlation with price perception. This suggests that frequency of use of a particular food may decrease with increased food price perceptions only for a very small subset of the foods we select.

Somewhat different findings from an ongoing study of elderly persons by the second author showed significant positive correlations, but again for only a few items. Squash and lettuce were found to be used despite perceived high price. In the same study the use of tea decreased when perceived price became too high. Finally, research in progress by a co-worker (George 1981) included a study of adolescent females, age 14 to 16 years, in Toronto high schools. Again, the usage of only two foods (doughnuts and liver), out of 48 studied were correlated with price. Doughnuts were eaten moderately frequently and liver infrequently, and both foods were perceived as relatively expensive. It has to be born in mind that the girls in this study rarely shopped for food, and it appeared that they were not very familiar with food prices. From these findings it does not appear that perception of price is an important factor in food selection of adolescent girls.

When the above three studies are considered in total, there does not appear to be good evidence supporting the common sense notion that frequency of food usage is tied to the perceived price of the food.

Price and Food Patterns. These Canadian data are not inconsistent with McKenzie's finding in the United Kingdom (McKenzie 1979) that price effects were not predictably linked to food patterning: indeed, they could work in a most haphazard fashion. Food consumption and expenditure data from the United Kingdom established that though a direct relationship exists between food price, family income, and the nature of consumption patterns in general, the effect of price on the use of specific food items is subject to large variations. Foods such as bread, flour, potatoes, sugar, jams, which are viewed as staple items, hold a static position regardless of income and price fluctuations. Significant consumption increases were observed for dairy, meat, fish, fruit and vegetable products when income increased. A reverse trend was demonstrated for condensed milk and margarine. A combination of high and low priced items, moreover, would be expected within any given food basket. The impact of higher prices on the food budget may be moderated by using high priced foods in smaller amounts or with reduced frequencies. This modification of food purchasing behavior in response to fluctuation of food prices is well summarized by McKenzie (1979).

Limited Budgets. When income level approaches the poverty line, and the balancing of the total budget for the needs of housing, clothing, transportation, and food is in question, price considerations may limit the range of foods used. Foods perceived to be too expensive for the budget will be eliminated and the foods selected will be mainly those required for the satisfaction of hunger and maintenance of life. The sensory, convenience, and prestige qualities may become secondary as choice determinants. When affordable (inexpensive) items are purchased, price considerations may not be as important in selecting food as the eating qualities or health aspects of the product (Monroe 1973).

Convenience of Foods and Their Usage. Generally, the term convenience is defined as anything that saves or simplifies work and adds to one's ease or comfort. More specifically, convenience foods are those that have services added to the basic ingredients to reduce the amount of preparation required in the home (Glicksman 1971). By using this definition as a standard, all foods, including raw, semi-processed, or completely processed items can be rated on an appropriate scale. Fewster et al. (1973) used a seven-point semantic differential scale to measure perceived convenience in terms of "ease" or "difficulty" of preparation. Reaburn et al. (1979) used a five-point scale ranging from 1 "takes very long and is difficult to prepare," to 5 "very quick and easy to prepare."

Who Uses Convenience Foods? Convenience-oriented consumption has been identified by Anderson (1971) as representing a focal point between rising affluence and the increasing significance of time (see also Mintz, this volume, Chapter 9). On this basis it could be hypothesized that people with time constraints would be more frequently inclined to choose foods perceived as highly convenient. Convenience as a food choice motive fluctuates in importance depending on age, sex, income, and education of the household head, as well as with location—rural or urban—of the household (Tinklin et al. 1972). The use of convenient snack foods, moreover, was reported by Buchanan (1974) to be greater in city homes, with children largely responsible for the regular use of snack foods in the household. Most North Americans under 25 years of age readily accept convenience foods, presumably because they were regularly exposed to them early in their lives and are familiar with their time-saving qualities.

Our studies have attempted to relate the convenience of specific foods to their use. An initial study (Reaburn et al. 1979) found that in only three foods (instant coffee, commercial cake, and turnip) out of 52 were the correlation coefficients significant between perceived convenience and usage. The reported use of commercial cake was very low and the negative association observed between usage and convenience is difficult to explain. It may be due in part to our observation that the perception of convenience was found to be subject to individual variation depending on the cooking skills, the enjoyment of preparing a particular food, and possibly age. When we (Lau, in preparation) studied the association between food use and convenience perception of elderly females, six foods out of 14 showed significant correlations, five of them negative. Although all six foods (skim milk powder, baked custard, macaroni and cheese, frozen fish fillet, beef liver, and lettuce) were rated as relatively convenient, only lettuce was frequently used (almost daily, compared to about one a month for the other five items). These results refute the hypothesis that as perceived convenience of food increases, so does its use. Obviously other factors, such as price and eating qualities may be relevant. Processed and prepackaged foods are more expensive and are subject to flavor losses as compared to their freshly prepared counterparts.

Factors Interacting with Convenience. Traub (1974) suggest that consumers' concern with respect to convenience foods includes (1) the added costs of the items, (2) the time actually saved by using the item, (3) the eating quality, and (4) the amount of fuel saved when using the item. Thus the determinants of price and taste qualities would have to be considered for a given food simultaneously with the convenience aspect before the food would be selected. The weak associations between convenience and food use that we found is compatible with other research findings. Davies and Macleod (1971) reported that when the price of a food is judged high, convenience loses its importance as a food choice motive. In addition, family preferences accounted for food choices of the majority of the women surveyed by Cooper and Wakefield (1975). Convenience along with price and appearance played only a minor role in individual food selection patterns in this particular survey.

Prestige of Foods and Food Usage

A food's prestige is some measure of the position of the food in a hierarchy relative to society's values. It is a difficult term to define and uniform criteria for the evaluation of prestige do not exist. Jelliffe (1967) categorized prestigious foods as those served to illustrious members of the community for important occasions (see also Lamb 1969; Niehoff 1969; Fewster *et al.* 1973; Lowenberg 1970). Cussler and deGive (1970) have proposed that people may seem to be motivated by a desire to consume foods that are prestigious rather than foods that are good for their health. Peer influence, as an external social cue, may induce changes in values and affect the rationale for assigning status value to foods. This would consequently change their use patterns. People tend to eat foods of the social group to which they aspire, and prestige foods can become an important attribute to vertical mobility. The consumption of prestige foods, however, obviously would not occur on a regular and frequent basis, if they are defined as those reserved for guests and for special occasions.

Prestige Unrelated to Usage?   In our research (Reaburn *et al.* 1979; Lau, in preparation) we have assessed a food's prestige as the appropriateness of the food for guests or for special occasions. With some variations between studies, "prestige of food" was measured by responses on a 5-point scale ranging from 1 "not at all appropriate for guests" to 5 "most appropriate for guests."

The influence of prestige on food was measured by associating the perceived prestige values of common food items with their use frequency. It was interesting to note that even within a list of common and inexpensive foods, different prestige values were represented. For example, low prestige value of beef liver was consistently indicated. Such fresh foods as juice, strawberries, homemade bread, and homo-milk are considered higher in prestige than the frozen or preprocessed varieties (Reaburn *et al.* 1979).

A summary of findings for three populations (young, adult, and elderly women) in which food use was correlated with the perception of prestige suggests that a food's perceived prestige plays only a minor role in influencing foods selected on a routine basis. For example, the perceived prestige of only two foods out of a total of 52 foods were found to be significantly associated with use in an adult female sample. Among elderly women, of the 14 foods studied, nine foods showed significant correlations between prestige and use. They included 2% milk, skim milk powder, baked custard, frozen fish fillet, apple juice, squash, canned creamed tomato soup, macaroni and cheese, and margarine. The positive correlations observed between the perception of prestige and food use may be interpreted to mean that the foods the elderly consume are judged to be highly suitable for their guests as well; that is, seniors may not distinguish foods in terms of prestige as do the younger age groups (Reaburn et al. 1979).

Among adolescent females, usage of 26 foods out of 48 foods examined have been found to be correlated with the perception of "comfortability when eaten in company" (George 1981). Only five of these foods (homogenized milk, eggs, carrots, soft drinks, and hamburgers) were used more frequently than once a week. These foods, then, could be designated as having a relatively high social status among young females and peer opinion would influence their continued usage.

Summary of Social Factors of Price, Convenience, and Prestige

From the preceding evidence it is apparent that the perceptions in the social category play a minor role in influencing the use of foods. The more influential factors, the perceived health belief and the perception of taste of foods will now be discussed.

THE RELATIONSHIP OF PERCEIVED HEALTH BELIEF, COGNITION, AND FLAVOR TO FOOD USE

Health Beliefs

Philosophically, among the Chinese, health belief is related to the life balance concept. Health, illness, and food are integrated into the dualistic concepts of Yin and Yang, sometimes loosely translated as Hot and Cold. Good health is thought to be a state of balance between the Yin and Yang elements of the body. Food, herbs, and medications are also classified as Hot or Cold. Attaching Hot or Cold qualities to food does not refer to thermal characteristics or to taste, but to specific innate qualities of the food (Caliendo 1979; Harwood 1971; Hsu 1974). There are many varieties of this Hot–Cold system related to food and health beliefs, including that of the Chinese (Hsu 1974), Malayans (Cosminsky 1975, 1977), Mexicans (Molony 1975), and Indians (Storer 1977).

The Judaic dietary prescriptions are best known in Western culture as religious health beliefs (see Simoons, this volume, Chapter 12). Among old cultures such as the Chinese, there seem to be no quantitative and objective nutritional standards and criteria comparable to the "recommended dietary allowances" of various Western countries. Feelings, and the subjective state described as "feeling good" would be the expected popular criterion of good nutrition (Hsu 1974). By contrast, today's consumer in the West believes a good diet takes rational planning and must provide daily adequate amounts of all known essential nutrients. The general public equates a balanced diet with foods containing particular nutrients. In a recent survey of nutrition concepts, for example, foods mentioned must frequently as healthy were vegetables (Health and Welfare Canada 1979A). Health beliefs are therefore associated with scientific knowledge about food and nutrition. In Canada, the most widely used nutrition references are Canada's Food Guide (Health and Welfare Canada 1979B) and the Canadian Dietary Standards (Health and Welfare Canada 1976). In the United States, the basic four food groups (Hertzler and Anderson 1974) and the Recommended Daily Dietary Allowances (National Academy of Sciences 1980) are used.

Role of Cognition.   Food and nutrition information, whether popular or scientific, is learned through cognitive processes. When it is accepted, either rationally or traditionally, it becomes a belief. Brown *et al.* (1978) documented the success of nutritionists in "selling protein." Stowell (1979) reported a decline in use of sweet foods and all meats and an increased use of nutritious snacks, poultry, homemade soups, and hot dishes due to changes in health beliefs. As previously mentioned, a survey carried out by Health and Welfare Canada (1979A) showed that nutrition concepts are viewed as important at older ages. In other words, the elderly perceive nutrition as important for maintaining good health.

Cognitive learning about foods is a continual process. This is particularly true in North America, where media—TV, radio, press—are important for promotional advertising. Written materials such as books, magazines, and bulletins are widely available on all aspects of nutrition and food selection. It is within the responsibilities and domain of the health care professional to provide appropriate protection for the consumer so that they will have access to reliable health/food/nutrition messages. In adults, food selection based on body needs and under the control of the hypothalamus may be obscured by information from the higher brain centers in the form of habit, customs, prejudices, social pressures, radio, or television (Lepkovsky 1973; see also Beidler, Åstrand, and Booth, this volume, Chapters 1, 2, and 4).

Research on Perceived Health Belief.   In our research (D. Lau, in preparation; George 1981) we have looked at the effect that perceived health belief about foods has on their usage. We have found that among older women, 93% of the foods they used correlated positively with their perception that the given food was good for them. Interestingly, among young consumers only 48% of the foods actually used were seen as being particularly healthy. For the elderly, the perceived health belief was correlated with usage much more often than was the price, convenience, or the prestige of foods. Indeed, only one other factor correlated more highly with usage than health belief, namely, that of taste of foods.

Taste As a Factor in Food Usage

Taste as a factor in food selection is a complex phenomenon which combines ontogenic, genetic, and learned components (see Weiffenbach 1978; Beidler, this volume, for overview). When applied to food selection, "taste" commonly is understood as "flavor," the latter term being a combination of taste and smell factors.

Flavor—a Most Important Factor.   The association between food use and flavor perceptions of foods is strongly indicated in our work. High correlations were observed in 14 out of 14 foods in the elderly, in 8 out of 10 foods in the single parents (Lau *et al.* 1979), and in 43 out of 48 foods in the adolescent (George 1981). These findings were not exactly unexpected. The ultimate test for acceptance of food is whether or not it will be put into the mouth and swallowed. The flavor of food provides the link between the biological senses and the initiation of immediate responses of the metabolic system—for example, in salivation and digestive enzyme secretion. Taste acceptance could be the last barrier a food has to cross before the two systems, food and man, can finally interact and ultimately integrate with each other.

"FIXED" AND CHANGING FOOD HABITS

In a recent marketing survey, almost 50% of the population reported changes in their eating patterns in the preceding two years. For them, the price of food appeared to be the strongest reason for change in eating patterns (Grocery Products Manufacturers of Canada 1979). An independent study by Health and Walfare Canada (1979A) reported that four out of 10 respondents admitted a change in food selection in the past year; the most frequently mentioned reasons were "for better health" and "to feel better." Cost was also reported to be important in food selection changes. A longitudinal study of 135 urban single-living elderly alone by one of our co-workers Wong (1980) showed that rising food prices caused a decrease in the use of some items. The food items most affected were beef steak, fruits, and vegetables.

CONCLUSION

From our research it appears that the social determinants of price, prestige, and convenience of foods are less important in the decision-making processes of food choice when compared to learned health belief (especially among the elderly) and flavor of foods. These and other social factors are definitely implicated in changing food habits. While the core of our food patterns may be resistant to change (see Beidler, this volume) imperceivably over time, through interactions with the changing environment mediated by social determinants, food habits do change.

The cultural anthropology model including food perceptions (see Fig. 8.1) has proved to be a useful beginning in the study of food selections and food use. The identification of both exogenous and endogenous determinants and perceptions related to social, cultural, psychological, and physiological experiences in the food use system of man will provide a greater appreciation of the fragility and complexity of the operative system in food selection. Environmental factors which affect changes in food practices are often under the control of man and because of their nutritional and health implications, man must assume the responsibility for ensuring that the system is operating in a positive manner in affecting food choice and ultimately changing food habits.

REFERENCES

ANDERSON, W.T.   1971.   Identifying the convenience-oriented consumer. J. Market. Res. *8*, 179–182.

BROWN, G.B., CELENDER, J.H., and SLOAN, A.E.   1978.   What the U.S. consumer knows, thinks and practices when it comes to nutrition. Food Prod. Dev. *12*, 35.

BUCHANAN, R.D.   1974.   Two marketing surveys reveal convenience food attitude and usage.   1974.   Food Sci. Market. *36*, 51–56.

CALIENDO, M.A.   1979.   Nutrition and the World Food Crisis.   MacMillan Publishing Company, New York.

COOPER, R.B., and WAKEFIELD, L.   1975.   Food choices of women.   J. Am. Diet. Assoc. *66*, 152–155.

COSMINKSY, S.   1975.   Changing food and medical practices in a Guatemalan community.   Ecol. Food Nutr. *4*, 183.

COSMINSKY, S.   1977.   Alimento and fresco: Nutritional concepts and their implications for health care.   Human Organ. *36*, 203–207.

CUSSLER, M., and DE GIVE, M.   1970.   Twixt the Cup and the Lip.   Consortum Press, New York.

DAVIES, L., and MACLEOD, M.   1971.   Are convenience foods acceptable to geriatrics?   J. Home Econ. *17*, 4–6.

GEORGE, R.S.   1981.   Food Selection Behaviour Analysis of Adolescents. M.Sc. Thesis, University of Toronto.   Toronto, Ontario, Canada

FEWSTER, W., BOSTIAN, L.R., and POWERS, R.D.   1973.   Measuring the connotative meanings of foods.   J. Home Econ. Res. *2*, 44–45.

GIFFT, H.H., WASHBORN, M.B., and HARRISON, G.G.   1972.   Nutrition, Behaviour and Change.   Prentice-Hall, Englewood Cliffs, New Jersey.

GLICKSMAN, M.   1971.   Fabricated foods.   *In* CRC Critical Reviews in Food Technology, Vol. 2, Chemical Rubber Company Press, Cleveland, Ohio.

GROCERY PRODUCTS MANUFACTURERS OF CANADA.   1979.   Food and Nutrition Survey Report.   Grocery Products Manufacturers of Canada, Toronto, Canada.

HARWOOD, A.   1971.   The hot-cold theory of disease.   J. Am. Med. Assoc. *216*, 1153–1158.

HEALTH AND WELFARE CANADA.   1976.   Dietary Standard for Canada. Health and Welfare Canada, Ottawa, Ontario, Canada.

HEALTH AND WELFARE CANADA.   1979A.   Report on Nutrition Concepts Evaluations Study.   Health Promotion Directorate, Health and Welfare Canada, Ottawa, Ontario, Canada.

HEALTH AND WELFARE CANADA.   1979B.   Canada's Food Guide Leaflet and Handbook Evaluation by Nutrition Professionals and Para-professionals. Health and Welfare Canada, Ottawa, Ontario, Canada.

HERTZLER, N.A., and ANDERSON, H.L.   1974.   Food guides in the United States.   J. Am. Diet. Assoc. *64*, 19–28.

HSU, L.C.   1974.   Nutrition: From China to the West.   Ecol. Food Nutr. *3*, 303–314.

JELLIFFE, D.   1967.   Parallel food classifications in developing and industrialized countries.   Am. J. Clin. Nutr. *20*, 279.

JEROME, N.   1977.   Taste experience and the development of a dietary preference for sweet in humans: Ethnic an cultural variations in early taste experience.   *In* Taste and Development: The Genesis of Sweet Preference. J.M. Weiffenback (Editor).   (Publ. No. NIH 77-1068) U.S. Department of Health, Education, and Welfare, Bethesda, Maryland.

KRONDL, M., and BOXEN, G.   1975.   Nutrition behavior, food resources and energy.   *In* Gastronomy: The Anthropology of Food and Food Habits.   M.L. Arnott (Editor).   Mouton and Co., New York.

KRONDL, M., and LAU, D.   1978.   Food habit modification as a public health measure.   Can. J. Public Health *69*, 39–43.

LAMB, M.W.   1969.   Food acceptance, a challenge to nutrition education: A review.   J. Nutr. Educ. *1*, 20–22.

LAU, D., HANADA, L., KAMINSKYJ. O., and KRONDL, M.   1979.   Predicting food use by measuring attitude and preference.   Food Prod. Dev. *13*, 66.

LEPKOVSKY, S.   1973.   Newer concepts in the regulation of food intake. Am. J. Clin. Nutr. *26*, 271.

LOWENBERG, M.E.   1970.   Socio-cultural basis of food habits.   Food Technol. *24*, 751–754, 756.

MCKINZIE, J.C.   1979.   Economic influences on food choice.   *In* Nutrition and Lifestyles.   M. Turner (Editor).   Applied Science Publishers Ltd., London.

MOLONY, C.H.   1975.   Systematic valence coding of Mexican "hot" and "cold" food.   Ecol. Food Nutr. *4*, 67.

MONROE, K.   1973.   Buyers subjective perception of price.   J. Market. Res. *10*, 70.

NATIONAL ACADEMY OF SCIENCES.   1980.   Food and Nutrition Board: Recommended Dietary Allowance, 9th Ed.   National Academy of Science, Washington, DC

NEWMAN, M.T.   1975.   Nutritional adaptation in man.   *In* Physiological Anthropology.   A. Damon (Editor).   Oxford University Press, Oxford, England.

NIEHOFF, A.   1969.   Changing food habits.   J. Nutr. Educ. *1*, 20–22.

REABURN, J., KRONDL, M., and LAU, D.   1979.   Social determinants in food selection.   J. Am. Diet. Assoc. *74*, 637–641.

SCHACHTER, S.   1967.   Cognitive effects of bodily functioning: Studies of obesity and eating.   *In* Biology and Behaviour: Neurophysiology and Emotion.   D.C. Glass (Editor).   The Rockefeller University Press, New York.

SCHUTZ, H.G., RUCHER, M.H., and RUSSEL, G.F.   1975.   Food and food-use classification systems.   Food Technol. *29*, 50–56; 60–64.

STORER, J.   1977.   Hot and cold belief in an Indian community and their significance.   J. Human Nutr. *31*, 33–40.

STOWELL, C.   1979.   Marketers to fight for declining in home sector as food consumption patterns change.   Food Prod. Dev. *13*, 95–97.

TINKLIN, G.L., FOGG, N.E., and WAKEFIELD, L.M.   1972.   Convenience foods: Factors affecting their use where household diets are poor.   J. Home Econ. *64*, 26–28.

TODHUNTER, E.N.   1973.   Food habits, food faddism and nutrition.   *In* Food, Nutrition and Health.   G.H. Bourne (Editor).   S. Karger, Basel, Switzerland.

TRAUB, L.G.   1974.   Convenience foods progress report evaluating factors that predict sales.   Food Prod. Dev. *8*, 22–27.

WEIFFENBACH, J.M. (Editor).   1977.   Taste and Development: The Genesis of Sweet Preference.   (Publ. No. NIH 77-1068) U.S. Department of Health, Education and Welfare, Bethesda, Maryland.

WONG, H.   1980.   Summative evaluation of a food habit modification program for the elderly.   M.Sc. Thesis.   University of Toronto, Toronto, Ontario, Canada.

Part III

Sociocultural Factors in Human Feeding Behavior

In Parts I and II we have viewed the food selection process from the perspective of the individual. We have seen that each of us inherits biological and psychological predispositions which make possible our feeding behaviors. The biological mechanisms include taste, smell, and visual receptors and other areas of the brain involved with feeding. These brain systems enable us to interpret which objects in the environment are suitable for ingestion. Selecting among and eating those foods replenishes the energy we expend.

Each of us, moreover, lives in a distinctive psychological food world comprised of our own peculiar likes and dislikes for particular foods. We have unique memories of prior feeding experiences. In large part these food memories form an individualized "nutritional wisdom" about our personal food experience. In our memory we know how each food item should look and taste, how "filling" it is (i.e., how calorically dense), when and under what circumstances it should be eaten (e.g., for breakfast, lunch, supper, or snack), and other information pertinent to ingestion.

In Part III the focus is shifted from the individual to groups of people—from nutritional wisdom to cultural wisdom about foods. Individuals select foods within a particular sociocultural framework, and in large measure it is the culture that delineates our range of choices and prescribes rules for food preparation and ingestion.

We begin Part III with a look at the American lifestyle's influence upon the way many of us eat. Sidney Mintz ("Choice and Occasion: Sweet Moments") proposes that schedules of work and play have produced feeding patterns that stress convenience, informality, and speed of consumption as well as flavor of foods—increasingly often at the expense of traditional "sit-down" type meals. He further notes that societal demands for convenience foods have in turn provided the impetus for America's food industries to generate new food products. As a result sugar now plays an expanded role in new food technologies, and Mintz discusses implications of these changes for our food selection strategies.

On the assumption that sociocultural factors play dominant roles in our personal food choices, we are justified in inquiring into the origins of and differences between cultures. Three papers in Part III directly address questions of cultural differences in food selection. The first of these ("Food, Behavior, and Biocultural Evolution") by Solomon Katz attempts to integrate present day genetic differences among humans with their food practices—all within an evolutionary framework. Katz and his colleagues have found, for example, that certain individuals have hereditary blood disorders that are aggravated by the consumption of fava beans. One might expect that fava beans would be eliminated from the diet of these individuals. In this instance, however, the individual's nutritional wisdom is overridden by "cultural" wisdom. Fava beans remain essential ingredients in their diets, and the continued fava bean consumption can be understood by noting that the blood disorder affords a degree of protection against malaria, a far more serious disease. Indirectly, then, fava bean consumption helps select for individuals resistant to malaria. Apparently, cultural practices interact with evolutionary processes in important, albeit highly intricate, ways.

Ethnic groupings are in part defined by the foods they eat, including their culinary behavior. Elisabeth Rozin ("The Structure of Cuisine") proposed that every cultural group, both modern and ancient, practices a unique and consistent set of food manipulations called cuisines. Cuisines in turn can be analyzed in terms of basic foodstuffs, cooking techniques, flavor principles, and psychological, social, or religious attitudes toward food and eating practices. As noted earlier by other contributors to this volume, Elisabeth Rozin's paper emphasizes that flavor principles are all important in defining culturally acceptable foods.

One might suspect that what each culture eats is determined primarily by availability—by the geographical distribution of foods. Indeed, tropical fruits have restricted availability and are "delicacies" as opposed to staples for those cultures not living near the equator. Frederick Simoons ("Geography and Genetics as Factors in the Psychobiology of Human Food Selection") informs us, however, that the distribution and availability of a food is not always the best predictor of its inclusion in a diet. In one culture he studied, for example, he notes that only about

50–75% of potentially edible plants are consumed. Simoons' research has sought answers to these curious limitations on cultivated plants and domesticated animals. Milk utilization within a culture, he has found, has a genetic component and can best be understood within the framework of "human ecogenetics."

In the concluding chapter Paul Rozin summarizes the complexities of human food selection ("Human Food Selection: The Interaction of Biology, Culture, and Individual Experience"). He illustrates these interactions with specific examples, including individual and cultural preferences for milk, sweets, spices, and meat. Rozin attempts to account for an individual's choices by proposing a flow of information about foods—initially from biology (nutritional requirements) then to cultural practices (cuisine) and finally to individual behavior (acculturation). While cognizant of the problem of historical reconstruction, Rozin suggests a plausible scenario to account for the incorporation of a specific item into a cuisine (e.g., chili peppers). In noting the biological, psychological, and sociocultural components of human food choices, this final chapter serves as a summary statement for the whole volume.

Choice and Occasion: Sweet Moments[1]

Sidney W. Mintz

This argument proceeds from the well-known fact that human beings do not eat only to live; eating is part of our social universe, as is most of the rest of our behavior. Anthropological literature is replete with eloquent demonstrations of the close relationship between ingestion and sociality, and of the way eating behavior takes on group-specific attributes, in terms of what is eaten, how, and when, in what company, and to what ends besides the simply nutritive. Though anthropologists seem to have a good deal of trouble in explaining what they mean by the term "culture," it certainly appears as if different human groups accomplish the same thing—nourishing themselves, say—in very variant ways, and using a wide variety of substances. What is more, they all seem disposed to invest in what they eat, and in the way they eat it, many complicated meanings, such that their lives, conscious and unconscious, are enriched by such symbolic activity. When we say, speaking of some contemporary event, that the condemned ate a hearty meal, or that what he ate was humble pie, or that he had to sing for his supper, or that the proof of the pudding is in the eating, we are employing scraps of such symbolic activity. But of course it is not merely in the discourse and reading of well-educated persons that food and eating figure so importantly. Any reader of the Scriptures knows how one's cup runneth over, why one casts bread upon the waters, and what manna from

---

[1] The writer is grateful to Dr. Sidney M. Cantor and to Professor Paul Rozin for the valuable criticisms of an earlier draft of this chapter. Persisting errors are the writer's responsibility alone.

Heaven is. And anyone in this society, our own, no matter what his/her social origins or lifestyle, is familiar not only with "bread" (which is money), and "corn" (which is hickish), but also with "honey," "honey-bunch," "sweetie pie," "sweetheart," "sugar," and "candy"—all of which are terms of affection.

CHOICE AND OCCASION

That our language and our consciousness are immersed in food metaphors and the rituals of eating is nowhere so dramatically illustrated in American society as in television advertising; and here, of course, there is ample subject-matter for a different paper. I shall restrict myself to just four points in this connection, the relevance of which will, I hope, eventually become clearer.

Television Advertising

Differentiation and Redifferentiation.   First of all, TV treatment of foods is intended to encourage consumption. As such, it is differentiated in order to reach many different (and segmented, but sometimes overlapping) populations, such as little boys and girls; adolescent males and females; adult singles, both male and female; families eating out; couples eating out; campers and travelers; single males in groups; athletic teams of both sexes; and so on. This design aims at reaching the widest possible variety of audiences, each on its own terms, but also at leaving room for continuous redifferentiation by subdivision (for instance, black male basketball players and white male basketball players; little girls and little boys, etc.) (Sahlins 1976), in order to perpetuate the sensation of innovation and of participatory membership upon which heightened consumption battens.

Making the product "right" for the consumer requires continuous redefinition and division of the groups in which he, as an individual consumer, defines himself. The deliberate postulation of new groups—often divisions between already familiar categories, as "pre-teens" were created between "teenagers" and younger children—helps to impart reality to what are supposedly new needs. "New" foods, as in the sequence skim milk : whole milk : half and half : light (table) cream : heavy (whipping) cream split differences in order to "create" new needs. New medicines, as in the treatment of daytime headaches and nighttime headaches or daytime colds and nighttime colds, seek to do the same.

Time-Saving Foods.   Second, TV treatment of foods emphasizes speed and efficiency of preparation and/or consumption. Whenever the greater expenditure of time is evoked as a positive value, it is the time spent by the maker or manufacturer in order to give the consumer maximum enjoyment in minimum time. The wine may remember, all right, but the consumer may hurry so much he forgets. Since the value of time is very high in this society, as unforgettably demonstrated by Linder (1970), multiple simultaneous enjoyment of consumable items— eating Fritos, while drinking Coca Cola, while listening to hard rock, while watching the Cowboys play the Steelers, while smoking a joint, while your girl sits in your lap—is called for. My improbable example is crudely plagiarized from Linder. But I think it is legitimate to argue that the high price of time in a society like this one—both really high and artificially heightened—explains why speed and efficiency of preparation and/or consumption are so highly touted.

Sociability of Ingestion. Third, such treatment usually emphasizes the sociability of ingestion, but there are at least two significant and interesting exceptions: the very young on the one hand, and the unattached, particularly the elderly, on the other. Yet these exceptions are not alike in most ways. The elderly commonly eat alone, and have no choice; appeals to them dare not stress a precious sociability that is not, in fact, available most of the time. To associate the product with good times in company could impart a negative valence to it. Little children are much less likely to eat alone, though the child fiddling with his dinner while the baby sitter fiddles with the TV is not unheard of. But below the age of five, children are rarely appealed to by stressing the fun of shared ingestion. Where similarities between the aged and the very young may be seen (at least, so far as the advertisers are concerned) is in pet food ads, where the sociability between single human being and animal is often dramatized. Though adults often take part by "teaching" the young child the supposedly different nutritive needs of infant, young, adult, and older cats and dogs—subdivisions again!—often a child and pet, or elderly person and pet, form a dyad. Here, art mimics life a little more faithfully, instead of merely idealizing it. In happy peer groups, consuming products in endlessly repeated demonstrations of Coca-Cola *agapē*, an illusory good fellowship is endlessly reimagined and reenacted.

Language of Attraction. Finally, TV advertising shares with other food advertising in this country an intemperate affection for adjectives of certain kinds, the contrastive meanings of which seem very consonant with other values in American life, but at subtle, profound, and even unconscious levels. One thinks here, on the one hand, of "crisp," "fresh," "wholesome," "refreshing," "vibrant," "energizing," and similar words.

And, on the other hand, one thinks of "juicy," "succulent," "luscious," "savory," "rich," and "finger-lickin' good." These two kinds of words are counterposed in the language of attraction, as are wet and dry, flesh and bone, hot and cold, and certain other familiar polarities that need not be pursued here. While their effectiveness in inducing or increasing consumption may be problematical, advertisers clearly desire to capitalize on the emotions and predispositions of potential consumers. I believe that the terminology they employ is consistent with an American feeling that food ought not to be dawdled over except in times of ritual excess—weddings and anniversaries, Christmas and New Year's, for instance. Its consumption at any one sitting should otherwise be terminated with a minimum of fuss. The emphasis is on succulence, freshness and convenience while eating; but on cleanness of the clothes, fingers, face, lips, and even the inside of the mouth, once the eating is done. "Finger-lickin' good" does not mean you do not wash your hands after eating deep-fried, breaded chicken!

Trends in Eating Behavior

My concern here is not with the advertising of foods, so much as with certain of the foods themselves, and the social meanings of the circumstances under which they are eaten. But because the advertising actively and importantly reflects what is actually happening among consumers—in this case, in the cultural arena of eating and food choices—it is relevant to the sociology of consumption. Three significant features of this arena deserve mention here.

The first is the increasing tendency of Americans to eat their meals outside the home. The National Advertising Bureau tells us that "the typical American eater"—whoever that may be—visits a fast-food restaurant nine times in any one month. One-third of all food dollars are spent on meals away from home, according to the *Wall Street Journal*. Of course, we need to know at what rates these trends are revealing themselves, and for what specific parts of the population, and over how long a time. But the multiplication of syndicated food dispensaries, so-called fast-food systems, since the Second World War and particularly in the last 20 years, is persuasive evidence in itself.

The second such feature is the increased consumption of ready-made or prepared foods in the home. There are immensely important sociological concomitants of this trend that cannot be dealt with here, but we may take note that the increase in consumption of such foods is paralleled by the heightened differentiation of the foods themselves, so that we get several different precooked and frozen veal dishes, for instance, packaged by the same manufacturer, but different in "style" (Milanese, marinara, limonada, oreganata, etc.).[2] The number of such foods that require nothing but temperature changes to be "prepared" has doubtless risen, proportionate to the total number of all such foods available. The variety of heating and chilling media, usually running on high-energy inputs (ovens, woks, steamers, bakers, cookers, deep fryers, etc.) has, of course, also risen sharply.

A third trend of a somewhat different sort has been remarked on by those having a special interest in sugars: increased consumption of sugars and fats, and decreased consumption of complex carbohydrates, as in wheat products. This tendency is of very long standing in the United States, however, and not a largely postwar phenomenon, as are those changes noted previously. Cantor and Cantor (1977), basing themselves in part on the work of Page and Friend (1974), and using the years 1909–1913 as their comparison base ($x = 100$), show that the average daily per capita consumption of sugars as a proportion of carbohydrates has increased in 60 years (1910–1970) from 31.5% to 52.6%. The total average daily per capita consumption of carbohydrates in that same 60 years has fallen from 500 g to about 380 g, while dietary fat has increased by 25% in that period to 155 g. Thus, complex carbohydrates have steadily given ground to both simple carbohydrates (that is, sugars), and to fats.[3] As Cantor and Cantor have pointed out, these two nutrient sources are associated with a certain "modern" lifestyle. Indeed, fats and sugars probably represent the two sides of the lexical compass used to orient the potential American consumer to consume appropriately, in terms of the constraints, real and contrived, under which he operates.

---

[2]It may be important to note that all samples of any one such style—like every can of the same kind of soup made by the same manufacturer—should be exactly the same in composition and taste; indeed, that is precisely what the manufacturer strives for. I am grateful to my colleague, Professor William C. Sturtevant, for pointing this out to me.

[3]The growing consumption of fats and sugars, which seems to have accompanied other changes in United States diet and social life during the last half-century, is paralleled by events in other countries, particularly (though by no means exclusively) in those that are industrialized or industrializing, such as England, The Netherlands, and Switzerland. Wretlind (1974), in presenting this information, notes that other observers (McGandy et al. 1967, Perisse et al. 1969) had earlier made the same observation, and later figures have simply confirmed the trend. According to a recent Associated Press story, George W. Kromer of the U.S. Dept. of Agriculture's Economics, Statistics and Cooperative Service, reports a sharp increase in the food fats disappearance (and, inferentially, consumption) in the period 1969–1979: from 126 lb per person to 135 lb per person. This would mean a yearly combined sugars and fats consumption in the United States of about 265 lb per person, assuming that the amounts "disappearing" are all ingested.

SUGAR USAGE

Now I wish to call attention to another well-known trend typical of American diet, stretching in its significance over half a century or more of sugar use, and developed in analysis most tellingly by Cantor in a series of wide-ranging papers (Cantor 1974, 1978; Cantor and Shaffer 1974). That is, the gradual displacement of sucrose from direct to indirect use, and its supplementation by ever-increasing use of certain other sugars, particularly corn sweeteners and, most recently, so-called high-fructose corn syrup (HFCS), which is not really a corn syrup. It is commonly recognized that while sucrose consumption in the United States has hovered for some time now around the 100 lb/year per person level, the consumption of other sweeteners has risen quite steadily for at least the last 70 years. This increase has pushed the per capita disappearance to nearly 130 lb/year. In 1979, HFCS distribution was 15 lb per capita (dry basis); sucrose, about 91.5 lb; regular corn syrup, 18.5 lb; and dextrose, 5.3 lb (Cantor 1981).

In this regard, however, we are dealing with several different processes at once. While sucrose consumption steadies, direct consumption of it falls. Meanwhile, consumption of other sweeteners rises; but most of that consumption is also indirect. And perhaps most important for the argument here, the indirect uses of sugar multiply as the unusual versatility of these foods is recognized.

Sweet Roles

Sugars are sweet, and that is why human beings like them. Beidler (1975; this volume, Chapter 1), Beauchamp et al. (1977), Rozin (1975, 1976), and other specialists have dealt imaginatively with the probable usefulness of sweetness in identifying edible foods during the evolution of mammalian, and perhaps particularly primate, forms. But certain sugars, notably sucrose, can be used to do more than simply sweeten. For instance, they can be used to preserve other foods, such as fruits. They supply what is called "body" to soft drinks, which taste "watery" without sucrose or dextrose. (Then "body" is usually supplied by gums such as arabic or algin or by suspending agents like carrageenin.) By serving as a medium for the yeast, sucrose has played a special role in baking; it also inhibits staleness in bread, and adds materially to shelf life. Sucrose can help to stabilize the chemical content of other foods, such as salt, and mitigate acidity in foods like catsup.

These varied uses are immensely important in understanding the quite extraordinary role that sugars have played in the diet of industrial peoples like ourselves. For clarification, a tentative use-typology may be attempted. Though other sugars and sweeteners besides sucrose may serve for some of the purposes covered by this classification, because of the complex chemistry and food technology involved, it is limited to sucrose only, our major refined sugar, manufactured from both sugarcane and sugarbeet.

Household Uses. The first category would be household use, but this refers only to the use of sugar for immediate consumption, as in the sweetening of tea or coffee, the baking of cakes, the making of icings, and the like. Such uses as the preserving of strawberries in jams or jellies are not included.

Preservation. The second category would be sugar use for preservation, as in the making of jams, either at home or in the factory; in the making of candies; and in other manufacture where the sucrose helps incidentally to conserve the food, even while sweetening it.[4]

Sugar as Stabilizer. The third category, however, is sucrose use in which the primary objective is not sweetening, but preservation, stabilization, or some other aspect of food technology not specifically connected with taste. In many of the modern uses of sugar in canning, baking, and otherwise, the actual taste of sweetness may play little or no role, as in artificial powdered substitutes for cream, dredging substances for deep-frying, and even many baking compounds. There is a good deal of fudging in this last category, of course. "Taste of sweetness" is a highly complex matter. Besides, so many different sugars are used in so many different processes in modern food technology that the category remains only very loosely specified. Nonetheless, it may have some initial utility because we are going to need to distinguish between sucrose uses wherein sugar tastes like sugar, its traditional place in human ingestion, and uses in which the issue of *what taste is* reveals itself as a highly complex one.

If we are told, for instance, that when sucrose is used in non-yeast-raised baked goods, ". . . texture, grain and crumb become smoother, softer and whiter . . . ," and "this tenderizing effect of sugars has long been recognized" (Pyler 1973), we are talking less about taste, and more about what is commonly called "texture." And when we are told that sucrose supplies "body" to soft drinks, because "a heavy liquid is more appealing to the mouth than water" (Sugar Association [1979?]), it is open to question whether it is taste that we are discussing. What needs

---

[4]Professor Paul Rozin has pointed out that when sugar is used to make jam at home, say, it is both sweetening and preserving, and hence combines two different functions in one. I have not attempted to revise my very inexact "typology," in spite of its many limitations, in the present chapter. In a book I have just completed entitled "Sweetness and Power" a fuller description of the historical uses of sugars is provided, however.

to be distinguished here is palatability as a coefficient of sweetness as such, and palatability derived from other characteristics of what is eaten (to which sugars may contribute), even if they are not experienced by the taster as sweet.

Sugar Uses Summarized. Finally, there remains a fourth category, which is purely residual: all other sugar uses not referred to previously. The main objective of these categories is to distinguish between sugars as directly consumed sweeteners; sugars as indirectly consumed (or deferred) sweeteners; sugars as nonsweetening (though apparently important) food processing components; and sugars in all other uses. Such a typology is meant only as a beginning approximation. Whatever its defects, perhaps it will allow us to think for a moment about the circumstances in which sugars are consumed. This means turning to the relationship between substance and event, between food and occasion.

The German historian Werner Sombart, with his conspiratorial view of world history, took pen in hand to argue that capitalism was the product of the love of luxury. Each of Sombart's theories has a villain and this theory's villain was womanhood. Not only did women give rise to capitalism; there was also, Sombart tells us, a clear ". . . connection between the consumption of sweets and feminine dominance" (Sombart 1967 [1913]). His discussion of the links between the production of plantation commodities—what I have elsewhere called "drug foods" (Mintz 1979)—and European eating habits is brilliantly insightful. But Sombart's view of the link between women and sweetness requires radical amendment. By discussing ingested substances in the context of place, time, and group, Sombart brings up the whole question of sweet moments. His association between women and the kitchen, one that some disciples of the philosophy he espoused would later turn into a hortatory slogan *("Kirche, Küche, Kinder")*, leaves something to be desired; and his view of foods (and especially sweets) as corrupters of a sane society, especially in the hands of women, requires many correctives.[5] But Sombart looked for connections between what is eaten, who eats it, and the circumstances under which ingestion occurs, and his ideas about food are provocative and original.

---

[5]In my recently-completed study of sugar consumption in the United Kingdom between 1650 and 1900, entitled "Sweetness and Power," I have tried to disaggregate the use of sugars among different social and economic groups at different periods. Though any thorough analysis is precluded by the inadequate data, it is certainly clear that the use of sugars as confectioneries percolated downward from the nobility and upper classes after 1650. Both among the nobility and the newly wealthy of the seventeenth and later centuries, sweetness was associated in many specific ways with women as opposed to men. But this association is a far cry from Sombart's assertions about female love of luxury, female dominance and the rise of capitalism.

A contemporary observer, the French semiotician Roland Barthes, has asked the question more precisely. Barthes, viewing all consumption as forms of communication, writes with particular regard to France; but much of what he says may be equally applicable to our own society. In his argument,

> . . . food serves as a sign not only for themes, but also for situations; and this, all told, means for a way of life that is emphasized, much more than expressed, by it. To eat is a behavior that develops beyond its own ends, replacing, summing up, and signalizing other behaviors, and it is precisely for these reasons that it is a sign. What are these other behaviors? Today, we might say all of them: activity, work, sports, effort, leisure, celebration—every one of these situations is expressed through food. We might almost say that "polysemia" of food characterizes modernities; in the past, only festive occasions were signalized by food in any positive organized manner. But today, work also has its own kind of food (on the level of a sign, that is): energy-giving and light food is experienced as a very sign of, rather than only a help toward, participation in modern life (Barthes 1975).

Implicit in Barthes' view is the idea that food has been transformed, by the emergence of modern society, from a substance that suits a certain ritual, atmosphere or mood, into a substance that epitomizes that for which it is supposed to stand. In his own words:

> . . . we are witnessing an extraordinary expansion of the areas associated with food: food is becoming incorporated into an ever-lengthening list of situations. This adaptation is usually made in the name of hygiene and better living, but in reality, to stress this fact once more, food is also charged with signifying the situation in which it is used. It has a twofold value, being nutrition as well as protocol, and its value as protocol becomes increasingly more important as soon as the basic needs are satisfied, as they are in France. In other words, we might say that in contemporary French society, *food has a constant tendency to transform itself into situation* (Barthes 1975).

Food as Love

Barthes' argument deserves additional reflection, in the light of what we recognize about modern societies generally. The creation of societies of the American sort, typified by mass-produced fast food and prefabricated food, by eating out, by eating in casual social groups, in groups that are not really groups at all, or solitarily, societies in which each individual is empowered to choose pretty much what he or she wants among the foods that are available, subject to food technology and pocketbook and the limitations of time, has materially altered the context within which occasion or moment can be identified or experienced.

The phrase "sweet moments" may seem to have a fairly specific meaning, and to be no more than a gentle pun—a sweet moment is figuratively (emotively) sweet, perhaps also (or instead of) gustatorily sweet. But suppose we agree with Barthes that food substance is constantly being turned into situation in the modern world? Then could candy take the place of feeling, rather than merely symbolizing it? Do we show our child love by giving it candy, or do we replace our feeling with a substance: *love* it by giving it candy? Implicit in such a question is the whole issue of time, and how it is differently conceived. If giving love means, among other things, giving time; if time is the more precious resource; if the value of time can be expressed exactly in the value of goods, then can the giving of goods be the giving of love itself? Such, at any rate, is the line of questioning Barthes' intuition suggests. But there is also another, more mundane, issue here, one rather prosaically concerned with the multifunctional roles of the sugars in the modern diet.

What Is a Meal?

Food availabilities in modern society have tended to "smooth out" or to eliminate the structure of meals and the calendar of diet in daily life. Coffee and Coca-Cola are now appropriate at any time and with any accompaniment. So, too, are breaded, deep-fried bits of protein (chicken, scallops, shrimp, ribs, pieces of fish), highly seasoned fat-covered slivers of starch, and certain other items, including synthetic juices that split the difference between the food faddists and the Pepsi Generation. These varied items now provide a nutritive medium *within which* social events occur, rather than the other way round. The meal, which once had a clear internal structure, dictated at least in part by the one-cook-to-one-family pattern, as well as by so-called "tradition," can now mean different items, and a different sequence of items, for each individual consumer. The week's round of food, which once meant chicken (or some equivalent) on Sunday or fish on Friday, is no longer so stable, not viewed as so necessary by the participants. And the year's round of food, which brought bock beer, shad, fresh dill, and new potatoes each in its turn, turkey twice a year, and fruit cake at New Years, survives only much reduced, finessed by turkey-burgers, year-round bock beer, and other modern wonders.

The transformations involved here have made ingestion a much more individualized and noninteractive process; but the choices are still made within ranges strictly predetermined, on the one hand, by food technology and, on the other, by the constraints of time, real or contrived. Accordingly, "sweet moments" is a phrase now acquiring rather different meaning from that it had 50 or even 25 years ago. In order to comprehend that difference, we need to put shifts in sucrose usage together with the broader, more general social changes referred to earlier. The rise in the use of prepared foods, the increase in meals eaten out, and the decline in the meal itself as a ritual (particularly of kin groups) have led to different patterns of sucrose usage, as well as to an increase in the consumption of sugars overall.

Changing Meal Patterns. Between 1955 and 1965, per capita use of certain sugars and sweets—candy, for example—actually dropped 10%. But during the same period, the per capita use of frozen milk desserts rose 31%; baked goods 50%; and soft drinks 78% (Page and Friend 1974). From these figures one infers an increased intervention in meal schedules by sweet moments, and these sweet moments were more substantial, if anything, than those formerly provided by candy bars. The sweet moments such consumption occasioned, though they may have been altering the very notion of what a meal was, were still recognizable as non-meals, but the effects they had on what was left of the dissolving mealtimes were substantial, nonetheless. The enlargement of the mid-morning and mid-afternoon snack, as would appear to follow from these increases, automatically tended to make the meals on either side more "snack-like."

Sugar Isn't Always Sweet

At the same time, the expanded use of prepared foods at home, together with the intensified patronage of fast-food outlets, has also meant a parallel increase in sugar consumption, in these instances often without sweetness. The high sucrose content of many foods that do not taste sweet (dredging flours, for instance, for baking and deep frying) is one such source of the increase. Even in foods such as peanut butters, Cantor and Cantor (1977) have pointed out, standard peanut butter formulas now allow up to 10% sugars. If a peanut butter "tastes better" when it is 10% sugar than when it is not, even if it does not "taste sweet," then we are plainly dealing with a different kind of sweet moment.

CONCLUDING REMARKS

It is the peculiar versatility of sugars that has led to their remarkable permeation through so many foods and into nearly all cuisines. But the subsidiary or additional uses of some sugars, and particularly sucrose, have become more important, not less, as prepared foods, both inside and outside the home, grow in popularity. Sweetness has not lost its importance by any means; but its role in the patterning of ingestion has changed, even while the nonsweetening uses of sucrose and corn sweeteners have expanded. It is because of the highly divergent functions of sugars in the industrial societies that a new typology of sugar use—a cultural typology based on the perspective of the users—is now much needed. The categories suggested here are crude. More important, they do not arise from the subjective perceptions of the users, which ought to be the principal guide to a solid understanding of sweet moments. It will probably be in the intersection of user response and a solid knowledge of the physiological bases of tasting sweetness that our next questions will arise; they will be better questions, even if the answers are every bit as elusive.

REFERENCES

BARTHES, R. 1975. Toward a psychosociology of contemporary food consumption. *In* European Diet from the Industrial to Modern Times. E. Forster and R. Forster (Editors). Johns Hopkins University Press, Baltimore, Maryland.

BEAUCHAMP, G., MALLER, O., and ROGERS, J.C. 1977. Flavor preference in cats (*Felis catus* and *Panthera* sp.). J. Comp. Physiol. Psychol. *91*, 1118–1127.

BEIDLER, L. 1975. The biological and cultural role of sweeteners. *In* Sweeteners: Issues and Uncertainties. National Academy of Sciences, Washington, DC.

CANTOR, S. 1974. The chemistry and technology of sugars. *In* Sugars in Nutrition. H. Sipple and K. McNutt (Editors). Academic Press, New York.

CANTOR, S. 1978. *In* Special Supplement—Feeding, Weight, and Obesity Abstracts. J. H. Shaw and G. C. Roussos (Editors). Information Retrieval, Inc., Washington, DC.

CANTOR, S. 1981. Sweeteners from cereals: the interconversion of function. *In* Cereals: A Renewable Resource. W. Pomerantz and L. Munck (Editors). American Association of Cereal Chemists, St. Paul, Minnesota.

CANTOR, S. and CANTOR, M. 1977. Socioeconomic factors in fat and sugar consumption. *In* The Chemical Senses and Nutrition. M. Kare and O. Maller (Editors). Academic Press, New York.

CANTOR, S. and SCHAFFER, G.E. 1974. Food consumption patterns: pressures toward a three-commodity sweetener system. Cereal Sci. Today *19*, 266–291.

LINDER, S. 1970. The Harried Leisure Class. Columbia University Press, New York.

McGANDY, R.B., HEGSTED, D.M., and STARE, F.J. 1967. Dietary fats, carbohydrates, and atherosclerotic vascular disease. N. Engl. J. Med. *277*, 186.

MINTZ, S. 1979. Time, sugar and sweetness. Marx. Perspect. *2*, 56–73.

PAGE, L., and FRIEND, B. 1974. Level of use of sugars in the United States. *In* Sugars in Nutrition. H. Sipple and K. McNutt (Editors). Academic Press, New York.

PERISSE, J., SIZARET, F., and FRANCOIS, P. 1969. The effect of income on the structure of the diet. Nutr. Newsl. *7*.

PYLER, E.J. 1973. Baking Science and Technology, 2nd ed. Siebel, Chicago, Illinois.

ROZIN, P. 1975. Psychobiological and cultural determinants of food choice. *In* Dahlem Workshop on Appetite and Food Intake. T. Silverstone (Editor). Dahlem Konferenzen, Berlin, Germany.

ROZIN, P. 1976. The selection of foods by rats, humans, and other animals. Adv. Study Behav. *6*, 21–76.

SAHLINS, M. 1976. Culture and Practical Reason. University of Chicago Press, Chicago, Illinois.

SOMBART, W. 1967. Luxury and Capitalism. University of Michigan Press, Ann Arbor, Michigan.

SUGAR ASSOCIATION, INC. 1979. Why Sugar? Sugar Association, Inc., New York.

WRETLIND, A. 1979. World sugar production and usage in Europe. *In* Sugars in Nutrition. H. Sipple and K. McNutt (Editors). Academic Press, New York.

10

Food, Behavior and Biocultural Evolution

Solomon H. Katz

Over the last 15 years a group of us at the University of Pennsylvania and the Eastern Pennsylvania Psychiatric Institute have investigated a number of cases where traditional cultural practices have overcome serious biological limitations naturally present in the foods being consumed (Katz and Foulks 1973; Katz *et al.* 1975; Katz 1977, 1979, 1981; Katz and Schall 1979). In this chapter I will present an analysis of this incompletely understood process which we have called "biocultural evolution."

MAIZE AND BIOCULTURAL EVOLUTION

It has been demonstrated that if maize (corn) is first treated with an alkali solution before consumption, the alkali liberates niacin from an undigestible complex and significantly improves the amino acid quality of the digestible protein fraction of the zein and germ (Katz *et al.* 1975). Since the presence or absence of this alkali processing technique may therefore have provided an important limitation in the nutritional efficacy of maize diets, we attempted to determine the degree to which American Indian societies traditionally depended on this technique in their consumption of maize. Specifically, we hypothesized that the use of alkali processing techniques would significantly increase the nutritional advantages to those American Indian societies that depended on this food resource (Katz 1977). We collected cross-cultural data from a study of over 50 American Indian societies in which we determined the relationship between the use of alkali processing techniques and the degree of production and consumption of maize (Table 10.1) in areas where it was ecologically feasible for this kind of agriculture (Fig. 10.1). We found a highly significant relationship between the degree of dietary and agricultural dependence on maize and the use of alkali processing (Fig. 10.2). The geographic distribution of alkali use and the relationships between consumption and production among alkali users and nonusers are shown.

These striking results led us to hypothesize further that such a sophisticated processing technique, which was discovered scientifically only in the last decade or two, was the product of an evolutionary process. We reasoned on the basis of a variety of evidence that this process was neither totally biological nor totally cultural in its development. Rather, it was the result of an incompletely understood interplay of both biological and cultural evolutionary factors.

Biocultural Evolution

We defined this process, in which biological evolution and adaptation is supplemented and complemented by a variety of cultural adaptations, as biocultural evolution (Katz *et al.* 1975). More specifically, we suggested that biocultural evolution involves a reciprocal feedback process between biological needs and cultural responses in which an effective

TABLE 10.1. THE RELATIONSHIP BETWEEN THE USE OF ALKALI FOR PROCESSING MAIZE AND THE EXTENT TO WHICH SOCIETIES CULTIVATE OR CONSUME MAIZE[1,2]

		Consumption			
Cultivation	Rating	None 0	Less than 1/3 Low 1	1/3 to 2/3 Moderate 2	More than 2/3 High 3
More than 2/3 of crops (High)	3			**** **** **b	**** ***
1/3 to 2/3 of crops (Moderate)	2		*	000c 00	
Less than 1/3 of crops (Low)	1		0000 0000 0000		
None	0	0000 0000 0000	*a 0		

Source: Katz *et al.* 1974.
[1] Key to symbols: *, Alkali treatment; 0, no alkali treatment. a, Crow society; b, Paez society; and c, Papago society.
[2] See Fig. 10.1.

FIG 10.1. MAP SHOWING THE LOCATIONS OF 51 SOCIETIES INVESTIGATED AS RE-PORTED IN KATZ *ET AL.* (1974)
For each society the manner of processing and consumption of maize were compared. See Table 10.1 for the comparison.

FIG. 10.2. MAP DISPLAYING THE RATINGS GIVEN TO EACH SOCIETY FOR MAIZE CULTIVATION AND CONSUMPTION AND THE USE OF ALKALI FOR COOKING CORN For each society, two numbers are shown. The first indicates the rating for maize cultivation. The second indicates the rating for maize consumption. Societies utilizing alkali processing techniques have circled numbers.

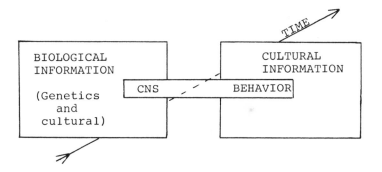

FIG. 10.3.   INFORMATION AND BIOCULTURAL EVOLUTION

dynamic equilibrium with environmental resources is established over time. Moreover, this reciprocal feedback process directly involves human behavior as the major link between the biological needs of the individual and accumulated traditional cultural patterns of adaptation of the population.

This concept is summarized in Fig. 10.3. It consists of a series of essential interactions among several components that underlie the adaptability of a human ecosystem over time. Specifically, the components underlying the essential interactions are (1) the biological information system consisting of the DNA of a particular human population; (2) the cultural information, which is the sum of the knowledge that particular society has accumulated—and is available for exchanging among its members; and (3) the human central nervous system (CNS) which is itself a biologically based information system whose principal evolved function in this model is to facilitate the communication and storage of individually and socially developed knowledge.[1]

Although it is obvious that other important sources of knowledge accumulate in this cultural information pool besides that knowledge associated with food, nevertheless, it is unquestionable that knowledge accumulated about food resources and consumption plays a major role in biocultural evolution. For example, if we examine Fig. 10.4, it is evident that population size—which is a major biological measure of the success of the genus *Homo*—has increased in a revolutionary or exponential

---

[1] While the mechanisms underlying the evolution of the genetic information changes are understood relatively well, and the mechanisms by which the human central nervous system receives, processes, creates, stores, and sends its information are being successfully investigated, I would argue that there is little systematic understanding about the analogous ways in which the sociocultural system develops, changes, stores, transforms and communicates (i.e., evolves) its information, particularly in response to the needs of the biological system.

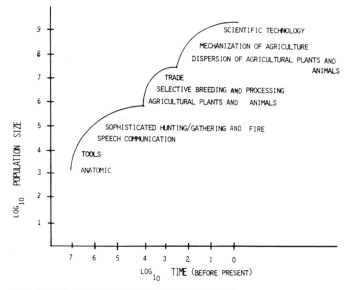

FIG. 10.4. POPULATION REVOLUTIONS AND FOOD

manner each time the mode of subsistence changed. Hence the major revolutionary increases in population size are closely associated with the solution of subsistence problems throughout human history (Katz 1978). Conversely, this close relationship between food and human evolution also suggests that a more comprehensive theory of biocultural evolution will ultimately allow us to develop a more complete theory of food and human behavior which includes a thorough understanding of the full role of food habits for both the individual and society.

FAVA BEANS, G-6-PD DEFICIENCY, AND MALARIA

Since we reasoned that the ways in which human populations solve their food resource problems are central to the evolution of modern societies particularly since the neolithic era, it was important to focus intensive investigation on other plant foods with properties different from maize. We also reasoned that those plant foods with particularly long post-neolithic histories may yield important clues both about the current process of biocultural evolution and the ways in which foods become established as important sources of nutrients. We began by investigating other major foods with significant and diverse limitations. One food source we investigated was fava bean consumption patterns. The use of these beans as a food can be traced archeologically all the way back to neolithic times and the folklore that surrounds their consumption has been termed the most extensive of all foods in Indo-

European history. In a geographic survey conducted much like that for maize, we found an unusual overlap (depicted on Fig. 10.5) between fava bean consumption, the occurrence of malaria, and the gene for glucose-6-phosphate dehydrogenase (G-6-PD) deficiency.

G-6-PD Deficiency.   G-6-PD deficiency is an X-linked genetic trait that renders the red blood cells of the hemizygous males and homozygous deficient females highly sensitive to the powerful hemolytic effects of the strong oxidant compounds found in fava beans (Katz 1979; Katz and Schall 1979). When consumed by these highly sensitive individuals, the beans lead to a rapid hemolytic anemic crisis resulting in a very serious illness or death.

G-6-PD Deficiency and Malaria.   While it was known that frequency of the G-6-PD deficient gene was closely and positively associated with the occurrence of malaria, it was not thought that this association of malaria and the G-6-PD gene was in any way tied to fava bean consumption. Generally, several reports suggested that the gene through some unknown mechanism was associated with resistance to this very important disease. In addition, it was also known that the ingestion of antimalarial drugs also produced a profound hemolytic anemia in these G-6-PD

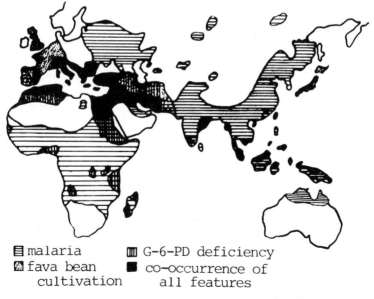

☰ malaria   ▥ G-6–PD deficiency
▨ fava bean   ■ co–occurrence of
   cultivation   all features

From Katz and Schall (1979)

FIG. 10.5. GEOGRAPHICAL DISTRIBUTION OF FAVA BEAN CONSUMPTION, MALARIA, AND G-6-PD DEFICIENCY

deficient individuals that was just like that produced by the consumption of fava beans.

This combination of data together with other evidence we developed in our laboratory led us to hypothesize that the consumption of fava beans by heterozygous females, who were carriers of the gene but not as sensitive to the toxic effects of the bean, were rendered more resistant to malaria via the pharmacological constituents of the beans. Likewise, normal individuals were also benefited. This resulted in a balance favoring the frequency of the G-6-PD deficiency gene in females and in the advantages of other genes that may have mitigated the effects of favism. This was particularly so in females such as in the case of β-thalassemia. Hence, a balance (Fig. 10.6) was established between the gene for deficiency and the continued use of a bean that was, on the one hand, deadly and, on the other, life saving. From the biocultural evolutionary perspective this suggested for the first time that the cultural support mechanisms for the continued consumption and selective avoidance of the beans were intricately involved in the biological evolution of a gene—a gene that represents the most common genetic disorder in the world.

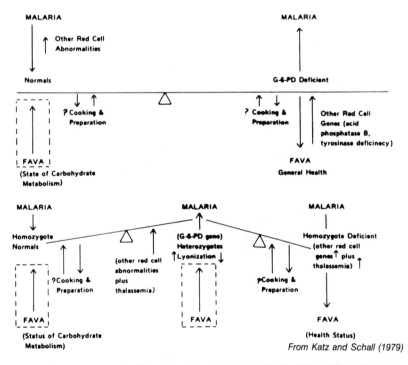

From Katz and Schall (1979)

FIG. 10.6.   FACTORS AFFECTING DISTRIBUTION OF 6-G-PD GENE FREQUENCY IN MALES *(TOP)* AND FEMALES *(BOTTOM)*

Fava Beans and Behavior. These findings have led to a number of further hypotheses about biocultural effects of the fava bean. It also led us to investigate important pharmacological properties of the beans. In this instance fava beans contain sufficient quantities of the L-DOPA (dihydroxyphenylalanine) (0.25%) to be its chief commercial source. Hence we hypothesized that the cultural data should in part reflect this psychologically important brain biochemical. Our analyses of a variety of ancient Greek, Roman, and later English texts all agree as to the sleep restlessness, heavy dreaming, and increased sexuality associated with their consumption (Katz 1979).

BITTER MANIOC

The biological findings on the relations of genetics, food pharmacology and disease led to an investigation of bitter manioc, another food with potent pharmacological effects. This extraordinarily productive and hearty root crop *(Manihot esculenta)* contain cyanate which is bound to glycosides distributed throughout the tuber pulp.

Any physical damage to bitter manioc releases a potent glycosidase which immediately acts to free small amounts of cyanide (HCN). Hence, bruising the pulp and squeezing it releases glycosidases, which in turn break the glycosidic bonds. This process frees the HCN and cooking the juice and pulp volatolizes the HCN into the air. In the event the bitter manioc is consumed without first squeezing and subsequent cooking, the probability of deadly toxic effects remain very high. In experiments with the traditional South American Amerindian preparation of bitter manioc into cassareep we found most of the cynate liberated (Mihalik and Katz 1981). However, a significant but not toxic quantity remain in the glycosidic form. During digestion this HCN is slowly liberated and the cynate fraction presumably is absorbed by the body.

Bitter Manioc and Sickle Cell Anemia

It has been demonstrated the cyanate (CN^-) chemically interacts with (carbamylates) hemoglobin S (HbS) in sickle cell anemia (SSA) and acts as an antisickling agent. Therefore, we recently hypothesized that the consumption of bitter manioc may be associated with sufficient intake of CN^- to ameliorate the effects of sickle cell anemia crises. First we tested the "cooked" form and found sufficient CN^- to have, at least theoretically, a small carbamylation effect on HbS (Mihalik and Katz 1981). However, the *in vivo* studies to determine the extent to which sickling crises are averted are not yet complete. What is striking, nevertheless, is the rapid manner in which this crop has spread throughout sub-Saharan Africa over the last 400 years in a broad band that is coincident with the distribution of SSA and malaria (Mihalik 1980). Hence, it is entirely possible that if this food lowered mortality rates due to sickle cell anemic crises, then it follows that the very rapid rise in the postulated gene frequency of HbS in Africa may in part be due to the enhanced selective advantage of recessive SSA provided by this food mechanism.

If we begin to add this and other cases of foods currently under investigation—such as the highly adaptive role of yeast in brewing and breadmaking (see AAAS 1981), or the significance of spices and herbs as antioxidants and pharmacologically active agents—then it becomes increasingly apparent that most human foods fit into some culturally evolved pattern. In this pattern there are multiple interactions among various aspects of the ecosystem, the cultural means of exploitation, and the genetic constitutions of the individual consumers (see also Simoons, this volume Chapter 1). In the following section I will present our current analysis of the biocultural factors involved in the exploitation of soybeans as a food source.

THE ORIGINS OF SOYBEANS IN CHINA

We recently investigated the origins and diffusion of soybeans (Katz and Ricci 1981). Soybeans are the leading cash crop of this country, which in 1979, according to USDA statistics, overtook corn for most acreage devoted to a single crop in the United States. Although soybeans provide an immensely important source of nutrition throughout Asia, (e.g., in Japan where soy goods are the leading source of protein in the diet) until very recently they have not been used as an important food resource in the United States or in any other Western countries where they are grown.

We have hypothesized that the principal reason for the lack of their incorporation into Western cuisine is the fact that without appropriate processing of an antinutritive substance within them they are essentially inedible. For example, as recently as the end of World War II soybeans were shipped in large quantities to Korea, Japan and Germany. The Asiatic populations thrived on them. The Germans kept getting very sick every time they ate them, consequently losing weight and suffering other ill effects. Finally, within a short period of time the United States had to stop shipping soybeans to post-World War II Germany.

Deactivating the Antitrypsin Factor

Further investigation by nutritionists indicated that soybeans contained a potent antitrypsin factor, which could only be deactivated at high temperatures or by prolonged boiling up to several hours. However, the heat destroyed much of the nutritive value of the beans. Since both of these techniques were impractical, further biochemical analyses were undertaken. We subsequently demonstrated that the antitrypsin factor could be separated from the other soy proteins by precipitation with a divalent cation such as magnesium or calcium (Katz and Ricci 1981). The antitrypsin factor remains in the supernatant and the high quality soy proteins in the precipitate.

This process appeared to the U.S. food scientists to represent a major breakthrough in cleaning up soy proteins, since the amount of cooking time was reduced by two-thirds and the product was highly nutritious. The food scientists quickly learned, however, that the Koreans were already using this process as a normal part of their reparation of *doufu* (soybean curd). It became immediately apparent, of course, that the same technique had been used for many centuries in China and Japan for making *doufu* and *tofu*, respectively (*doufu* is generally a calcium precipitate and *tofu* is usually a magnesium precipitate). This led us to two lines of investigation. First, was there an association between this and other traditional processing technologies and the optimal exploitation of soybeans; and second, how did this technology for optimal processing evolve?

Cultural Processing of Soybeans

In the first instance, we examined all food data on 60 societies listed in the region within the Human Relation Area Files (HRAF) and expanded this source with data from all nutritional sources that we could locate (Katz and Ricci 1981). Several findings emerged from this survey.

1. The vast majority of soybeans were consumed as bean curd throughout Asia. An exception is Indonesia, where a *Rhizopus* mold is introduced to the beans that ferments them into *tempeh*. The latter deactivates the antitrypsin factor and also enhances the production of vitamin B_{12}, which is usually lacking in vegetarian diets.
2. Other means of fermentation were also used to treat the soybeans—particularly molds—to produce soy sauce, which is widely used as a condiment throughout Asia.

From Katz and Ricci (1981)

FIG. 10.7.   THE ORIGINS AND DIFFUSION OF SOYBEANS

3. Other traditional usages, including sprouting and production of soymilk were apparent.

4. Finally, it also became clear that only populations that had had extended contact with China and Buddhism utilized soybeans as a food resource. Essentially, a line could be drawn around China and the rest of Asia showing the circumscribed exploitation of this resource as a human food through modern times (see Fig. 10.7). This led us to hypothesize that the origins of soybeans as a food for human consumption was closely associated with efficient deactivation of this antitrypsin factor.

Soybeans in Chinese History

In testing this hypothesis we were fortunate to have available written records from Chinese history that helped us to document much of the entire soybean usage phenomenon. Soybeans are thought to have originated prehistorically as a food in Mongolia in Northern China. Neolithic cave dwellings have yielded archeological evidence showing that soybeans were roasted. While this process probably deactivated the antitrypsin factor, the intensity of flame for roasting is associated with significant decomposition of the amino acids, thereby lowering their nutritional value. The first mention of soybeans in Chinese history is in the Materia Medica of the Chinese Emperor, Shang Nung, in 2838 BC. However, most scholars of Chinese history currently believe that Shang

Nung was the mythological conception of later Han Dynasty historians (Ho 1975).

Soybean's First Usage. This and other data recorded that Chinese agriculture was already established by the time that soybeans were introduced and that they were first recorded as a medicine rather than as a food. In addition, soybeans were added as the fifth of the sacred grains of China in the Chou dynasty. This group included rice, barley, wheat and millet. Yet there is no evidence in the Chinese literature that the magnesium and/or calcium precipitation into bean curd was practiced at this time or earlier. Beside the evidence of earlier roasting, the only method of deactivating the soybean antitrypsin factor was the use of fermentation in the preparation of the *miso* and soy sauce first appearing in the Chou dynasty (1134–246 BC). The first mention of *doufu* after the Chou dynasty appears in several instances in the Han dynasty (205 BC to 220 AD). However, even this interpretation has recently been discredited by Yuan Han-ch'ing (1981), who has suggested that this is merely legendary. Hence, there is an apparent discrepancy between their widespread use in the Chou dynasty and the absence of an efficient means of extracting an optimal nutritional profile. This problem is heightened further by the fact that the first extensive descriptions of soybeans appear in agricultural reports either coincident with the Chou dynasty (Hymowitz 1970) or predating it by over a thousand years. Hence, we conclude that optimal processing of soybeans via the divalent precipitation method did not accompany their early exploitation as a food resource. This leads us to question how soybeans were utilized and established as ultimately one of the sacred grains before the development of what now appears to be the best method of traditional processing.

Nonfood Usage of Soybeans? The first mention of the soybean is in an agricultural context. We therefore reasoned that initially their advantage to these early agriculturalists may lie in the fact that they provided a more important role as a necessary link to the productivity of the other cereal grain crops rather than as an important source of protein. That is, unlike other cereal grains soybeans are unique in that nitrogen-fixing bacteria extensively invade their root structure, providing a natural means of fertilizing the surrounding soil. Hence, soil nitrogen depleted by other cereal grains could be replaced by appropriate planting of soybeans.

There is evidence in support of this interpretation. As will be seen in Fig. 10.8 the Chinese characters for the sacred grains all emphasize their seed-bearing qualities by depicting the seeds and differentiation of the top of the plant. However, for the fifth plant, soybeans, the emphasis

From Ho (1975)

FIG. 10.8.   CHINESE CHARACTERS FOR CEREALS
The upper characters are symbols for soybeans and demonstrate strong emphasis on the nodules attached to the roots. The lower row are symbols for cereal grains and emphasize the upper seed-bearing portions of the plant and minimize the lower root structure.

is exactly reversed, emphasizing the bacterial nodules on the root struc- ture rather than the bean pods, which would have been the source of food (Ho 1975). Hence, the earliest Chinese characters for soybeans provides evidence in support of the hypothesis that soybeans were used initially more as a means of increasing cereal crop productivity than as a major food resource. After optimal processing methods evolved, it is likely that the emphasis shifted toward soybeans as an important source of food.

Obtaining the Divalent Cation

The above analysis does not indicate how the technology for obtaining the necessary divalent cation evolved. It is evident that the calcium used in central China was abundantly available in the form of gypsum, a calcium sulfate compound. However, in China, Korea, and Japan a magnesium salt is used when gypsum is not available. Magnesium salt is the principle ingredient of *nigari*, whose preparation further demon- strates the often complex technology added over time to the optimiza- tion of soybean foods.

Nigari.   The first step in making *nigari* is to evaporate seawater to sea salt. The latter is placed in cloth sacks and hung on the rafters of the house. When allowed to equilibrate there with humid air, the sea salt becomes selectively hydrophillic and slowly dissolves into a liquid that is differentially rich in magnesium, the divalent cation found in seawater. These drippings of *nigari* are collected in a container and make an ideal precipitating solution (Shurtless and Aoyagi 1975). In general, this process represents a remarkable technological innovation for extracting high concentrations of magnesium and possibly contributing other trace elements to the salt.

CONCLUSIONS

These remarkable sequences and data on the agricultural origins of soybeans and the technology for extracting the divalent cation, magnesium, from sea salt raise further questions about biocultural evolutionary processes as they pertain to human subsistence. Most importantly, they suggest that an examination of the entire human food chain is necessary in order to answer questions about human behavior and food.

It appears to be necessary but not sufficient to deal with food production, on the one hand, and nutrition, on the other. Under traditional circumstances, there are many intervening steps and processes that have evolved over time and play crucial roles in maintaining a balanced equilibrium between the biological needs and the cultural prescriptions for their solution. For example, to propose that soybeans are highly limited as a source of food because of their antitrypsin factor is apparently a necessary but not sufficient explanation for their early use in China. Likewise, to generalize on the specific limitations of maize without the nutritional complementarity that exists when consumed with lysine-rich beans—or the consumption of methionine rich rice with methionine deficient soybean curd—limits our understanding of the traditional role of cuisine in the regulation of balance in dietary nutrients. Hence, on the basis of these and other data, we have concluded that over the time interval since the domestication of plants those populations that became increasingly dependent on an agricultural mode of production evolved a series of equilibria that stabilized along each step of the human food chain—spanning from alterations of the environment to the consumption of the food. A diagram of this food chain can be seen in Fig. 10.9, which attempts to organize the major multiple interacting factors that underlie the connection between the culturally developed solutions and the biological needs of the population. In each of the cases, we have explored and tended to take advantage of the immense knowledge and scientific information available at the biological level to generate our hypotheses about particular foods. These are culturally

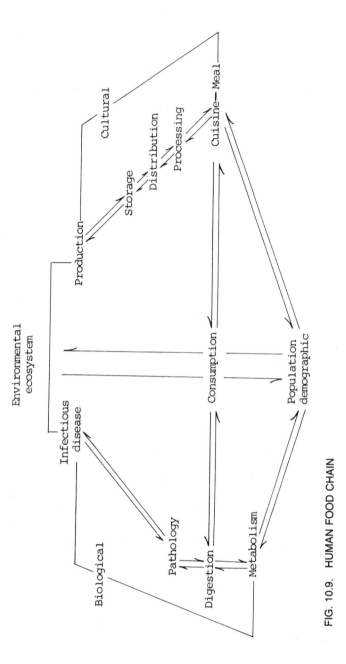

FIG. 10.9. HUMAN FOOD CHAIN

prescribed and adapted transformations of foods that appear to be universally practiced, ranging from production, through storage, distribution, processing and cuisine to consumption. While we know a great deal about the genetics, biochemistry, physiology and pharmacology of various nutrients, antinutrients, toxicants, allergens, stimulants, depressants and other psychoactive effects, we know very little about the feedback relations with practices which have evolved over many centuries. We know even less about how these processes systematically influence cuisine patterns and how they in turn influence the cultural aspects of human behavior as it relates to food consumption. However, if we do recognize the intrinsic nature of the interactions of these kinds of variables, we can easily go on making very limited generalizations about behavior and food. The latter may fit a particular population. But, as we have seen all too frequently, specific food practices do not fit the conditions in other populations when food is distributed across boundaries of cultural traditions. If we are going to move toward a more comprehensive theory of food and human behavior we must begin to consider a holistic model that considers the entire food chain in both time and space. Thus we need to develop a new science that deals with human food and behavior—a social nutrition, which takes the basic knowledge of metabolism and digestion and the neurological controls underlying feeding behavior, and integrates it with a thorough anthropological understanding of the origins and evolution of food at the biocultural level.

REFERENCES

AAAS 1981. Symposium on Religion and Food. American Association for the Advancement of Science, Washington, DC.

HO, P.T. 1975. The Cradle of the East. Chinese University of Hong Kong and the University of Chicago Press, Hong Kong.

HORBATH, A.A. 1927. The Soybean as Human Food. Peking Union Medical College, Chinese Government Bureau of Economic Information, Peking.

HYMOWITZ, T. 1970. On the domestication of the soybean. Econ. Bot. 24 408–421.

KATZ, S.H. (Editor). 1975. Biological Anthropology: Selected Readings from Scientific American. W.H. Freeman, San Francisco, California.

KATZ, S.H. 1977. Toward a new concept of nutrition. In Malnutrition, Behavior, and Social Organization. L. Greene (Editor). Academic Press, New York.

KATZ, S.H. 1978. Toward a new science of man. Zygon 10, 12–31.

KATZ, S.H. 1979. Fava bean consumption and human evolution. Social Commun. (Paris) 26, 47–69.

KATZ, S.H. (Editor). 1981. Nutrition Policy Planning and Anthropology. Cambridge University Press, New York. (in press).

KATZ, S.H., and FOULKS, E.F. 1973. Calcium homeostasis and behavioral disorders. Am. J. Phys. Anthropol. *32*, 299–304.

KATZ, S.H., and RICCI, J. 1981. The soybean and traditional processing techniques. *In* Nutritional Policy Planning. S.H. Katz (Editor). Cambridge University Press, New York. (in press).

KATZ, S.H., and SCHALL, J.I. 1979. Fava bean consumption and biocultural evolution. Med. Anthropol. *3*, 459–476.

KATZ, S.H., HEDIGER, M., and VALLEROY, L. 1975. The anthropological and nutritional significance of traditional maize processing techniques in the New World. *In* Biosocial Interrelations in Population Adaptation. E. Watts, B. Lasker, and F. Johnston (Editors). Biosocial Interrelations in Population Adaptation. Mouton, The Hague, Netherlands.

KATZ, S.H., HEDIGER, M.L. and VALLEROY, L.A. 1974. Traditional maize processing techniques in the new world. Science *184*, 765–773.

MIHALIK, G. 1980. SS anemia and bitter manioc. M.A. Thesis. University of Pennsylvania, Philadelphia, Pennsylvania.

MIHALIK, G., and KATZ, S.H. 1981. Bitter manioc cynate and sickle cell hemoglobins. Submitted for publication.

SHURTLESS, W., and AOYAGI, A. 1975. The Book of Tofu. Autumn Press, Inc., Brookline, Massachusetts.

YUAN, HAN-CH'ING. 1981. On the question of the origin of bean curd. China Historical Materials of Science and Technology *2*, 84–86. (Chinese).

11

The Structure of Cuisine

Elisabeth Rozin

In the dusty streets of rural villages, in the dingy rooms of city tenements, in the furtive clearings of sweating jungles, in the secret, sacred precincts of three-star restaurants, it is going on. Listen, and you will hear it: the clatter of pans, the slapping of dough, the pounding of grain. Sniff, and you will smell it: the roasting meat, the newly baked hot bread, the aromatic sauce. Look, and you will see it: the quick stirring of a pot, the delicate folding of a triangle of dough. . . . Wherever you may wander, among those of the human kind, you will find them preparing their food, expending enormous quantities of time, energy, and attention on the homely activity we call cooking.

CULINARY BEHAVIOR

Man is a unique creature, and one of his most unique attributes, indeed one of the things that brands him as quintessentially human, is the fact he has from his very beginning rejected omophagia (the eating of raw food). Culinary behavior, the voluntary or deliberate manipulation or processing of a foodstuff for the purpose of altering it in some predictable fashion, can be shown to exist in all cultures throughout human history. Although culinary behavior can be found in the animal world, it exists in limited ways and under very limited circumstances; while the rudiments of true cooking can be faintly glimpsed in non-humans, it is always on a level that is motivationally and technologically simple (Kawai 1965). The complexity of human culinary behavior means not only that we are willing to put up with long delays between obtaining our food and eating it, but that many of us are willing as well to spend a good part of our lives transforming potential food into real food. There are many and diverse solutions to the problem of transforming food, but the inclination and the ability to deal with it appear to be universal.

CUISINE

Culinary behavior, or what we more commonly call cooking, is practiced not just occasionally or under special limited conditions, but with a frequency and a regularity that are true of very few other activities. Yet, while all people do it, they all do it differently. Within the broad universal practice we call cooking there is an almost limitless set of individual practices. People who define themselves as a group express or interpret the general human practice in their own individual terms, and it is this individual style or expression of universal culinary activity that we call *cuisine*. Every culture cooks, but each is intimately bound to its own unique and individual culinary practice. In order to assess the nature of the relationship between a culture and its cuisine, we must attempt to determine, if only at first in very broad terms, the specific acts and processes that comprise the activity of cooking, and to describe the salient choices of foods and manipulations involved in the formation of a cuisine. It is hoped that these seemingly simple descriptive elements will provide us with a preliminary framework of analysis for an extraordinarily rich and complex area of human behavior.

Basic Foods

The first crucial element in any cuisine must be the food itself, the basic foodstuffs that are selected for culinary preparation and consumption. What people eat, the foods they select, is the first important variable in cuisine because there are noticeable and describable distinctions between the foods of different groups of people, foods that produce different sensations when they are consumed, in addition to whatever nutritional or physiological factors may be involved. The meat of a cow tastes significantly different from the meat of a sheep and both are distinguishable from the meat of a pig. Similarly, there is no confusing boiled rice with boiled corn, either in taste, odor, appearance, or texture, just as there is no confusing goat cheese with cow cheese.

All cultures make such selections of foodstuffs, whether in the dark recesses of the tropical jungle or in the spacious aisles of the suburban supermarket. Even, indeed, in areas that are considered "marginal" for human habitation, where one might assume that people would eat almost anything, such selections are rigorously made. The bushmen of

Botswana, in the northwest corner of the Kalahari desert, face droughts and ensuing lean periods every 2 or 3 years. Yet, of the 223 species of animal that inhabit the region, the Bushmen consider only 54 to be edible (Lee 1968).

The general rule seems to be that everyone eats some things, but no one eats all things, and the basis for the selection of foods by a culture is dependent on a wide variety of factors: availability, environmental variables, ease of production, nutritional costs and benefits, palatability, custom, and religious or social sanction. In any case, whatever the reason for the choice, a selection of foods is made by all peoples and forms the basic underpinning of all cuisines. Different foodstuffs produce varying sensations of flavor, aroma, appearance, and texture, all of which seem to be critical factors in the human eating experience.

MANIPULATIVE TECHNIQUES

Assuming, then, that we can describe with reasonable accuracy what foods a given culture eats and with what frequency, or, in other words, to compose a dietary, we are still far from understanding the cuisine, with all its inevitable intricacies and subleties. We must now begin to analyze what it is exactly that people do to or with their basic foods in order to transform them from their raw to a cooked state. It should be clear that in this context the term "cooking" is used in its widest sense, to cover any and all culinary manipulations performed to alter a foodstuff in some predictable fashion, and not in its more narrow sense of applying heat. In this wider sense of the word, a salad of raw greens is "cooked" when it is tossed with a dressing or sauce; the original substance is transformed or altered by the deliberate addition of other ingredients.

It is not immediately obvious how to classify all cooking techniques, as the ingenious human, throughout culinary evolution, has devised no small number of food manipulations involving a variety of processes and motives. It is useful to attempt a comprehensive scheme or taxonomy of culinary techniques, however, because none, to my knowledge, has been devised, and it would be of obvious value in any descriptive analysis of cuisine.

Processes That Involve Physical Changes in Size, Shape or Mass

Particulation. The process of particulation is of inestimable culinary importance, in that it effectively reduces a food substance into smaller and smaller elements. Applied to flesh or fibrous plant foods the basic technology would include such processes as cutting, slicing, dicing, mincing, pounding, chopping, and pureeing. Applied to seeds, grains, and some other kinds of plant foods, it would include grinding, milling, grating, rasping, sifting, and pulverizing.

Incorporation.   Incorporation is a process by which a food substance is altered by having another substance mixed with or incorporated into it, utilizing techniques such as mixing, stirring, beating, or whipping. A raw egg white, when beaten, changes from a runny mucoid substance to a white fluffy mass, which increases in volume as air is incorporated into it. That white fluffy mass, when mixed into yet another substance, causes an alteration in its texture, making it less dense and less compact (as, for example, in a mousse or a soufflé). So, too, the simple mixing of wet and dry substances produces striking modifications: milled grain mixed with water can, depending on the fineness of the milling and the amount of the liquid, result in a porridge or gruel, or in a batter or dough.

Separation or Extraction.   Distinct elements within a foodstuff may be separated one from another. In its simplest form it may be the separation of the edible part of the substance from the inedible part, i.e., peeling a banana. In more complex forms it may be applied to foods whose separable elements are not always discrete or visually evident, such as the extraction of oils from plants, or the rendering of fat from meats. The concept of separation or extraction may be dependent on other processes, such as particulation or the application of heat, and may itself give rise to other processes such as squeezing, pressing, straining, skimming, and the introduction of chemical or bacterial agents that can cause separation.

Processes That Involve Manipulation of Water Content

Marination.   A food substance may be immersed in liquid for varying amounts of time. Depending on the nature of the liquid medium (marinade) and the length of the immersion, different culinary results can be achieved.

1. Brief marination.   A relatively short process of hours or days can produce striking alterations of taste and texture. In the Peruvian–Mexican dish *ceviche*, fish or seafood is literally "cooked" by a few hours' immersion in citrus juice. The texture of the marinated fish is more or less indistinguishable from the texture of fish to which heat has been applied. The acid in the citrus juice breaks down the connective tissues in flesh much as heat does. Brief periods of marination can be used as well to effect desired alterations in flavor or to increase the water content of a substance.

2. *Extended marination or curing.* Longer periods of immersion (weeks or months), in which the natural water content of a substance is totally replaced by the marinating liquid, can cure foods, that is, prepare them for longer periods without spoilage. Although the technique of marination can theoretically employ almost any flavored liquid, the curing process, where preservation of food is the primary motive, utilizes two basic marinating media. The first is a salt liquid, or brine, which preserves for longer periods by inhibiting the growth of bacteria. The second basic curing medium is acidic in nature, using primarily vinegar or citrus juice. Such a marinade is called a "pickle" and, like brine, retards the growth of bacteria.

3. *Soaking or leaching.* Most substances absorb water: when soaked, their tissues swell and become soft. Soaking in water is a useful culinary process, then, for softening items that are quite hard, like dried beans or certain grains. The process may also be necessary to initiate processes like fermentation. Beer cannot be produced unless the grain is soaked in water; this process softens the grain and permits the growth of microorganisms.

Leaching is fundamentally a cleansing process in which undesirable material is washed out of the food. Such material can range from relatively harmless but unaesthetic dirt, to actual poisons that must be removed if the foodstuff is to be edible. Many groups in tropical South America, Africa, and the West Indies rely for their basic diet on the starchy manioc (cassava) root, which may contain fatal amounts of prussic acid. These groups have developed lengthy and elaborate techniques for leaching the poison from the manioc, resulting in an edible tapioca (Sturtevant 1969).

Dry curing. Dry curing is a process in which the water content of a food is gradually reduced, either by salting or by exposure to air and/or smoke. Salt dehydrates organic substances by causing them to exude their natural water content, while exposure to air or smoke causes dehydration by evaporation. The technique of dry curing offers two distinct advantages. First, by reducing the moisture content of food the possibility of harmful bacterial growth is lessened and the food can be stored for longer periods without spoiling. Second, the removal of water significantly alters the bulk and the weight of food, making it lighter, more compact, and thus easier to transport. The jerky and various pemmicans of American Indian tribes are classic examples of dry-cured foods.

Freezing. Freezing is a simple process of preservation in which the water content of foods is altered by lowering the temperature to the point where bacterial growth is significantly retarded. The use of this technique has been extended in modern times for the production of more elaborate culinary items such as ice cream, sherbet, and other frozen confections.

Processes That Involve Direct Chemical Changes

Application of Heat. Probably the most pervasive and most commonly used of all culinary techniques, heating foods involves a number of distinct processes (Lehrer 1969).

1. Dry heat (dry cooking)
    a. Indirect—bake, parch, toast
    b. Direct—roast, barbecue, broil, grill, charcoal-broil
2. Wet heat (cooking with liquid)
    a. Indirect—steam
    b. Direct—boil, parboil, simmer, poach, stew, braise
3. Fat or oil cooking—deep fry, fry (pan fry), saute, stir-fry.

Fermentation. "Fermentation" is a catch-all term to describe a large number of culinary processes in which food substances are altered by the action of microorganisms, including yeasts and molds, which are spore-producing fungi, and bacteria of various kinds. The critical variables of time, temperature, and variety of microorganism can yield a myriad of culinary products, and every culture has its own standard and judgment as to what is regarded as ripe (good) or rotten (bad). The process of fermentation is central to the production of such diverse items as alcoholic beverages, leavened bread, condimental sauces such as soy sauce and various fish sauces, and all cultured dairy products.

Taken together, the processes described above form part of the basic structure of culinary practice. Taken individually, any of the processes can develop from very simple origins to very complex technologies, but the fundamental process remains the same. It is critical to note that even though there appears to be a limited number of techniques or processes that humans use to cook their foods, every culture makes a selection from among them. In the preserving of fish, for example, the Indians of the northwest coast of America smoke their salmon, while the Portuguese salt their cod, and the Scandinavians pickle their herring.

FLAVORING FOODS: FLAVOR PRINCIPLES

We have described thus far two essential elements in the structure of cuisine: basic foodstuffs and the manipulative techniques used to transform these foods in predictable ways. There remains one essential factor, what may well be the most crucial act in human culinary behavior—the specific alteration of the flavor of food.

Any manipulation of food, even some of the very simple processes we have described, can be said to affect flavor in some way, and no doubt the great human tradition of seasoning foods began not with the addition of specific flavoring agents but more likely with the use of cooking processes themselves. Cow flesh has a taste that is significantly altered by direct exposure to fire, just as a sun-dried raisin has a flavor very different from the original unprocessed grape. The flavor of yogurt is not really very similar to the flavor of the fresh milk from which it is made, and the difference in taste between the two products is achieved not by seasoning additives but by the culturing process itself. So cooking can effect desired changes in taste while at the same time performing perhaps more vital functions of improving digestibility, removing toxic materials, preventing spoilage, and so forth. Still, cooking processes themselves do not seem to have been effective enough in the specific role of altering or enhancing the flavor of foods, since, as far back as the records go, people have been using specific seasoning agents to manipulate the taste of food.

From studies of fossilized plant remains, for example, comes evidence that the Indians of central Mexico have been spicing their food with chili peppers for many thousands of years, and sophisticated botanic studies have at least begun to show how a wild indigenous plant was gradually domesticated specifically for its seasoning properties (Pickersgill 1969). So too in China, where unfortunately the paleontological record is not so complete, the root of the ginger plant seems to have been used as a common kitchen herb for as long as can be remembered.

It is clear that people go to some trouble to flavor their foods, and have done so from very early times. Moreover, there seems to be a fairly widespread tendency for groups of people to season their foods in unique and characteristic ways, such that the same flavoring agents or combination of agents is used over and over again within any given cuisine. I have elsewhere (Rozin 1973) called these unique flavoring combinations *flavor principles*, and these must be considered, along with basic foods and cooking techniques, as one of the critical elements in the structure of cuisine.

Description of Flavoring Practices

It is almost impossible to overestimate how very critical flavoring is as a marker, a defining characteristic of cuisine. If one says, for example, that a certain group of people eats pork, that tells us something, but not very much, about who those people are. But if one says "soy sauce," there is an almost instantaneous equation or identification with orientals and oriental food. That is because soy sauce, the seasoning agent, is so ubiquitously used in oriental cooking, imparting its own unique and characteristic flavor to food, that it acquires some sort of intense symbolic value as a culinary marker. Orientals use soy sauce in their food and other people do not; to put soy sauce into food is to say that that food *is* in some sense oriental and is *not* Russian or French or Algerian.

Moreover, the somewhat general soy sauce–oriental equation can be broken down into yet smaller and more discrete units that are markers of distinguishable cuisines that exist within the larger soy sauce context. If, to the basic soy sauce, you add garlic, brown sugar, sesame seed and chili, you will obtain a seasoning compound that is definably Korean, because it is this very combination of flavoring ingredients that is used ubiquitously in Korean cooking and in no other. Similarly, if you add garlic, molasses, ground peanuts and chili to the basic soy sauce you will inevitably create a taste that is characteristically and definably Indonesian; this combination of ingredients forms the unique flavor of a sauce that is used on everything from rice to broiled meat to vegetable and salad preparations. And even though these two groups of flavor ingredients may look very similar, and indeed are very similar, they nontheless produce tastes that are distinguishably different from one another.

Even within national or geographic boundaries these flavor principles can be further delineated into smaller regional principles. So, for example, a basic flavor principle in Chinese cuisine is the combination of soy sauce, rice wine, and gingerroot. It forms a classic and fundamental seasoning sauce used widely throughout China. But various regions have added to it their own unique and characteristic ingredients, further individualizing the flavor and thus producing a distinct marker for the cooking of their particular region or group. The cooking of Canton (southern China) is frequently characterized by the addition of fermented black beans and garlic, while the regional cooking of Peking (northern China) is more frequently than not characterized by the addition of soy bean paste, garlic, and sesame oil. In the area of Szechuan (west central China) the basic principle is individualized by the characteristic addition of a "hot" element provided by Szechuan pepper (brown peppercorns) or chili pepper incorporated into a hot bean paste or oil.

The same kinds of flavor principles characterize cooking styles of cuisines throughout the world, and they seem to function equivalently in all cuisines, differing from one another only in the details of the specific ingredients. So another great bond of flavoring ingredients is the combination of olive oil and tomato, which occurs throughout the Mediterranean. The eastern Mediterranean (Lebanon, Greece, the Balkans) individualizes the taste by the frequent addition of cinnamon and/or lemon, while the central Mediterranean (southern France and Italy) leans toward a preference for garlic and various herbs such as oregano, basil, and thyme. In the Iberian peninsula, large amounts of onion and bell pepper are added, while in some areas of Spain the unique flavor of saffron is employed.

One could go on describing equivalent kinds of flavor combinations that appear to operate as distinct taste markers for individual cuisines: the wine−herb principle of French cooking, the onion−lard−paprika principle of Hungarian cooking, the chicken fat−onion principle of eastern European Jewish cooking, the sweet−sour principle that appears independently in many cuisines from China to Germany. What we see is a very widespread tendency for people to select a small number of flavoring ingredients and to use them in combination so frequently and so consistently that they become a clearly defining factor in that particular cuisine.

Functions of Flavoring Practices

The definition that flavoring provides is both inclusionary and exclusionary; it imparts a culinary identification and a sense of familiarity for those individuals who create and share in the tradition, while providing as well a defining marker for those outside the group who do not participate in it or who do so only occasionally. What we do not often realize is how powerfully these flavor markers shape our notion of what a cuisine is. Cover any food, no matter what, with a sauce made of tomatoes, olive oil, garlic and herbs, and we identify it as Italian; what is more, Italians will identify it as Italian. Be it dromedary hump or acorn meal, its culinary identification will ultimately be determined by the way in which it is flavored.

It is clear that the taste of food is a critical factor in cuisine, and that people will go to quite extravagant lengths to attain the means of providing what they regard as a good or proper flavor. Much of the history of the Western world was determined by a desire for seasoning ingredients. The need for flavorings, more than anything else, opened up the spice trade and gave impetus to the age of exploration. It was above all a culinary quest that mirrored in large the quest of most human beings to season their food. J.H. Parry, the distinguished historian of the age of reconnaissance, has pointed out that even more than the shimmering silks and brocades, the precious metals, and all the luxury goods of the east, Europe craved the pepper, the cinnamon, the ginger and cloves that grew in remote and exotic corners of the world. As it became possible to obtain these spices and aromatics, though at great cost in both lives and money, European demand for them seemed insatiable (Parry 1963).

The customary explanation for this extraordinary desire is that spices and seasonings were necessary to "cover" or disguise the taste of tainted meat. There may be some truth in this notion, although the impression it conveys is that most of Europe was subsisting for several centuries on an unremitting diet of spoiled meat. This can hardly have been the case, since for most people meat was then, as it is now, a luxury, and the common diet was composed primarily of grain, cereal, and vegetable foods. It is far more likely that because meat was a desirable and more expensive food, more care and interest were exercised in preserving it. Unfortunately, the preservative techniques that were commonly in use, brining in salt or pickling in vinegar, were likely to result in products that were very unpalatable. The demand for some of these spices can then be more plausibly interpreted as a desire to modify or enhance the flavor of preserved meats. It is the fact that even today exotic spices that are not indigenous to Europe (with the notable exception of pepper) are largely reserved for use in the preparation of preserved meats—sausages, wursts, etc.—rather than in other culinary preparations.

Of course, not all people set sail on treacherous and unknown seas in order to find ways of making their food taste more pleasant. Other people in different cultural and ecological circumstances may go to other lengths quite astonishing to us; human ingenuity in discovering and exploiting the potential flavor possibilities of individual habitats is impressive indeed. The Maidu Indians of California, not dissimilar in this respect from the French or the Thais or the Moroccans, prefer their salad greens enhanced with an acidic flavor. Since they have neither vinegar nor citrus juice, they place the leaves of wild lettuce near the nests of a species of red ant. The ants scurry all over the lettuce, leaving behind a sour secretion much like vinegar. The ants are then shaken off and the lettuce leaves are consumed, quite literally, with relish (Raab 1959).

It must at this point be noted that although characteristic combinations of seasoning ingredients are very widely used throughout the world, they are not universal; there are cultures that depend on one single pervasive flavor. Many of the peoples of Oceania rely almost exclusively on cocoanut to flavor their foods, while the Plains Indians of the United States relied rather heavily on the unique taste of the juniper berry. And again, there are cultures that do not appear to use any particular seasoning in any consistent fashion, or who use cooking techniques themselves to provide alterations in the taste of their food, without adding any specific flavoring ingredients. If a generalization is to be made, it is that people whose diet emphasizes animal foods tend to season less consistently than people whose diet is composed primarily of plant foods. And, in what may well be a related factor, cultures in northern or temperate climates do not use seasoning ingredients with the same regularity as people in southern or tropical climates. Indeed, the great flavor principle cuisines of the world today may be seen to have originated in the great agricultural centers of antiquity: Mexico, Southeast Asia, India, the Mediterranean, and the Middle East.

SOURCES OF VARIATION IN CUISINE

The apparent necessity to manipulate or modify or enhance the flavor of foods by adding various seasoning ingredients seems to be a very consistent and characteristic feature of much of human culinary practice. Moreover, the very salient character of flavor principles and the regularity with which they are used by individual cuisines affirm their importance as one of the great structural elements in culinary style.

This hypothetical construct of culinary structure based on three fundamental elements, basic foodstuffs, manipulative techniques, and seasoning practices, looks rather simple, and indeed is a fairly easy way to begin to assess culinary styles. But is this structure really as simple as it looks? In some ways it is; that is, valid distinctions and descriptions can be made on the basis of these three general elements. But when one begins to look somewhat closer, one sees the incredible variability that exists even within the apparent limits of a seemingly simple element.

Variability in Basic Foods

Take the category of basic foodstuffs, for example. One might say, with apologies to Gertrude Stein, that a cow is a cow is a cow. But this is certainly not the case, and particularly from the culinary point of view. There are many different varieties or breeds of the general class of animal we call cow, and these varieties produce different kinds of beef. Furthermore, the kind of herbage that the animal eats has strong effects on the taste of the flesh and on the flavor of the milk. Indeed, this is the preliminary distinction in the production of a huge number of cow-milk cheeses, all of which are describably different from one another. Again, one may speak of rice as a basic foodstuff, but this seemingly simple element has many varieties—long grain, short grain, fluffy, glutinous, sweet—all of which result in different eating experiences. It should be obvious, then, that this "simple" structural element of basic foods is not really simple at all, and that a large variety and richness of distinction exist within any class of food substances.

Variability in Mainipulative Techniques

The same kind of complexity and variability can be found in the framework of the second structural element of cuisine, manipulative techniques. For even though there are a limited number of techniques or processes by which humans characteristically manipulate their foods, any given technique does not inevitably produce the same result. Variations in technology for the same general process can substantially affect the finished product. For example, a steak cooked over a direct fire of hickory wood will be distinguishably different from a steak cooked over a direct fire of dried cow dung, though the cooking technique for both is essentially the same. That notion of the potential variability of similar cooking techniques was clearly realized and richly described by Ishi, the last surviving member of a tribe of California Indians, the Yahi, who existed on a cultural level comparable to that of stone-age people. Said his biographer (Kroeber 1967) of Ishi:

> The white man's stove he found good for roasting and broiling as in his own earth oven or open-fire cooking, but he considered that the modern stove ruined boiled food. Said Ishi, "White man puts good food in pot full of boiling water. Leaves a long time. Food cooks too fast, too long. Meat spoiled. Vegetables spoiled. The right way is to cook like acorn mush. Put cold water in basket. Place hot rocks in water till it bubbles. Add acorn meal. It cooks *pukka-pukka*. Then it is done. Same way, make deer stew. Or rabbit stew. Cook *pukka-pukka*. Not too long. Meat firm, broth clear, vegetables good, not soft and coming apart.

This vivid description of Ishi's comparing two different applications of the same technique, boiling or stewing, indicates clearly how culinary variations can arise from what appear initially to be simple processes. Boiling a foodstuff in water is a cooking process that from both a theoretical and practical point of view is simple to perform and easy to comprehend. But from the point of view of the differences in technology and the differences in their application and interpretation (Ishi said, "Not too long." How long is long?), a seemingly simple process is capable of generating a myriad of results. This potentially limitless variability has been richly exploited and expressed in the diversity of human culinary practice.

Variability in Seasonings

It should not be surprising, then, to discover that a similar variability occurs in seasoning practices, and even within the bonds of flavor principles. We cannot speak of soy sauce, for example, without indicating the incredible richness of this general class of condimental sauces. Soy sauce is used as a flavoring agent by a number of oriental cuisines and each has its own particular version of the sauce. Indonesian soy sauce is generally sweeter and more viscous than Chinese soy sauce, while Japanese soy sauce is thinner and more delicate. But even within the bounds of Chinese cuisine itself there are many varieties of this basic seasoning ingredient. There is light (or thin) soy sauce, dark (or heavy) soy sauce, sweet soy sauce, mushroom-flavored and shrimp-flavored soy sauce. And all of these soy sauces can justifiably be subsumed under the label of a specific flavoring agent, while at the same time they produce different and describable variations in flavor.

In Mexican cuisine, one of the great flavor principles is the ubiquitous bond of tomatoes and chili peppers. It is used as a sauce or relish on other foods, mixed into salads, cooked into soups and stews. Yet, even these apparently simple ingredients are used with surprising variability. There are red tomatoes and green tomatoes, and they may be eaten raw or cooked. There are hundreds of varieties of chili peppers: some are used fresh, some dried; some are red, some orange, some green; some are violently pungent, others less so, and they differ widely in the type of "burn" or hotness that they produce in the lips, mouth, and throat of the eater. So, too, both the tomatoes and the chili peppers may be used in different proportions and in different combinations for different preparations; these many culinary products can all then be described as flavored by the tomato–chili principle, while at the same time exhibiting a great variety and subtely of flavor.

If, as I have proposed, seasoning ingredients, whether single or in combination, act has a marker or label for a given cuisine, how then can we account for this incredible variability within the bounds of a specific culinary tradition? We have argued elsewhere (Rozin and Rozin 1981) that these flavor variations on a general theme may serve to introduce subtle variety into a fixed (and therefore potentially boring) flavor experience. For just as humans apparently have a need to brand their foods with a well-liked and familiar taste, so have they also an opposing need for interest and variety in dining. To the naive taster all red wines taste alike, while to the experienced taster the differences may be subtle or gross, but they are distinguishable.

CUISINE AS A CULTURAL SYSTEM

All cuisines, like other cultural systems, are sets of rules or prescriptions about how to organize our knowledge or beliefs of human behavior. Cooking, like language or architecture or hair style, depends for its outcome on a socially determined, communally accepted set of rules. These rules determine the elements of the system and structure their arrangement, both spatially and temporally. Thus, before any action is initiated ("I think I'll bake a cake."), its outcome is in some sense determined or prefigured by an underlying structure that shapes the sequence and character of events and the relationship of the elements to one another. We are under most circumstances unaware of these rules, just as we are unconscious of the rules of syntax that govern our utterances. It is only when we attempt to teach or describe an act of cooking (or of speaking, etc.) to another human that we become intensely aware of the necessity for learning the rules that underlie any culturally transmitted system or tradition of behavior.

The scheme I have proposed for analyzing culinary style offers two advantages. First, it allows for a general overview of a prevalent, typical or representative tradition. Second, it permits a closer view of the details of that tradition, so that the variations and subleties that exist within the larger theme can be picked out and examined.

The analysis of culinary practice that results from this scheme takes the form of recipes—whether written or orally transmitted—actual recipes for actual food eaten by actual people. Recipes are sets of rules that determine the ingredients and the appropriate sets and sequences of manipulative techniques that transform the food into a culturally acceptable edible. The scheme therefore deals with the food itself and the means by which it is prepared for eating. This scheme is limited in the sense that it does not provide access to those more intangible factors that also have a large influence on culinary tradition. What we do not learn from this scheme (or may learn only incidentally) is what the symbolic value of any food preparation may be, by whom it may or may not be eaten and on what occasions, its place in ceremonial, festive, or religious life, where it is used in the sequence of foods in a meal, and what its value or significance may be beyond its existence as a food.

When we consider how much time and energy human beings spend in the preparation of their food, that fact alone should be enough to convince us of the profound significance of culinary tradition in human society. It is a curious and wonderful thing that, given the apparently simple structure of cuisine, people have managed to develop an amazing number of individual varieties, each of which is distinctly and definably different from the next. It is this that we call style, and human ingenuity in exploring and exploiting the potentials of culinary style cannot be overestimated; where once our ancestors lounged in the tree-tops munching bananas, we now spend a good part of our waking lives thinking about, preparing for, and actually practicing those critical manipulations that seem to be so crucial to the human food experience.

For their disobedience, God banished Adam and Eve from a fruit-filled nonculinary paradise, and from that time on their descendents (mainly the female ones) have been compelled to grind and knead, to stir and salt. But perhaps that metaphorical departure from innocence and ease was not without its rewards, for had it not occurred, Homo sapiens would perhaps not have found his destiny as Homo culinarius, the creature who smacks his lips and says, "A little more garlic, maybe?" Or perhaps paradise is really the place where potato kugel and fettucine Alfredo grow on trees.

REFERENCES

KAWAI, M. 1965. Newly acquired precultural behavior of the natural troop of Japanese monkeys on Koshima islet. Primates 6, 1–30.

KROBER, T. 1967. Ishi. University of California Press, Berkeley, California.

LEE, R.B. 1968. What hunters do for a living: Or, how to make out on scarce resources. In Man the Hunter. R.B. Lee and I. Devore (Editors). Aldine, Chicago, Illinois.

LEHRER, A. 1969. Semantic cuisine. J. Linguis. 5, 39–56.

PARRY, J.H. 1963. The Age of Reconnaissance. Mentor Books, New York.

PICKERSGILL, B. 1969. The domestication of chile peppers. In The Domestication and Exploitation of Plants and Animals. P.J. Ucko and G.W. Dimbleby (Editors). Gerald Duckworth and Co., London.

RABB, P.V. 1959. The nutrition of the Maidu and the Maya Indians: A comparison. M.S. Thesis. University of Texas, Austin, Texas.

ROZIN, E. 1973. The Flavor Principle Cookbook. Hawthorn, New York.

ROZIN, E. and ROZIN, P. 1981. Culinary themes and variations. Nat. Hist. 90, 6–14.

STURTEVANT, W.C. 1969. History and ethnography of some West Indian starches. In The Domestication and Exploitation of Plants and Animals. P.J. Ucko and G.W. Dimbleby (Editors). Gerald Duckworth and Co., London.

Geography and Genetics as Factors in the Psychobiology of Human Food Selection

Frederick J. Simoons

I was invited to the conference to be one representative of the sociocultural perspective, to cast light on human belief systems as they influence selection among the vast array of edible substances available for consumption. When, however, I sat down to think about what contribution I might make, I found that my interests cannot neatly be categorized. Two decades ago they were purely cultural or—more specifically—culture historical, but they have come to range, however timidly, into the biomedical realm. It would seem that for this book I might best start by explaining how I got into food habit research at all, for this is not a usual field for geographers. I would also, however briefly, like to identify a few of the more interesting areas of investigation in the culture historical sphere as they bear on human food selection, and then to show how my research has led me into the biomedical questions with which I am becoming further involved. Before turning to the above questions, however, I would like to make a few remarks about culture as it relates to human food selection in general, and in the United States and Western world in particular.

Range of Foods Selected

I would first emphasize the point that human groups around the world generally consume quite a limited range of the edible substances available to them. Anthropologist Richard B. Lee in field work in Botswana in the 1960s, found that the !Kung Bushmen of the Dobe area—hunters and gatherers without agriculture or animal husbandry—identified 54 wild animal species as edible, yet regularly hunted only 10 of these, all mammals, for food (Lee 1969). Similarly, though 85 plant species were considered edible, a half to two-thirds of the entire plant diet, by weight, was from a single plant species, the mongongo (*Ricinodendron rautaneii* Schinz), which yields an edible nut (see also Lee 1973). The ecological and socio-cultural factors involved in the choice of food by the Dobe Bushmen need not concern us here, but it should be emphasized that peoples all over the world utilize only a portion of the edible items readily available to them. Some human groups use a broad range of the available edible substances. Others tend to be quite restrictive. Of the world's major population groups, the Chinese might be singled out as broad ranging in their dietary selection (Chang 1977), and Hindu Indians, especially those of the upper caste, as restrictive.

Restrictive American Diets. The United States has seen astoundingly rapid acculturation of most immigrant groups. Along with acculturation, traditional foods have been lost, have become dishes eaten only on special occasions, or have, often in modified form, become part of an amorphous American cuisine. Some observers, in light of the above, suggest that Americans are experimental, eager for innovation, ready for change, people who eat according to availability and cost. In one sense this may be true. By the Chinese standard, however, Americans are quite restrictive in the range of available edible products they consume. This is well-illustrated by Calvin W. Schwabe who in his fascinating book "Unmentionable Cuisine" (1979), identifies and provides recipes for preparing a broad range of foods of animal origin that are utilized in other parts of the world, but little, if at all, in the United States. The restrictive aspect of American and European food behavior is further illustrated by a scoffing at and discouraging of the consumption of certain foods, insects, for example, that Westerners do not consume, a sort of "dietary imperialism" that has tended to reduce the range of foods available to other peoples.

Are American Food Patterns Atypical? One must also caution against viewing the American food selection scene as typical of mankind. We live in one of the most highly urbanized regions of the world, with perhaps half of our people living in communities of 20,000 persons or more. Urbanization and rapid social change enhance the opportunities for immigrant groups to take up new foodways. The socio-cultural factors acting for change in food selection in this country often derive from large-scale commercial campaigns that appeal to convenience, time-saving in a daily life that tends to be hectic. Ours, however, is a situation in which youth are not merely acquiescing to the appeals of advertisers, but are following the patterns of their age groups rather than that of their elders. I am suggesting that however important it may be to study the socio-cultural factors that influence what foods Americans choose to eat, and however significant the inroads Western ways are making elsewhere, the non-Western world today remains largely rural (80% or more in China, India, and most of sub-Saharan Africa), and generally more committed to the traditional belief systems that are the major concern of the culture historian.

CULTURE DEFINES FOOD CHOICES

My first acute awareness of the importance of culture in determining what foods are eaten or not eaten was brought on during doctoral field work in Ethiopia in the early 1950s. Nicolai Vavilov, the Russian botanist, had identified Ethiopia as one of the world's centers of plant domestication, and my concern was with domesticated plants and animals, agriculture and animal husbandry, in one of the northern provinces, Begemder and Semyen (Simoons 1960). That province was dominated by the Amhara, a Christian Semitic people, but other groups lived there as well. There was a large population of native Moslems, the Jabarti; a significant minority of Falasha, the so-called Black Jews of Ethiopia, who were noted iron-workers, potters, and weavers; the pagan Kamant and other Cushites, last remnants of the pre-Semitic occupants of northern Ethiopia; and, along the Sudan border, various Negro tribes. What struck me there was the curiously limited range of food plants cultivated, domesticated animals kept, and foods eaten.

Lowly "Ensete Eaters". Though Ethiopia is not far from Iran, a great center of fruit and nut tree domestication, such products were of virtually no importance in indigenous agriculture or diet. About the only fruit one could obtain in the bustling daily or weekly markets was the lemon. Also striking was the Amhara's lowly opinion of certain Cushitic groups of southern highland Ethiopia who cultivate ensete (*Ensete edule*), a banana-like plant. With the ensete it is not the fruit that is eaten, but the false stem and young shoots, which, prepared in various ways, are comparable in food value to manioc and other starchy tropical roots and tubers. Plantations of ensete provide high yields, so that areas of ensete monoculture in the south have among the highest densities of rural population in Ethiopia. Why then, did the Amhara and other cereal cultivators of the north refer disparagingly to "ensete eaters?" Clearly theirs was a concern with enhancing their own social status, with relegating the Cushitic "ensete eaters" to a lower level. The food had become representative of a group, a symbol, in the minds of

Amhara, of the Cushites' lesser status. Equally impressive to me was the north Ethiopian interest in cereals and pulses, and lack of interest in green vegetables and roots and tubers.

Pig, Hippopotamus, and Fish Taboos. In the animal realm, the nearly universal view of all ethnic groups, Christian and pagan as well as Moslem and Jewish, was that the pig was unclean, not to be kept or eaten. That view was extended to the pig's distant relative, the hippopotamus, which was once numerous on Lake Tana, and remains so today along the Blue Nile, which drains the lake. The Wayt'o, a hunting and gathering people who, by tradition, hunted and ate hippopotamus, were, as a result, pariahs of very low status. One Cushitic people, the Agow, even though they lived along a major river with fish readily available, did not eat fish. Travelling across Africa after a year in Ethiopia, I was struck by the fact that other readily available flesh foods were not consumed. I decided to write an article on the use and avoidance of certain flesh foods in Africa: pork, fish, horse, donkey, chicken and eggs, and dogflesh. The result was a book on the avoidance of certain flesh foods in all of Eurasia as well as Africa (Simoons 1961). What had initially been observed in Ethiopia seemed to be a widespread trait: that avoidance of a particular animal food is often linked to concerns with maintaining ritual purity and avoiding pollution, and that use and avoidance of such foods are often ethnic and religious markers.

RELIGION AND FOOD SELECTION

Pork Avoidance

The best-known examples of links between food and religion are pork in the Near East and beef in India. In Egypt at the time of the Greek historian Herodotus (fifth century BC), there was an inferior class of swineherds. If an Egyptian should accidentally brush against a pig, he would immediately—Herodotus insisted—cleanse himself by jumping, clothes and all, into the Nile. The view that the pig was unclean and pork a food to be rejected thus long preceded the Islamic conquest of Egypt in the seventh century AD. One cannot even safely ascribe the origin of pork avoidance to Southwest Asia, whether to Jews or other groups there. Pork avoidance occurs across a broad region from India to East and South Africa, and in some places is an ancient custom.

"Ecological Niche" Theory. One cannot determine with any certainty how the rejection of the pig and pork may first have developed. Anthropologist Carleton Coon (1951) has suggested an "ecological niche" theory, that in the early Near East and Mediterranean the pig fit well into the ecology because the region contained abundant oak and beech woodlands where they fed. With population increase and clearing for cultivation, Coon suggested, the pig's ecological niche was destroyed. Therefore a ban of pork was instituted to keep insensitive individuals from continuing the now inappropriate practice of pig-keeping. A similar view has since been championed by Marxist anthropologist Marvin Harris (1972, 1973, 1974).

Pork Avoidance and Politics. An alternative position is that of Diener and Robkin (1978), who suggested that the Islamic ban on pig-keeping and pork-eating derives from deliberate political and economic self-serving by early Moslems, whose base was urban. If this view were applicable more widely in the region, the lowly position of pig and pork in the Near East would be part of a long struggle for dominance by urban centers over a balky peasantry. There are other possibilities as well, that negative attitudes toward pig and pork in the Near East derive from pastoral nomads. Nomads do usually look on the pig as an alien creature, unclean, unsuited for dietary purposes. By this hypothesis nomadic influence, which was important at various times in the Near East, was taken up by one or another religious sect.

There remained, throughout the Near East, groups who continued to keep pigs, for suitable ecological niches remained. One was the Nile Valley of Egypt, which produced sufficient garbage to sustain pigs in considerable numbers. Another was the Atlas Mountain region of Northwest Africa, where sufficient woodland remained to provide feed for swine. The pressures against pigs and pork, however, became powerful with the rise of Islam. The result was a decline in pig-keeping and, since people continued to require animal protein, an increase in numbers of other animals. The goat, a voracious feeder and destroyer of young shrubs and trees, gained prominence. To some historians and geographers (de Planhol 1959) the goat is a villain, a major contributor to the appalling destruction of woodland and forest in the Mediterranean and Near East since classical times.

Beef Avoidance in India

In the case of the cow in India, a high ritual status explains rejection of its flesh by humans. I have considered that matter in detail elsewhere (Simoons 1961, 1973B, 1974, 1979), and here I would simply emphasize that beef use and rejection in Hindu India is linked both with the ritual position of the cow and with human concerns about ritual purity and pollution. Beef in India cannot, therefore, be understood apart from the sacred cow concept, which has many other manifestations in Hindu culture, behavior, and ecology as well.

Limits of Research on Religion and Food Selection

Acknowledging the importance of religious belief in human food selection, one may legitimately ask whether there have been broader, more comprehensive studies of the impact of major religions on food use. I can think of no major study of that sort. Most studies so far focus on one or another of the more spectacular impacts of a religion on food selection, as with Hinduism and beef-eating.

HUMAN USAGE OF MILK

Nonmilking Groups

In 1954 I published an article on nonmilking in Africa, which included a map of the geographic limits of the practices of milking animals and consuming their milk (Simoons 1954). That paper had been made necessary by the skepticism I encountered from faculty and other graduate students in a seminar at Berkeley when I spoke of African peoples who possessed goats and sometimes other herd animals suitable for dairying purposes, but did not milk them. As it turned out, we were not dealing with a scattered handful of nonmilking groups, but with a phenomenon typical of a large part of the continent at the time of first European contact (see Fig. 12.1). The zone of nonmilking was centered on the Congo Basin, but extended eastward across the Cameroons and in a belt embracing the southern portions of the Guinea Coast states as far as Sierra Leone. To the south, nonmilking peoples were found well into Angola, and they also occurred in a strip extending from the southern Congo to Mozambique.

Accounting for the Nonmilking Groups

Since dairying was practiced in Africa in quite ancient times, 4000 BC or earlier (Simoons 1971), the question was immediately raised "why had it not been taken over by all peoples of the continent in the several millennia since?" and "why had some groups come to keep domesticated animals for their flesh but not for dairy purposes?" Perhaps it should first be noted that most, but not all, of the nonmilking groups occur in areas where tsetse flies occur and African sleeping sickness is endemic. Because horses and most types of common cattle suffer high mortality from sleeping sickness, that disease constituted a real barrier to the invasion of fly zones by pastoral peoples who might have been expected to introduce dairying. Though sleeping sickness would have been a deterrent to invasion by pastoral nomads, this cannot have been solely responsible for the persistence of the zone for nonmilking. People living

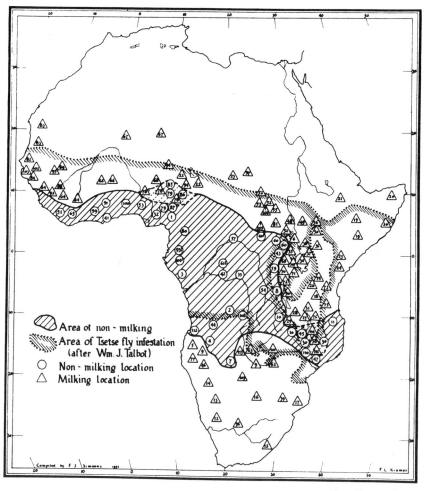

Area of non - milking
Area of Tsetse fly infestation
(after Wm. J. Talbot)
O   Non - milking location
△   Milking location

Compiled by F J Simoons   1951

F L Kramer

From Simoons (1954)

FIG. 12.1.   THE NONMILKING AREA OF TROPICAL AFRICA

in the zone of nonmilking did possess herd animals well-suited to dairy purposes. Sheep and goats were kept by many groups and, in some fly areas along the Guinea Coast, resistant breeds of common cattle—the dwarf and Ndama breeds. Yet they were not milked but kept only for meat and other purposes. Why?

Innate Conservatism.   Some (Sauer 1952) have suggested that non-milking groups had remained so because of their innate conservatism, reluctance to take up the strange practices of milking animals and consuming animal milk. That explanation did and still does make sense, for, when asked, nonmilking persons would point out that manipulating the udder of an animal was indeed a strange procedure. They also noted that the end product of milking was a white animal secretion, a substance that, when consumed, could make a person ill. It was suspected that such illness was psychosomatic in origin, an understandably strong reaction to an alien and somewhat revolting food.

Other Nonmilking Groups

My interest in the history and geography of dairying continued, and in the late 1960s, I assembled the data on a similar zone of nonmilking that traditionally included all of Southeast and East Asia (see Fig. 12.2) (Simoons 1970B). One notes in that part of the world a striking difference between India, most of whose people value milk and milk products highly and who consume as much of these as availability and cost permit, and China, whose people, except during a few periods of dominance by pastoral nomads, made little or no dietary use of animal milk. Nonmilkers of Southeast and East Asia, like those of Africa, looked on the practice of milking an animal as unnatural, and also raised similar objections to drinking milk. In addition, some Southeast Asian groups insisted that for humans to take animal milk for their own use was stealing, with possible adverse effects on the nursing animal and its mother.

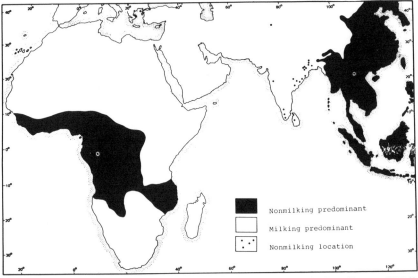

Nonmilking predominant

Milking predominant

Nonmilking location

From Simoons (1970A)

FIG. 12.2 TRADITIONAL AREAS OF MILKING AND NONMILKING IN THE OLD WORLD

LACTOSE MALABSORPTION

At about the time the above article was completed, I became aware that medical researchers, initially at Johns Hopkins (Cuatrecasas *et al.* 1965; Bayless and Rosenweig 1966) were finding striking differences among ethnic groups in prevalence of primary adult lactose malabsorption (LM). These and later studies found American blacks to have quite high prevalences of LM, usually 70–80% of the persons tested, whereas American whites had quite low prevalences, usually 6–25%. Similar ethnic differences were being found in other parts of the world (see Table 12.1), and I sought to determine what relationship, if any, there might be between prevalences of LM and patterns of milk use, contemporary and historical.

The Consequences of Lactose Ingestion

Lactose, a polysaccharide and the principal carbohydrate of the infant's diet, occurs in the milk of all other land mammals as well as in humans. When ingested, lactose is hydrolyzed in the small intestine by the enzyme lactase into the monosaccharides glucose and galactose,

TABLE 12.1   PREVALENCE OF PRIMARY ADULT LACTOSE MALABSORPTION (LM) AMONG ETHNIC OR RACIAL GROUPS

Category a	Hunting and gathering peoples (N = 287; with LM, 247; prevalence of LM, 86%)
Category b	Agricultural peoples from the traditional zones of nonmilking and their relatively unmixed overseas descendants (N = 1311; with LM, 1186; prevalence of LM, 90%)
	In North and South America (N = 167; with LM, 162; prevalence of LM, 97%)
	In sub-Saharan Africa (N = 311; with LM, 270; prevalence of LM, 87%)
	In Southeast and East Asia (N = 829; with LM, 750; prevalence of LM, 90%)
	In the Pacific Region (N = 20; with LM, 20; prevalence of LM, 100%)
Category c	Agricultural peoples whose ancestry lies in the traditional zones of nonmilking but who migrated into an adjacent zone, to become milk-users at a relatively recent date (N = 226; with LM, 199; prevalence of LM, 88%)
Category d	Peoples, including some of pastoral tradition, who have consumed large amounts of milk and lactose-rich dairy products for a long historical period and have lived under conditions of dietary stress (also their relatively unmixed overseas descendants) (N= 3489; with LM, 376; prevalence of LM, 11%)
	In Africa and the Near East (N = 101; with LM, 10; prevalence of LM, 10%)
	Europeans and their overseas descendants (N = 3269; with LM 344: prevalence of LM, 11%)
	In India and Pakistan (N = 119; with LM, 22; prevalence of LM, 18%)
Category e	Peoples who have used milk since antiquity but who do not meet conditions of strong selective pressures against LM (N = 716; with LM, 514; prevalence of LM, 72%)

Source: Simoons 1981B. Used with permission of the publisher.

which can readily be absorbed. The amount of intestinal lactase activity determines how much lactose is hydrolyzed and absorbed. That activity is high during an infant mammal's nursing period, but for most land mammals, including most human groups, lactase activity drops at weaning to low levels that prevail throughout life. The older child or adult who has insufficient lactase activity, moreover, commonly becomes ill when he or she consumes lactose or lactose-rich dairy products. The symptoms are identical with those reported by some persons from the zone of nonmilking when they drank milk: stomach gas, flatulence, intestinal discomfort, and sometimes cramps, diarrhea and even vomiting.

Lactose Malabsorption and Zones of Nonmilking

My initial effort focused on determining the distribution of high and low prevalences of primary adult lactose malabsorption among the world's peoples. The pattern that emerged, and that has been confirmed over the past decade, is that all groups with origins in the traditional zones of nonmilking have high prevalences of LM, usually from 70 to 100% of individuals tested. Outside the nonmilking zones all people of hunting and gathering tradition, who lacked herd animals to provide them with milk, have similar high prevalences. The three principal areas of the Old World where low prevalences (30% or less) of LM occur are Northern Europe, Saudi Arabia, and the Northwest of the Indian subcontinent. In addition, certain African pastoral peoples—the Fulani of Nigeria, the Hima and Tussi of East Africa, and the Beja of the Sudan—have low prevalences. All groups with low prevalences of LM consume milk and milk products in large amounts.

Induction Hypothesis. Though there were clear links between patterns of milk consumption and prevalences of lactose absorption and malabsorption, the nature of the association remained a mystery. Some medical researchers (Bolin and Davis 1970, 1972) favored an "induction hypothesis," which held that milk consumption induced lactase activity. By that hypothesis the geographic occurrence of high and low prevalences of LM merely reflected differences in present-day patterns of milk consumption. Adherents of the induction hypothesis argued that if a person, even one from a nonmilking group, were given milk continuously from early infancy onward, he or she would continue to experience high lactase activity. Subsequent efforts at inducing lactase activity in infant and adult humans failed, however, and it has become clear that an individual's developmental pattern of lactase activity is primarily under genetic control. The problem, then, becomes one of attempting to explain why some groups diverged genetically from most of humanity and from other land mammals by experiencing consistently high lactase activity through life. This led me to a "geographic" or "culture historical hypothesis" (Simoons 1969, 1970A, 1973A).

Culture Historical Hypothesis. The hypothesis is that all human groups in the hunting and gathering stage, when milk was normally consumed by only the nursing infant, experienced a drop in lactase activity at weaning. Low lactase activity was then typical of adults in all human groups. With the origins of dairying, the aberrant person who experienced high lactase activity through life would, under certain conditions, enjoy a survival advantage. This would occur among groups who consumed significant amounts of milk and milk products in lactose-rich forms and for whom these were dietary essentials. Under those conditions, by the hypothesis, the adult lactose absorber would be better off nutritionally because he would consume more milk and perhaps better be able to utilize its nutrients. The genetic trait of persistence of high lactase activity through life would thus make such lactose absorbers more fit and would come to typify such a milk-using group.

Enhanced Calcium Absorption. Subsequent studies, which I reviewed in recent articles (Simoons 1978, 1981B), support the culture historical hypothesis in most ways, and I remain convinced of its essential correctness. In addition to a generalized selective advantage, however, there may, in one geographic region or another, have been specific selective advantages enjoyed by the lactose absorber. Flatz and Rotthauwe (1973, 1977; Flatz 1976) suggest that in Northern Europe, one of the major regions with high prevalences of lactose absorption in adults, the prevailing cloud cover reduced the body's ability to produce vitamin D and, thus, to absorb calcium. Since animal experiments suggest that calcium absorption is enhanced by lactose hydrolysis, the argument is that the milk-using lactose absorber, who enjoyed greater ability at lactose hydrolysis than the malabsorber, would better be able to absorb calcium. This reduced the likelihood of calcium deficiency, especially among the poor who may have had diets deficient in vitamin D, and kept the lactose absorber free of rickets and other problems deriving from calcium deficiency. As a result, the lactose absorber would be favored in survival terms, and lactose absorption would become a common trait in the adult population. A second specific hypothesis is that the lactose absorber, because of his enhanced ability at absorbing water would better be able to survive cholera and other epidemics (Cook and al-Torki 1975; Cook 1978).

Whatever the merits of the above hypotheses in setting down specific selective advantages in one region or another, they cannot be applied to all geographic situations. The African, Indian, and Arabian groups characterized by low prevalences of lactose malabsorption live in areas of abundant sunshine, a situation far different from Northern Europe. This leads one to the likelihood that a lactose absorber, under the conditions set down by the culture historical hypothesis, enjoyed a generalized selective advantage that may, from place to place, have been supplemented by specific advantages.

HUMAN ECOGENETICS

In the matter of genetic differences among humans as they contribute to differing responses to lactose-rich dairy products, we are dealing with a branch of "human ecogenetics" (Brewer 1971). Human ecogenetics focuses on the contrasting responses of individual humans to chemical agents, other than drugs, in the environment, and on explaining why some individuals are adversely affected by such agents and others not. Basic to the concept of ecogenetics is the view that biochemical differences among individuals may contribute to their differing reactions to environmental agents. Aside from the case of milk as it relates to lactase deficiency, only a few foods have convincingly been implicated as significant ecogenetic problems (Vogel and Motulsky 1979). One is the horse bean or fava bean *(Vicia faba)*, consumption of which, in persons with deficiency of the enzyme G-6-PD (glucose-6-phosphate dehydrogenase), can lead to the disease favism. A second is wheat which, in genetically predisposed individuals, can lead to celiac disease (gluten enteropathy, nontropical sprue).

Celiac Disease

Celiac disease involves intestinal damage, malabsorption, and wasting brought on by consumption of wheat, rye, and, though they are less toxic to celiacs, barley and oats. Celiac disease has long been recognized as having a familial basis. What is inherited is a predisposition that may or may not be reflected in clinical symptoms. There is no simple Mendelian type of inheritance, and one present view (Mann *et al.* 1976; Falchuk *et al.* 1978; Albert *et al.* 1978; Peña *et al.* 1978A, B) is that multiple genes with high heritability are involved. The celiac's sensitivity is to gluten, and more specifically to the prolamins, the alcohol-soluble subfractions of gluten. How damage to the intestinal mucosa, characteristic of celiacs, develops—whether through a peptidase deficiency or in some other way—has not been determined. Before the early 1950s, when Dutch researchers (Dicke 1950; Dicke *et al.* 1953; van de Kamer *et al.* 1953) identified wheat, rye, and oats as toxic to celiacs, a surprisingly high percentage, perhaps 15%, of celiac patients, seem to have died (Hardwick 1939). Now, with proper diagnosis and removal of offending cereals from the diet, the disease is rarely fatal.

Genetic Marker for Celiac Disease. Few good studies of incidence of celiac disease exist outside Europe, but one is helped in determining the likely occurrence of the disease by the fact that an unusually high percentage of celiacs possess a single genetic marker, the HLA-B8 antigen. In Western Europe, from 79 to 90% of adult celiacs have that genetic marker, and one group of researchers (Svejgaard *et al.* 1975) estimated that a person with HLA-B8 has ten times the likelihood of developing celiac disease that other persons have.

If one maps the prevalence of HLA-B8 in Old World populations, so far as this has been studied, one sees that high prevalences occur mainly in two areas, Northwest Europe and Northwest India (see Fig. 12.3). These are also the regions (at the outer limits of wheat cultivation in Eurasia) where celiac disease seems to be most common (Fig. 12.4). There is, moreover a regular, consistent decrease in the prevalence of HLA-B8 in populations from the Near Eastern center of wheat domestication across Western Europe (see Fig. 12.5). One suspects that this may be related to the length of time that wheat was cultivated, with persons sensitive to the gluten of wheat gradually eliminated from wheat-consuming populations—more so in the early areas of wheat consumption than in the later ones.

My work on celiac disease is being presented in detail elsewhere (Simoons 1981A) and here I merely call your attention to it as another case in which consumption of particular types of food, as in the case of milk, may have led certain human populations to diverge from others genetically.

Milk Ingestion–Cataract Relationship

An equally intriguing hypothesis, for which I have just assembled evidence (Simoons 1982), is that consumption of large quantities of milk by some human populations, especially those characterized by high lactase activity through life, contributes to high incidences of senile cataracts among them. It has long been known that if normal rats consume large amounts of lactose or galactose (25–70% of total dietary intake) they develop cataracts (McLaren and Halasa 1975). Richter and Duke (1970), moreover, found that normal rats fed an exclusive diet of yogurt develop cataracts, which they presumed to be galactose-induced; and Stephens *et al.* (1974A, B, 1975) found that kangaroos and other herbivorous Australian marsupials, which are deficient in galacto-kinase and transferase (the enzymes by which galactose is metabolized

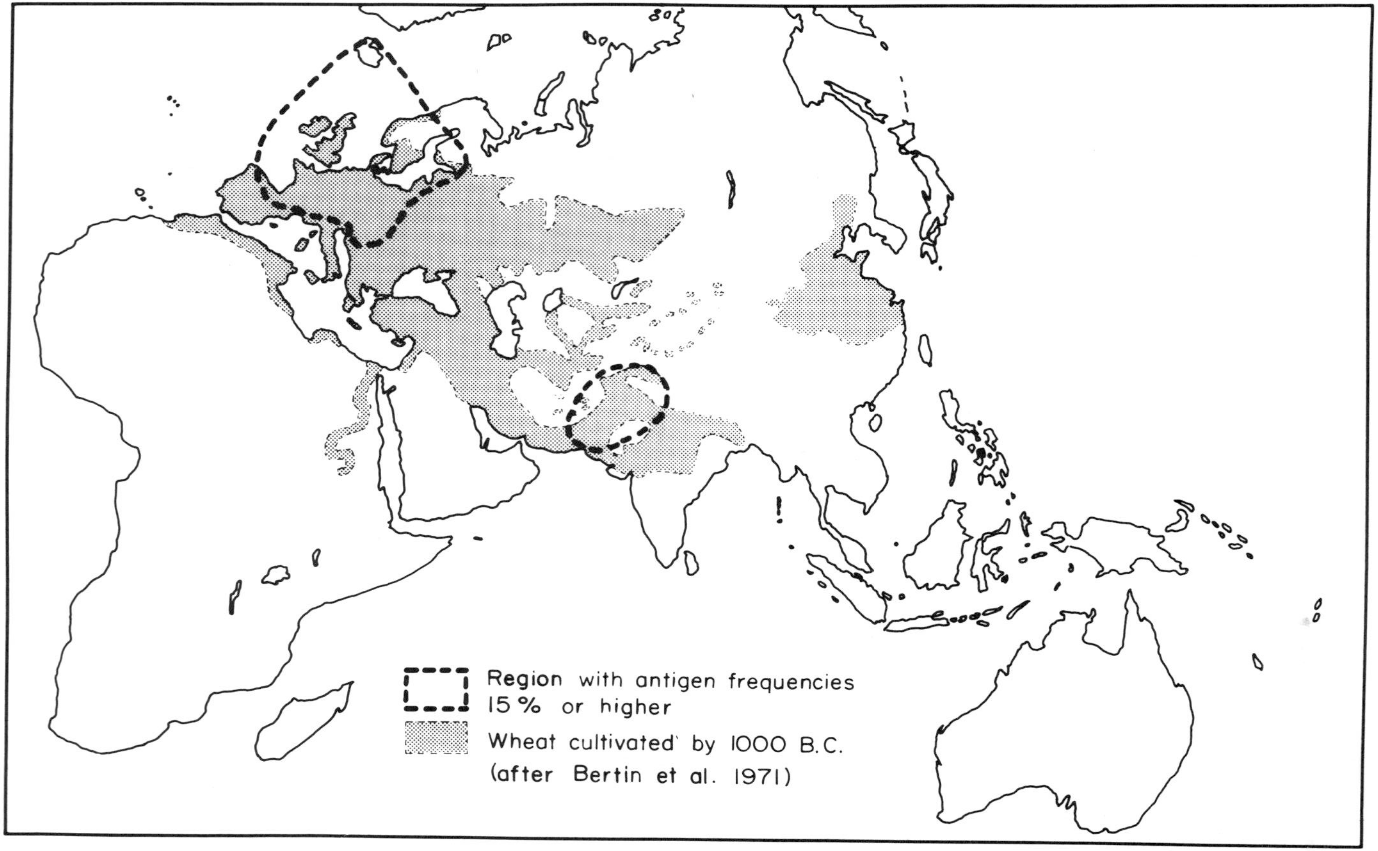
Region with antigen frequencies 15% or higher
Wheat cultivated by 1000 B.C. (after Bertin et al. 1971)

From Simoons (1981A)

FIG. 12.3. HIGH HLA-B8 FREQUENCIES AND WHEAT CULTIVATION

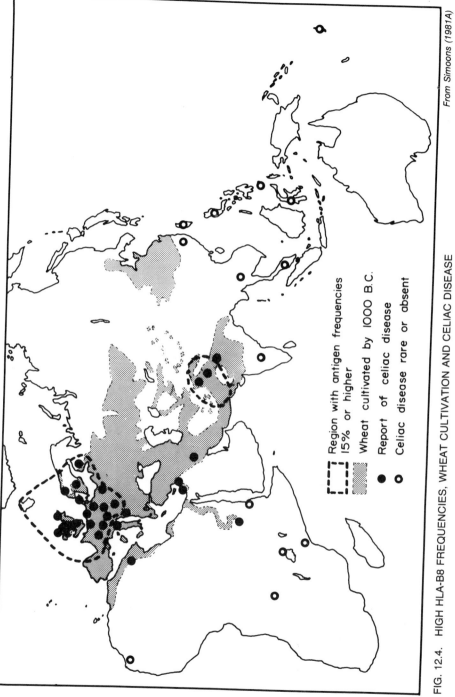

Region with antigen frequencies
15% or higher

Wheat cultivated by 1000 B.C.

● Report of celiac disease

○ Celiac disease rare or absent

FIG. 12.4. HIGH HLA-B8 FREQUENCIES, WHEAT CULTIVATION AND CELIAC DISEASE

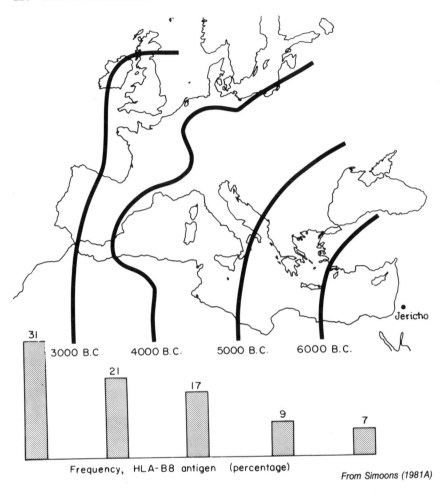

Frequency, HLA-B8 antigen   (percentage)

From Simoons (1981A)

FIG. 12.5.   HLA-B8 FREQUENCIES AND THE SPREAD OF EARLY FARMING IN EUROPE
Each arc indicates a 1000-year interval. (Spread of farming after Ammerman and Cavalli-Sforza 1971.)

by the normal pathway) develop cataracts when fed cow's milk. Galactose-induced cataracts also occur in humans who have deficiencies of galactokinase and transferase, but what I am suggesting is that persons with normal activity of these enzymes through repeated challenges involving high milk consumption and galactose absorption over several decades, may develop senile cataracts.

This suggestion is based on evidence that whether or not a person's intestinal lactase activity declines at weaning or remains at high levels throughout life, galactokinase activity in the adult seems to be only one-third to one-fourth that of the infant (Tedesco *et al.* 1972; Bayless *et al.* 1974). Since a much higher percentage of ingested lactose is hydrolyzed in the small intestine of a person with high lactase activity, he or she would absorb larger amounts of galactose and presumably be at greater risk of galactose-induced senile cataracts. If the hypothesis is right, one would expect to find high incidences of senile cataracts among populations characterized by high intestinal lactase activity and high milk consumption. In the Old World such groups are found in Northwest India, Northern Europe, and elsewhere among pastoral groups such as the Fulani, Hima, Tussi, and Bedouin Arabs. We are looking at the distributional evidence now. If the hypothesis does ultimately prove correct, what may have occurred historically is that with the origins of milking, certain human populations which used abundant dairy products underwent a genetic change involving persistence of high intestinal lactase throughout life. That persistence favored young and adult lactose absorbers in providing them with a generally superior nutritional state compared to persons who were lactose malabsorbers. That genetic change, however, also led the milk-using lactose absorber to have continually high galactose absorption through life, and in later years to a greater risk of senile cataracts. What had been an advantage in youth, could become a disadvantage in old age.

Conclusion

Further research is needed before we have answers to the question of what role, if any, milk consumption and lactase activity play in the formation of senile cataracts. The more general proposition, however, seems assured, that whatever elements in psychobiology direct humans in their selection of foods, that selection, at least in a few cases, may have significant genetic implications for their descendants.

REFERENCES

ALBERT, E., HARMS, K., BERTELE, R., ANDREAS, A., MCNICHOLAS, A., KUNTZ, B., SCHOLZ, S., SCHIESSL, B., WETZMÜLLER, H., REISSINGER, P., and WEESERKRELL, C. 1978. B-cell alloantigens in coeliac disease. *In* Perspectives in Coeliac Disease. B. McNicholl, C.F. McCarthy and P.F. Fottrell (Editors), pp. 123–129. MTP Press, Lancaster, England.

AMMERMAN, A.J., and CAVALLI-SFORZA, L.L. 1971. Measuring the rate of spread of early farming in Europe. Man *6*, 674–688.

BAYLESS, T.M., and ROSENSWEIG, N.S. 1966. A racial difference in incidence of lactase deficiency. J. Am. Med. Assoc. *197*, 968–972.

BAYLESS, T.M., ROTHFELD, B., BACK, C., TEDESCO, T.A., MILLER, K., and MELLMAN, W.J. 1974. Association between intestinal lactase activity and erythrocyte galactokinase in blacks. Gastroenterology *66*, A179–833.

BOLIN, T.D., and DAVIS, A.E. 1970. Primary lactase deficiency: Genetic or acquired? Am. J. Digest. Dis. *15*, 679–692.

BOLIN, T.D., and DAVIS, A.E. 1972. Primary lactase deficiency: Genetic or acquried? Gastroenterology *62*, 355–357.

BREWER, G.J. 1971. Human ecology, an expanding role for the human geneticist. (Annotation.) Am. J. Human Genet. *23*, 92–94.

CHANG, K.C. (Editor.) 1977. Food in Chinese Culture. Yale University Press, New Haven, CT.

COOK, G.C. 1978. Did persistence of intestinal lactase into adult life originate on the Arabian peninsula? Man *13*, 418–427.

COOK, G.C., and AL-TORKI, M.T. 1975. High intestinal lactase concentrations in adult Arabs in Saudi Arabia. Br. Med. J. *3*, 135–136.

COON, C.S. 1951. Caravan. Henry Holt and Co., New York.

CUATRECASAS, P., LOCKWOOD, D.H., and CALDWELL, J.R. 1965. Lactase deficiency in the adult. Lancet *1*, 14–18.

DE PLANHOL, X. 1959. The World of Islam. Cornell University Press, Ithaca, N.Y.

DICKE, W.K. 1950. Coeliac disease: A study of the harmful effect of some cereals on patients with coeliac disease. M.D. Thesis, University of Utrecht, Utrecht, The Netherlands. (Dutch).

DICKE, W.K., WEIJERS, H.A., and VAN DE KAMER, J.H. 1953. Coeliac disease II: The presence in wheat of a factor having a deleterious effect in cases of coeliac disease. Acta Paed. Scand. *42*, 34–42.

DIENER, P., and ROBKIN, E.E. 1978. Ecology, evolution, and the search for cultural origins: The question of Islamic pig prohibition. Curr. Anthropol. *19*, 493–540.

FALCHUK, Z.M., KATZ, A.J., SCHWACHMAN, H., ROGENTINE, G.N., and STROBER, W. 1978. Gluten-sensitive enteropathy: Genetic analysis and organ culture study in 35 families. Scand. J. Gastroenterol. *13*, 839–843.

FLATZ, G. 1976. Lactose tolerance: Genetics, anthropology, and natural selection. *In* Human Genetics. Excerpta Med. Int. Congr. Ser. No. 411. Excerpta Medica, Amsterdam, The Netherlands.

FLATZ, G., and ROTTHAUWE, H.W. 1973. Lactose nutrition and natural selection. Lancet *2*, 76–77.

FLATZ, G., and ROTTHAUWE, H.W. 1977. The human lactase polymorphism: Physiology and genetics of lactose absorption and malabsorption. *In* Progress in Medical Genetics, New Series, Vol. II, pp. 205–249. A.G. Steinberg, A.G. Bearn, A.G. Motulsky, and B. Childs (Editors). Saunders, Philadelphia, Pa.

HARDWICK, C. 1939. Prognosis in coeliac disease: A review of 73 cases. Arch. Dis. Child. *14*, 279–294.

HARRIS, M. 1972. The riddle of the pig. Nat. Hist. *81*, 32–38.

HARRIS, M. 1973. The riddle of the pig, II. Nat. Hist. *82*, 20–25.

HARRIS, M. 1974. Cows, Pigs, Wars, and Witches: The Riddles of Culture. Random House, New York.

LEE, R.B. 1969. !Kung Bushman subsistence: An input-output analysis. *In* Environment and Cultural Behavior. A.P. Vayda (Editor), pp. 47–79. The Natural History Press, Garden City, N.Y.

LEE, R.B. 1973. Mongongo: The ethnography of a major wild food resource. Ecol. Food Nutr. *2*, 307–321.

MANN, D.L., NELSON, D.L., KATZ, S.I., ABELSON, L.D., and STROBER, W. 1976. Specific B-cell antigens associated with gluten-sensitive enteropathy and dermatitis herpetiformis. Lancet *1*, 110–111.

MCLAREN, D.S., and HALASA, A. 1975. Nutritional and metabolic cataract. *In* Cataract and Abnormalities of the Lens. J.G. Bellows (Editor). Grune and Stratton, New York.

PEÑA, A.S., MANN, D.L., HAGUE, N.E., HECK, J.A., VAN LEEUWEN, A., VAN ROOD, J.J., and STROBER, W. 1978A. B-cell alloantigens and the inheritance of coeliac disease. *In* Perspectives in Coeliac Disease. B. McNicholl, C.F. McCarthy, and P.F. Fottrell (Editors), pp. 131–133. MTP Press, Lancaster, England.

PEÑA, A.S., MANN, D.L., HAGUE, N.E., HECK, J.A., VAN LEEUWEN, A., VAN ROOD, J.J., and STROBER, W. 1978B. Genetic basis of gluten-sensitive enteropathy. Gastroenterology *75*, 230–235.

RICHTER, C., and DUKE, J.R. 1970. Cataracts produced in rats by yogurt. Science *168*, 1372–1374.

SAUER, C.O. 1952. Agricultural Origins and Dispersals. American Geographical Society, New York.

SCHWABE, C.W. 1979. Unmentionable Cuisine. University Press of Virginia, Charlottesville, Virginia.

SIMOONS, F.J. 1954. The non-milking area of Africa. Anthropos *49*, 58–66.

SIMOONS, F.J. 1960. Northwest Ethiopia: Peoples and Economy. University of Wisconsin Press, Madison, Wisconsin.

SIMOONS, F.J. 1961. Eat Not This Flesh. University of Wisconsin Press, Madison, Wisconsin.

SIMOONS, F.J. 1969. Primary adult lactose intolerance and the milking habit: A problem in biological and cultural interrelations I—Review of the medical research. Am. J. Digest. Dis. *14*, 819–836.

SIMOONS, F.J. 1970A. Primary adult lactose intolerance and the milking habit: A problem in biological and cultural interrelations II—A culture historical hypothesis. Am. J. Digest. Dis. *15*, 695–710.

SIMOONS, F.J. 1970B. The traditional limits of milking and milk use in southern Asia. Anthropos *65*, 547–593.

SIMOONS, F.J. 1971. The antiquity of dairying in Asia and Africa. Geogr. Rev. *61*, 431–439.

SIMOONS, F.J.   1973A.   New light on ethnic differences in adult lactose intolerance.   Am. J. Digest. Dis. *18*, 595–611.

SIMOONS, F.J.   1973B.   The sacred cow and the Constitution of India.   Ecol. Food Nutr. *2*, 281–295.

SIMOONS, F.J.   1974.   The purificatory role of the five products of the cow in Hinduism.   Ecol. Food Nutr. *3*, 21–34.

SIMOONS, F.J.   1978.   The geographic hypothesis and lactose malabsorption: A weighing of the evidence.   Am. J. Digest. Dis. *23*, 963–980.

SIMOONS, F.J.   1979.   Questions in the sacred cow controversy.   Curr. Anthropol. *20*, 467–493.

SIMOONS, F.J.   1981A.   Celiac disease as a geographic problem.   *In* Food, Nutrition, and Evolution: Food as an Environmental Factor in the Genesis of Human Variability.   D. Walcher and N. Kretchmer (Editors), pp. 179–199. Masson Publishing, New York.

SIMOONS, F.J.   1981B.   Geographic patterns of high and low prevalence of lactose malabsorption: A further interpretation of evidence for the Old World.   *In* Lactose Digestion: Clinical and Nutritional Consequences. D.M. Paige and T.M. Bayless (Editors), pp.23–48.   Johns Hopkins University Press, Baltimore, Maryland.

SIMOONS, F.J.   1982.   A geographic approach to senile cataracts: Possible links with milk consumption, lactase activity, and galactose metabolism. Digest. Dis. Sci. *27*, 257–264.

STEPHENS, T., IRVINE, S., MUTTON, P., GUPTA, J.D., and HARLEY, J.D. 1974A.   The case of the cataractous kangaroo.   Med. J. Aust. *2*, 910–911.

STEPHENS, T., IRVINE, S., MUTTON, P., GUPTA, J.D., and HARLEY, J.D. 1974B.   Deficiency of two enzymes of galactose metabolism in kangaroos. Nature *248*, 524.

STEPHENS, T., CROLLINI, C., MUTTON, P., GUPTA, J.D., and HARLEY, J.D.   1975.   Galactose metabolism in relation to cataract formation in marsupials.   Aust. J. Exp. Biol. Med. Sci. *53*, 233–239.

SVEJGAARD, A., PLATZ, P., RYDER, L.P., NIELSEN, L.S., and THOMSEN, M.   1975.   HL-A and disease associations: A survey.   Transplant. Rev. *22*, 3–43.

TEDESCO, T.A., BONOW, R., MILLER, K., and MELLMAN, W.J.   1972. Galactokinase: Evidence of a new racial polymorphism.   Science *178*, 176–178.

VAN DE KAMER, J.H., WEIJERS, H.A., and DICKE, W.K.   1953.   Coeliac disease IV: An investigation into the injurious constituents of wheat in connection with their action on patients with coeliac disease.   Acta Paed. Scand. *42*, 223–231.

VOGEL, F., and MOTULSKY, A.G.   1979.   Human Genetics: Problems and Approaches.   Springer-Verlag, Berlin and New York.

13

Human Food Selection: The Interaction of Biology, Culture and Individual Experience

Paul Rozin

This paper consists of a critical analysis of the idea that biological factors are primary determinants of cultural food-related practices (cuisine) and that cultural processes are primary determinants of individual food choice. Cases are discussed where biological behavioral biases in food selection come to be represented, either directly or indirectly, in cuisine. However, such cases are rare. More commonly, "meabolic," as opposed to behavioral characteristics provide the motivation (adaptive values) for institutionalization of aspects of food selection or processing in culture. In at least some cases, the presumed adaptive value of technologies is not within the awareness of current users. There are many exceptions to the biology-to-culture "information" flow: some aspects of cuisine have the effect of reversing biological behavioral biases (e.g., the preference for chili pepper). In some cases, the biology-to-culture causal chain is reversed (e.g., the evolution of lactose tolerance in adults). In most of the cases discussed, it is very difficult to reconstruct actual historical sequences of discovery and adoption because of the importance of unique events in these sequences. The transition from culture to the individual is discussed, with primary emphasis on the ways that cultural "information" or "values" are internalized in individuals. Culture acquisition of aspects of cuisine often occurs in two stages: in the first, cultural forces maintain individual behaviors, such as ingestion of a food, constituting a form of "forced" exposure. For many foods, this stage is followed by a second one, in which a food preference is internalized, in that the motivation for ingestion is no longer dependent on cultural forces. This internalization process is accomplished in a number of ways, including motivation by desire for the consequences of eating the food, or development of a liking for the taste. This latter affect-based internalization seems to be a widespread and powerful means of enculturation. It causes children to come to like the foods that are valued by the culture.

INTRODUCTION

There is something fundamentally biological about food and eating. They are closely linked to survival, and at the most general level, involve activities that we share with other animals. However, over the course of human evolution, food selection has become more and more embedded in cultural systems.

The attention of those most interested in culture has centered on human social relations, rather than culinary behavior. Yet, for one interested in the biological origins of what has become culture-determined behavior, the domain of food may be more promising. We know much more about the basic biology and psychobiology of food and nutrition than we know about social behavior. We can identify with some precision the food needs of humans and other animals, so that we know the fundamental functions that food selection must serve. There are few, if any, well-established social parallels to dietary requirements. Food selection has its special incorporative organ, the mouth, through which all potential food must pass. And through decades of research on the laboratory rat, an omnivorous animal with nutritional requirements similar to ours, we have valuable insights into the biologically based behavioral predispositions of at least one omnivore. For these reasons, it should be profitable to try to unpack the relations among biology, culture and individual experience. The human omnivore did not invent solutions to the problem of discovering food sources in the world. It came equipped with the potential to discover new foods and vastly extended the power of its biological system with the accumulated wisdom of culture.

Although our species eats just about everything edible somewhere in the world, any particular group uses only a small percentage of the possible available nutrient sources. This limitation results in substantial part from economic and ecological factors that act to control availability of possible foods. Within the range of available foods, culture produces a further narrowing. Of course, culture also extends the range through increasing availability, by domestication or importation, or by rendering edible some previously inedible items in the environment, through processing techniques. Notwithstanding the importance of biological predispositions, there is no doubt that the best predictor of the food preferences, habits and attitudes of any particular human would be information about his ethnic group (and hence, native cuisine), rather than any biological measure that one might imagine.

I will examine human food selection as a set of phenomena determined by biological factors, culture and individual experience. Biological factors, including both behavioral predispositions to interact with foods in certain ways (e.g., to avoid bitter tastes) and nutritional or metabolic characteristics, set limits and create biases in the human organism (Rozin 1976A). Culture, on the other hand, restricts the possible set of food experiences and provides a great deal of information about foods. Within the constraints of both biology and culture, each individual amasses a particular set of experiences that are unique. The uniqueness probably comes primarily from the fact that the individual's exposure to the culture is filtered through his family's interpretation of that culture, and because unique and specific food experiences just happen to occur to individuals (e.g., consuming a piece of food contaminated with a pathogenic organism). I recognize, of course, that the division into biology, culture and individual experience is somewhat forced, and that clear distinctions can rarely be made. However, I find the distinctions useful, especially if one refers to specific mechanisms or causes, rather than more general ones. Obviously biological factors are a precondition for everything. But it is forcing things a bit to claim that the drinking of $15 bottles of Burgundy, the eating of spoiled milk (as cheese), or the rejection of insects as food have strong and direct biological roots.

I would like to begin with a simple sequence that will serve in part as a "straw scheme." As with the case of the perhaps more familiar straw man, this scheme will encompass some of the truth, and will reveal its flimsiness only as one tries to extend it to a broadly general principle. The scheme is historical in nature and represents a sequence of information transfer from biology to the individual to culture and then back to the individual (see Fig. 13.1). More specifically, the idea is that certain biological features of the human omnivore, in their expressions in individuals, can become incorporated into culture. As parts of culture, they may be reintroduced into each new generation of individuals. This sequence borders on being trite; however, its interest lies in the fact that it is sometimes valid and can be a base for many variations. I plan to trace out some of the variations and illustrate cases where it will not work at all.

There is no doubt that food selection in humans is intricately tied up with other aspects of culture. When this happens, as it does, for example, when food becomes involved in religion, social status and social interac-

FIG. 13.1 "STRAW SCHEME" REPRESENTING THE HISTORICAL INFORMATION FLOW
It originates in biological features and proceeds through expression in individuals, institutionalization in culture, and transmission to individuals in each generation.

tion, the picture gets extremely complex. For the most part, I will try to deal with simpler sequences and focus on food as food. My strategy will be to examine six pairs of foods. The straw scheme will be explicated for each member of each pair, and a particular contrast will emerge for each pair. From each contrast, I will extract general statements (here called lessons) about the interaction of culture, biology and individual experience.

TRANSFORMATION OR AMPLIFICATION OF BIOLOGICAL TENDENCIES BY CULTURE: SUGAR VERSUS FLAVOR PRINCIPLES

Sugar

Our species, and many other mammalian generalist or omnivore species, have an innate preference for sweet substances (Steiner 1974; Desor et al. 1973; Crook 1978; reviewed in Rozin 1976A). This taste bias presumably has its adaptive basis in the fact that the sweet taste is characteristic of energy sources (sugars), particularly fruits, in the world of Nature. Hence, it is a predictor of nutritive (energy) value. This innate liking for sweet tastes motivates the discovery of sweet edibles in the environment. Once discovered, because they are liked and usually nutritive, such items tend to be widely used and to become part of the acceptable foods of the culture. Thus, by accumulating and transmitting the individual discoveries of new sweet sources in the environment and by improving techniques of finding and cultivating such items, the culture can increase their availability. Furthermore, since the biology of the system is "the sweeter the better," individual discoveries that enhance the sweetness of available foods would be incorporated into the technology of the culture (see Fig. 13.2). Both the refining of sugar (with the associated agricultural and sociopolitical developments, see Mintz 1979) and the development of artificial sweeteners are so motivated. This is a particularly clear case, because the innate predisposition is openly recognized by individuals and appears explicitly as a directing force in cultural change (Mintz 1979). The transition from culture to

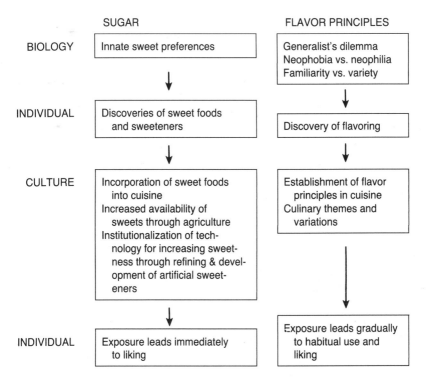

FIG. 13.2. BASIC SCHEME APPLIED TO SUGAR AND FLAVOR PRINCIPLES
In both cases, a biological behavior bias is transmitted through culture to individuals. In the case of sugar, the biological tendency is amplified, while for flavor principles, it is transformed.

individual is extremely straightforward. Only exposure is necessary, since people like the taste as soon as they experience it.

The sugar story is about as direct a path as one can imagine. Of course, it gets terribly complicated as sugar becomes involved in sociopolitical issues, but the basic line of causation remains clear. Furthermore, one must recognize the counter strength of culture (perhaps with its own biological roots); after all, even when sugar is generally available, few cultures use it indiscriminately. It is infrequently a *principal* ingredient in main dishes, as with meat or grain staples, and in some culture including our own, is usually considered inappropriate in such contexts.

Flavor Principles

I have written elsewhere of the basic dilemma of the omnivore or generalist[1] (Rozin 1976A, 1977): the opposing tendencies to explore new

---

[1]The critical feature is acceptance of a wide variety of foods. The wide variety may all be parts of plants. Hence, the inclusion of "generalists," as preferable to "omnivore."

sources of foods and to fear new foods as possible poisons. This results from the difficult problem that each omnivore or generalist must solve: 0the discovery of a variety of foods from among many potential foods, some nutritive, others not, some highly toxic, others mildly toxic, others toxin free. Each potential new food is a possible new source of energy or nutrients, a part of the broad spectrum of acceptable foods that make omnivores or generalists so versatile. Yet, the very act of sampling a potential food involves a risk to health or life, as it may be toxic. The generalist's dilemma can be seen in humans, manifested as preferences for familiar foods and at the same time desire for variety (Rozin 1976B; Siegel and Pilgrim 1958; B. Rolls 1979, this volume, Chapter 6).

I believe a case can be made (though it is surely more indirect than the case for sugar) that cultural practice—that is, cuisine—represents and mediates this basic biological conflict. As pointed out by Elisabeth Rozin (1973, this volume, Chapter 11), most of the world's cuisines are characterized by the repetitive use of a particular combinations of flavorings, or *flavor principles*, on virtually all basic food dishes. These flavor principles may function to provide a familiar and reassuring flavor for foods, and thus to blunt the fear of the new (Rozin 1976B, 1978). They may also function to promote wide acceptance of a new food, once it has been accepted by some members of a culture, by the process of preparing the new food with the highly familiar and reassuring flavor principle.

But we now face the other horn of the dilemma. Doesn't the clothing of all food in a monotonously repeated group of flavorings frustrate the desire for variety? A close examination of cuisines with clear flavor principles shows that there is a substantial amount of variety within the limits of the flavor principles (Rozin and Rozin 1981). The monotony is in the mouth of the outsider and is equivalent to the belief of the novice wine drinker that all wines taste the same. The ubiquity of chili pepper (part of a basic flavor principle) in Mexican food is misleading: many different types and combinations of different tasting chili peppers are used from day to day, and from dish to dish. And the same can be said for variations in the spices that make up "curries" in India. So it appears that there is a culinary flavor theme, but that there are many variations (Rozin and Rozin 1981). The conflict between desires for variety and familiarity is *transformed* into culinary themes and variations, in the culture.

This linkage is admittedly speculative. Furthermore, I do not pretend that, even if valid, this is the only virtue of characteristic food flavorings. They might well serve group identity functions, like costume, and the specific flavoring components may have nutritive or pharmacological values (Rozin 1978). It should also be noted that although there is at least a recognizable analogy between the generalist's dilemma and culinary themes and variations, the variation within cuisines does not serve the same ultimate function as variety seeking in animals: the discovery of new foods. However, this ultimate function is manifested in rats and humans by a desire for variety, and this desire may motivate the variety in the use of flavor principles.

The transition from culture to individual is by exposure to the flavors in the odors of the home and the food of the family. This exposure typically leads to an acquired liking for and attachment to these flavors (Rozin 1976B) (see Fig. 13.2).

Lesson 1A

In both the cases of flavor principles and sugar, innate aspects of food selection are passed on through culture and back to the individual. There is no change in function in these transitions. In the case of sugar, the role of culture is to increase availability and *amplify* the basic biological bias by providing sweeter foods. The *form* of the biological bias, seeking sweetness, remains the same through all transitions. In the flavor principle example, however, the *form* of the generalist's dilemma, as expressed in a nonhuman animal, is profoundly modified; there is nothing like systematic and voluntary variation of basic flavorings in nonhuman creatures. In this case, culture *transforms* the omnivorous animal's solution, but preserves its proximal function (balancing desires for novelty and familiarity). The examples illustrate different ways in which the transition through culture can affect the form of a biological (or incidentally, individually invented) tendency or program: in these cases, amplification, increased availability and transformation were cultural mechanisms.

Lesson 1B

A cultural practice with an adaptive biological basis need not itself be adaptive. The adaptive liking for sweets, as they occur in nature, can be turned into a maladaptive over-reliance on sweets, through increased availability and increased sweetness.

Lesson 1C

It would be nice to continue analyses of sequences starting with biological biases or programs. Unfortunately, the straw in our straw scheme is already beginning to show. There are precious few other examples of this sort. Perhaps one could find some in culturally based avoidances of innately unpalatable bitter substances, or in cultural adaptations to increase the amount of meat in the diet, if we consider the possibility of an innate desire for the flavor and texture of meat in our species. But the list is not long. Relatively few culinary practices can be traced back to biologically based behavior patterns. Of course, other *nonbehavioral* aspects of human biology have substantial effects on cuisine. "Nutritional anthropologists" have shown many adaptive links between cultural practice and nutritional needs. In such cases, the biological basis for cultural practice does not lie in behavior. We turn next to two examples.

REPRESENTATION OF NUTRITIONAL ADAPTIVE FUNCTION IN THE MINDS OF CONTEMPORARY INDIVIDUALS: MANIOC VERSUS CORN

Manioc

Bitter manioc contains high levels of cyanide (cyanogenic glucosides), and is therefore a very toxic food plant (see Fig. 13.3). The "biology" in this case is simply that cyanide interferes with basic life processes. The cultural response to this conjunction of nutrient and toxin in the same plant is the development of a technology that presses and/or rinses out the cyanide, yielding a valuable starch staple (Jones 1959; Sturtevant 1969).

Because the effects of the cyanide in manioc can be quite noticeable, it is not hard to imagine that individuals could associate them with the ingestion of manioc. It is harder to understand why anyone would persist with manioc use long enough to discover the elaborate detoxification procedure. Perhaps, the extensive pressing and rinsing in the traditional procedure was already used for another food. Alternatively, manioc may have been domesticated for reasons other than its nutritive value. For example, it may have served as a source of poison for use in fishing (Sauer 1970). Furthermore, the discovery of a successful process may have been aided by the fact that this same process removes the unpleasant bitter taste that comes, at least in part, from the toxic cyanogenic glycoside.

Although we do not know how it happened, given the salience of the toxic effects of untreated bitter manioc, and its undesirable bitter taste, we expect that individuals involved in the gradual discovery of the detoxification procedures knew that they had made progress; that is, they knew the value of what they were doing. Their efforts produced, at once, less toxic and better tasting manioc. This technique is taught to future cooks in the home, and becomes a habitual practice, as manioc becomes part of the transmitted cuisine (Fig. 13.3). It is likely that

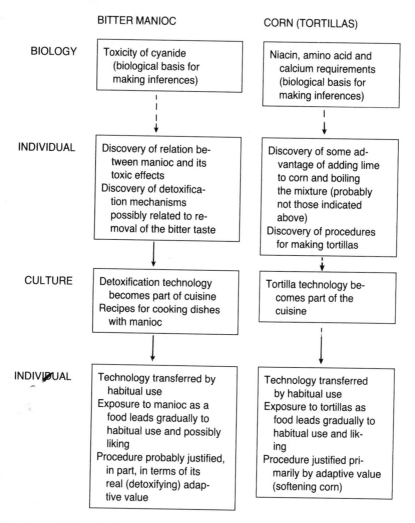

FIG. 13.3. BASIC SCHEME APPLED TO BITTER MANIOC AND CORN (TORTILLAS)
In both cases, the biological tendency that shapes the cultural practice is a metabolic characteristic, rather than behavior. For manioc, the biological adaptive value is probably within
the awareness of current users, while current tortilla makers are not aware of the nutritional
advantages of the tortilla technology.

current users of the leaching technique, who have acquired it through
their culture, understand its fundamental adaptive function: that it
renders the food edible by destroying a toxin and/or makes the food taste
less bitter.

Corn (Tortillas)

There is a complex technology associated with the making of tortillas in Mexico and other Latin-American countries. A detailed analysis by Katz and his colleagues (Katz *et al.* 1974) indicates a variety of nutritional advantages of the practice of boiling corn in lime (calcium hydroxide) before grinding it to make tortillas. This practice makes the corn much more suitable as a staple food (more compatible with the biology of the organism) by (a) introducing more calcium into an otherwise low calcium diet; (b) increasing the availability of bound niacin in the corn; and (c) improving the amino acid balance in the corn.

Katz *et al.* have made a convincing case, on the adaptive side, for the value of this technology. But the pathway to this solution is totally obscure. Were these effects responsible for initial use and the cultural adaptation of the tortilla technology? We do not know. We do know that current users of the technology do not carry this adaptive explanation in their heads. When I asked residents of a traditional Mexican village, who made their tortillas at home, why they use lime in tortillas, almost all responded that it made it easier to roll out and handle tortillas. They claimed that without lime, the corn would be hard to grind and the tortillas would break easily. In general, the opinion was that the lime treatment softened the corn. Three women willingly made tortillas for me from corn cooked without lime. It was clearly harder to crush the corn into meal *(masa)*. Although the tortillas could be rolled out (much to the surprise of two of the women), and held their shape in some cases, they seemed more brittle.

However the technology was originally established in culture, once it happened, the transmission of the technology and the liking for the resulting tortilla present no special problems (see Fig. 13.3).

Lesson 2A

In both of these cases, culture has institutionalized a procedure through which health is improved by removing a toxin or increasing the nutritive value of a food. No specific innate *behavioral* biases are necessarily involved, though removal of the bitter taste in manioc may engage such a bias. Rather, nutritional or metabolic features of the organism, possibly combined with the human's general capacity for inference, may account for the origin of these culinary procedures.

Lesson 2B

The contrast is this: in the case of manioc, it is highly likely that the basic adaptive function of the leaching process was obvious from the start, and is likely to be within the awareness of contemporary leachers. The biological and nutritional adaptive value of this practice may be a conscious source of motivation for using this process today. On the other hand, the contemporary tortilla-maker justifies her performance on grounds different from those that we suspect to be the "true" adaptive value.

The question is whether the essential nutritional adaptive value of a culinary practice is represented (manioc) or not represented (tortillas) in the head of the user. A second question is whether these same adaptive values played a direct role in the origin of the cultural practice. After all, given the three impressive advantages of lime processing of corn, why not add a fourth more prosaic and more apparent one: softening the dough? This is the most likely advantage to be noticed and to support adoption. Other adaptive aspects might then help to support and maintain the cultural practice, through general contributions to the well-being of the technology users.

This contrast raises an issue of central importance in the explanation of culinary adaptation. In biological evolution, it goes without saying that function is blind to mechanism. Any genetic changes that would lead to an adaptive end may be selected for. How they work is irrelevant. There are usually a number of alternative solutions to problems. The one chosen in any particular line of evolution is constrained by the limitations of the existing structure of the organism and genome and by the accidents of mutation or recombination. Many culinary practices, tortilla-making being a fine example, have multiple effects, like the pleiotropic effects of genes. Only one of these effects need be critical in establishing the practice, and this is likely to be the effect that is most apparent, and thus most likely to be appreciated when the practice first arises. Yet, the other effects may be critical to maintenance of the practice, and the success of the culture, though they never enter into the consciousness of any individuals.

Perhaps the clearest example of this would be cooking. Heating food has many biological advantages, in terms of increasing digestibility, killing microorganisms, destroying toxins, etc. These are powerful advantages for any culture that possesses the technology. Yet, it is most likely that more prosaic aspects of cooking are responsible for its widespread use: it may be a flavor enhancer, and it makes food easier to chew. The immediate effects of increasing the pleasures of eating are likely to be the causes of the origin of cooking traditions, and are the most likely explanations in the heads of contemporaries.

AMPLIFYING OR REVERSING BIOLOGICAL BIASES: SUGAR VERSUS CHILI PEPPER

Sugar

I have already discussed sugar, as a case of amplification by culture of an innate preference (see Figs. 13.2 and 13.4).

Chili Pepper

In contrast to sugar, there are some substances for which there are negative biases. Among the most prominent are the innate rejections of foods that cause painful or irritating sensations in the mucous membranes of the mouth, nose or pharynx. And yet, in almost every culture (Rozin 1976B, 1978), at least one innately unpalatable substance becomes an important part of food or drink. Acquired preferences for strongly irritant or bitter foods are rare in animals (Rozin et al. 1979), suggesting that this human phenomenon is associated with culture in some way.

Most innately unpalatable substances are distasteful for a reason. Those that might actually be consumed in natural environments are almost always parts of plants. The bad (usually bitter) sensations are usually associated with toxic substances presumably evolved by the plant to deter consumption by animals. The bad tastes serve as a warning signal to animals. But not all innately unpalatable substances are harmful. Perhaps, in at least some of these cases, a bad tasting substance evolves in the plant to deter animal consumption, even though it is not associated with a toxin. Plants with such chemicals are described as mimics of truly toxic plants. Chili pepper, for example, is quite safe to eat. Unlike many other innately unpalatable "edibles" (e.g., tobacco and coffee), it has only minor pharmacological effects (Maga 1975; Rozin 1978).

The adoption of chili pepper as a food in pre-Columbian American cultures, and its rather rapid adoption by many (especially tropical) cultures following the Age of Exploration remain real puzzles. Many hundreds of millions of people in the Old World now eat it on a daily basis. When one thinks of it, it is highly unlikely that such unpleasant stuff should ever make it through the early stages that must be prerequisite for entrance into a cuisine. Given the relatively firm resistance by many Old World cultures to corn and tomatoes, the success of chili is all the more remarkable. The widespread adoption in the Old World may have facilitated by a type of "preadaptation" (Mayr 1960). Black pepper was already popular in many parts of the Old World, but it was very expensive. Chili pepper is cheaper, and provides a similar irritant

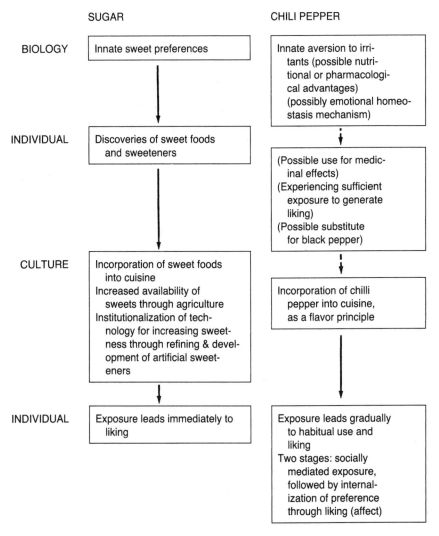

FIG. 13.4. BASIC SCHEME APPLIED TO SUGAR AND CHILI PEPPER
Sugar represents a biological behavior tendency that is amplified in culture. Chili pepper is innately unpalatable. The liking for chili pepper by people in many cultures represents a culturally mediated reversal of a biological bias.

sensation. But this, of course, only postpones the problem. We will eventually have to supply an explanation for the original popularity of black pepper (see Sass 1981, for some interesting suggestions).

As in the case of tortillas, we must take care in distinguishing presumed adaptive value from cause of adoption, either by the culture or by young individuals in each generation. From an adaptive point of view, it could be argued that as a participant in many flavor principles, chili pepper serves the functions described above for flavor principles. But there are other things that could be used that do not taste so bad at first. Chili pepper is a rich source of vitamins A and C. It activates the digestive system, causing salivation, gastric secretion, and gut motility, for which it was used for medicinal purposes after being brought to the Old World. The co-occurrence of chili use and bland, mealy, starch-based diets suggests a role for salivation. The same type of basic diet also leaves open the possibility that chili is used to add "zest" or "mouthfulness" (see Rozin 1978 for a discussion of these and other possibilities).

Reconstruction of the historical events leading to the initial use of chili pepper in the New World, or its institutionalization in cuisine in either the New or Old World would be purely speculative at this time. Such speculations are exercised in Fig. 13.4. However, the acceptance of this innately unpalatable substance occurs in tens of millions of children every year, in chili-eating cultures. This phenomenon should be subject to scientific analysis.

The preference for chili pepper is not motivated primarily by a desire for the consequences of eating it; that is, people do not eat it in spite of its bad taste, for example, as a vitamin supplement. Rather, they show a true affective shift; they come to like the same "burn" that they used to dislike (Rozin and Schiller 1980). There is very little information in the psychological literature about the mechanisms of such affective shifts (Rozin and Fallon 1981). It is clear that acquired likings for innately unpalatable substances take time to develop (Rozin and Schiller 1980), and almost invariably involve some mediation by culture. They tend to occur in two stages: the first stage involves "forced" exposure, under some sort of social pressure, and allows processes to work to produce a more enduring, second-stage preference (see page 247). The cause of this transition to a second stage for chili pepper is the issue at hand. We have suggested many possible mechanisms (Rozin 1978; Rozin and Schiller 1980), including flavor enhancement, social reinforcement, and "thrill seeking." I would like to consider one possibility here in some detail, because it involves a basic biological mechanism as an explanatory device in the overcoming of a biologically based rejection. It shows how cultural mediation can engage a biological system in a context for which it was not "designed."

Evidence has been growing for the existence of an "emotional homeostasis" system, whose function is to maintain an organism at a relatively even emotional level. Departures from normality (e.g., as produced by an arousing stimulus) may be neutralized by the internal development of an opponent process that opposes the stimulated affect

(Solomon and Corbit 1973; Solomon 1977). Thus, for example, the euphoria produced by heroin is reduced over time by an internally generated "negative affect" opponent. It has been suggested that the opponent process becomes strengthened with use: each exposure to a stimulus arousing a given affective response recruits a stronger (earlier onset, higher amplitude, longer lasting) opponent. This analysis has been applied very effectively to the understanding of opiate addiction and readily accounts for the phenomena of tolerance and withdrawal (Solomon 1977).

Now such a system should be engaged by the painful oral stimulus produced by chili pepper. A pleasurable opponent should be induced. Normally, one or a few experiences with chili pepper would cause it to be avoided, but culture-based social pressures support continued ingestion. This could allow the pleasurable opponent to continue to grow, and possibly to overshoot, resulting in a net pleasurable feeling—a liking for chili pepper.

It is notable that the chili-liker seems to experience about the same sensation as he did when he first tasted chili, but has changed his affective evaluation of this sensation. The parallel with the effects of morphine is suggestive, for morphine's primary effect seems to be to alter the interpretation (affective value) of pain, rather than its sensory properties. Recent research has revealed that the brain contains its own (endogenous) opiates. These are presumably involved in the modulation of chronic, repeated pain (Snyder 1980; Schull et al. 1981). It is conceivable that secretion of these endogenous opiates constitutes the opponent process to pain (Schull et al. 1981) and is involved in the development of a liking for the painful stimulation produced by chili pepper (Rozin et al. 1982).

This is, of course, a hypothesis. However, it illustrates how a cultural process can cause a basic biological mechanism to operate outside the context for which it was designed, with interesting results. It is quite likely that an emotional opponent system would not have a design feature to prevent overshoot, simply because one would expect an animal to avoid a situation producing negative affect long before such an overshoot might occur.

Lesson 3

Although culture can amplify biological tendencies, it is strong enough to reverse them. Cultural forces may recruit other biological mechanisms, not normally brought into play in the context in question, as part of this reversal process. The reversal may result in a net biological advantage: the nutritional or pharmacological advantages of consuming an innately unpalatable substance may outweigh any of the risks associated with toxin ingestion, as may be the case with the use of coca. Alternately, the original biologically based rejection may not have been based on any real risks, as seems to be the case with chili pepper. In this way, cultural processes allow correction of an inappropriate biological bias. For the case of chili pepper, this could be described as the discovery of a case of mimicry. Finally, it is possible that the reversal of an innate rejection may result in a net biological disadvantage, as perhaps is the case in the use of tobacco.

BIOLOGY TO CULTURE AND CULTURE TO BIOLOGY: CULTURED MILK VERSUS RAW MILK

Cultured Milk Products

Milk is not a natural food for adult mammals. Access is normally restricted to nursing young. For almost all mammals (with the exception of some relatively small groups of humans), lactose, or milk sugar, is not digestible after the period of weaning (see Johnson et al. 1974 for a review). This unique milk sugar is made of glucose and galactose. The gut enzyme, lactase, splits lactose into these two components, which, unlike lactose, can be absorbed. The enzyme drops to very low levels at about the time of weaning. Without lactase in significant amounts, lactose remains in the gut. It draws in water by osmotic forces, and forms a substrate for growth of gut flora. Following the ingestion of substantial amounts of milk (lactose), the results are cramps, gas, diarrhea, and loss of the energy value of unabsorbable lactose, the only carbohydrate in milk. The reduction in enzyme level makes sense: it can be seen, from one point of view, as a conservative mechanism to prevent investment of energy into making an enzyme for which there would be no substrate. It may also be a mechanism for facilitating weaning from milk, by supporting the development of an aversion to milk based on negative gastrointestinal symptoms (Pelchat and Rozin 1982A).

For the adult human, milk has some of the properties of manioc: it has substantial nutritive value, but also contains something that causes discomfort and compromises its nutritional value. As in the case of manioc, humans discover processes to "detoxify" milk. Since the symptoms of lactose intolerance occur within hours of drinking milk, it would not be unreasonable to assume that humans could make the connection between drinking milk and the symptoms. The problem of detoxification is much easier to solve with milk than with manioc. For bacteria that would in the normal course of events get into milk have the ability to break down lactose into its component sugars. Culturing milk renders it much more nutritional and digestible by reducing the level of lactose and replacing it with digestible glucose and galactose. Culturing can occur in many ways, including the placement of raw milk in animal skins for a few days, as was the case in some nomadic groups, or just leaving the milk around at normal outdoor temperature. This route of culturing could easily have been discovered by chance, especially in a world without either refrigerators or a germ theory. The result, with the establishment of some control over the type and action of the microorganisms, is yogurt, cheese or other cultured milk products (Fig. 13.5).

There is no problem with the establishment of culturing technology in culture, or its transmission to each new generation. Through exposure, each new generation would come to consume these products, by habitual use and by development of a liking for them (Fig. 13.5).

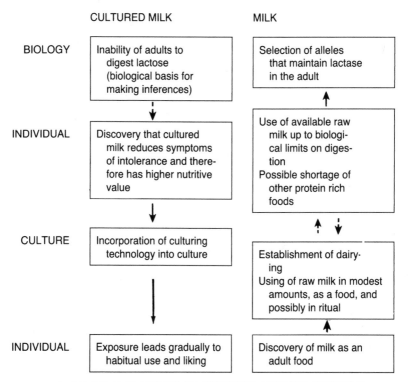

FIG. 13.5. BASIC SCHEME APPLIED TO CULTURED MILK AND RAW MILK
The case of cultured milk, like manioc, illustrates how culture finds ways to make a food biologically more suitable, through processing techniques. With raw milk, on the other hand, the causal arrow is reversed. Cultural practices exploiting raw milk as a food cause selection pressures which change the biology, in terms of the frequencies of the genes governing retention of the enzyme, lactase, into adulthood.

Milk

Most humans in cultures relying on cultured milk remain lactose intolerant. However, there are some groups that retain high levels of lactase into adulthood. This "deviant" trait seems to be under genetic control (Simoons 1969, 1979, this volume, Chapter 12), and is probably the result of a single dominant allele. Contemporary lactose tolerant groups have a racial history of substantial raw milk use. They are descendants of dairying cultures, most notably Northern Europeans and some pastoral groups in Asia and Africa (Simoons 1970, 1979). The most likely hypothesis is that use and later reliance on milk established a selective advantage for the ability to digest lactose. Presumably, extent of milk use and incidence of lactose tolerance co-evolved. It is very difficult to recreate, with present evidence, the steps that occurred in the sequence(s) from no milk use and lactose intolerance to extensive dairying and raw milk drinking and lactose tolerance. Lactose intolerant humans can consume moderate amounts of milk (usually in the 4- to 8-oz range) without symptoms.[2] Although they do not get full utilization of this milk (lactose constitutes about 40% of cow milk solids), they could assimilate minerals, vitamins, and milk fat and protein. Thus, perhaps by analogy with the nursing child or animal, some milk drinking may have occurred in lactose-intolerant individuals. Milk drinking may also have entered into ritual activities (Simoons 1970). But one would think that large-scale dairying would only be supportable if milk in some form (raw or cultured) were a substantial portion of the diet.

Given the ease of accidentally discovering the value of cultured milk, it is surprising that some cultures drank substantial amounts of raw milk. Of course, it is possible that some raw milk drinking cultures initially used cultured milk, and later switched to raw milk. But if cultured products were not discovered or, more likely, were avoided for some reason (e.g., odor), we can presume that milk might have been drunk up to biological limits. Increase in lactose tolerance could then be selected for, since it could extend those limits (Fig. 13.5). Perhaps a shortage in high protein foods over an extended period of time (many generations) provided additional selection pressure. Whatever the precise sequence of events, it is clear that individual and cultural food practices increased the desirability and availability of milk and established the selection pressure for genetic changes. The genetic basis for

---

[2]The relation between levels of lactase activity (determined by direct assay or levels of glucose in the blood following a lactose load) and symptoms of lactose intolerance is yet to be fully explicated. There are many instances in both animals and humans of high lactose tolerance (ability to drink substantial amounts of milk without symptoms) associated with very low lactase levels.

this selection would appear to present no problems: even among current lactose-intolerant groups that do not use milk products, there is a small percentage of the population that shows lactose tolerance. Therefore, according to the most likely genetic hypothesis, the frequency of the dominant allele is well above zero before selection for maintenance of lactase production into adulthood.

In addition to motivating the genetic changes, culture would operate in this case to establish a source of milk, by development of dairying (see Fig. 13.5). The transmission of milk drinking to new generations would be a straightforward matter, since milk seems highly palatable to humans (e.g., Meiselman *et al.* 1971). People could easily learn to modulate their intake so as not to induce symptoms. Occasional overdoses would probably not seriously affect the liking for milk; at least it appears that some lactose-intolerant Americans like milk and simply control their intake (Pelchat and Rozin 1982B).

Lesson 4A
The biology to culture "arrow" can be reversed. Although we do not know the details of the pathway, the end product (lactose tolerance under genetic control) suggests that the cultural practices of drinking raw milk and dairying provided the selection pressure for genetic change. Therefore, it is possible to go from culture to biology. This is in some ways analogous to the "Baldwin" effect in evolutionary biology: the influence of experience ("learning") on the gene pool (Baldwin 1896; Simpson, 1953).

Lesson 4B
There are many ways to milk a cow. Humans have solved the problem of utilizing milk as adults in two entirely different ways: changing genetically under selective pressures produced by culture so as to be able to digest lactose, or digesting the lactose externally through development of milk culture, a culturally transmitted technology.

AFFECTIVE OR COGNITIVE BASES FOR ACQUISITION OF CULTURE: POISONOUS MUSHROOMS VERSUS INSECTS

Poisonous Mushrooms

Some mushrooms contain deadly toxins. They usually produce some rather rapid symptoms, and later, more devastating results. It would not be surprising that humans could discover this and avoid those mushroom species that cause harm. One can imagine this individually acquired information spreading to other individuals, and eventually becoming part of the culture. In each generation, youngsters are warned not to eat certain kinds of mushrooms and possibly taught how to identify them. Given the threatened consequences, they appropriately refrain from doing so. This is a straightforward and highly plausible sequence (see Fig. 13.6).

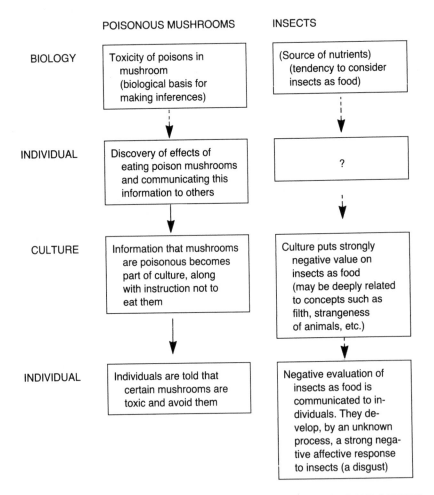

FIG. 13.6. BASIC SCHEME APPLIED TO POISONOUS MUSHROOMS AND INSECTS
Both represent culturally transmitted avoidances. However, in the case of poisonous mushrooms, the transmission to individuals is accomplished by communicating the dangers involved in consuming mushrooms; no affective response (dislike of the taste) results. For insects, the cultural prohibition takes the form of a strong negative affective response.

Insects

Like poisonous mushrooms, insects are widely rejected as food in many cultures. However, they *are* a valuable source of nutrients. Once again, as with chili pepper, we seem to be working against biology. There is no reason to believe that there is an innate bias against insects. Insects are consumed in quite a few cultures (Bodenheimer 1951), and it is a common observation, even in cultures that reject insects, that very young children eat them.

It is hard to imagine how a rejection of insects developed in individuals, or how a prohibition arose and was maintained within the culture. Explanations of this and similar widespread prohibitions, which almost always involve animals, have centered around ideas like filth or strangeness (e.g., Douglas 1966; Rozin and Fallon 1981). Somehow, this prohibition is passed on faithfully to each generation and results in a strong negative affective response or "disgust" reaction to even the thought of eating insects. This affective response dominates reactions to disgusting potential edibles. Even though information (cognitions) may be available to people, indicating the safety, nutritive value, and perhaps palatable taste of a disgusting item, they cannot bring themselves to eat it. There is an irrational aspect to disgust (Rozin and Fallon 1981).

Lesson 5

In both of these cases, culture causes rejection of a substance never (well hardly ever!) eaten by contemporary members of the culture. There is an information transfer in both cases. But in one case, poisonous mushrooms, the information serves merely to guide behavior; there is no affective response. Poisonous mushrooms are neither offensive nor distasteful; they are simply dangerous (Rozin and Fallon 1980, 1981). If one could extract or destroy the poison, the mushrooms would be good to eat.

On the other hand, the insect avoidance is affect-laden. People are sure that insects would taste bad, and they are offended by the thought of eating them. We call this the disgust response (Angyal 1941; Rozin and Fallon 1980, 1981). It is a potent and almost irreversible reaction to potential foods. Through an as yet not understood process, the information on insects provided through culture ties into a powerful affect system, whereas it does not for poisonous mushrooms. The cause of this critical difference is not known. This is an unsolved problem in the mechanism of culture acquistion and preference development. The end result is that reactions to foods or potential foods that are initially based on information transfer (cognitions), can be maintained on cognitive and/or affective bases.

MULTIPLE OR UNITARY PATHWAYS TO ENCULTURATION: CHILI PEPPER VERSUS TOBACCO OR COFFEE

Chili Pepper

I have discussed this sequence already (Figs. 13.4, and 13.7). The critical issue here is that in the transition from culture to the individual, chili eating is established in individuals because they come to like the taste. Virtually all chili eaters explain their consumption in terms of liking the mouth sensations that chili produces (Rozin and Schiller 1980). This is not to say that the processes through which a chili-liker comes to like chili are unitary or simple. On the contrary, it is likely that there are multiple pathways in the transition from dislike to like (Rozin 1978; Rozin and Schiller 1980). But, the end product is "unitary."

Coffee or Tobacco

Coffee and tobacco are unpalatable, at first (although in some cases coffee is introduced with enough sugar and milk so that its innately unpalatable bitterness is overwhelmed). As with chili, culture operates in some way as to incorporate these substances in the broad domain of acceptable ingestants, and widespread consumption is induced in each generation in many cultures. Also, as with chili, acquisition occurs in two stages. The first is "forced" exposure. For cigarettes, and to some extent coffee, the social motivation for the first stage is clearer than is the case for chili pepper: peer pressure and being "adult." This leads to the second stage of established preference (see Fig. 13.7).

There are two critical differences from chili pepper. First, unlike chili pepper, both tobacco and coffee have potent pharmacological effects, and both can support addictions. Although it is not clear how anyone, without cultural support, could get hooked on these innately unpalatable substances, salient positive pharmacological effects make the case more plausible than the case for chili pepper. Second, at the level of culture acquisition, we can identify the operations of more ways of maintaining consumption in the second stage. Analyses of smokers (Ikard and Tomkins 1973; Russell *et al.* 1974) and coffee drinkers (Goldstein and Kaizer 1969; Rozin and Cines 1982) indicate multiple motivations that support these behaviors (see Rozin and Fallon 1981 for a general discussion of this issue). Summarizing these studies (Fig. 13.8), each of the following different pathways occurs:

First-Stage: Exposure

1. Initial consumption is under social pressure, but consumption ceases with the onset of adulthood.

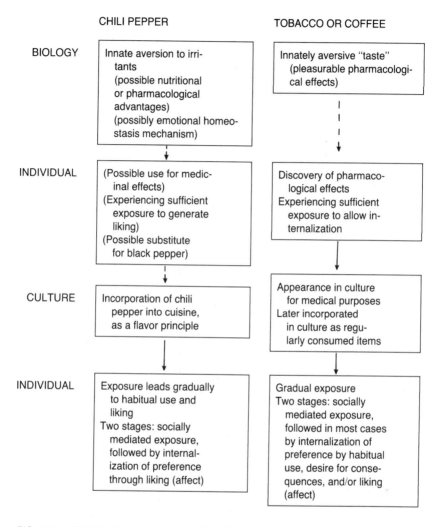

FIG. 13.7. BASIC SCHEME APPLIED TO CHILI PEPPER AND TOBACCO OR COFFEE
All three instances involve reversal of negative biological biases. For chili pepper, the reversal takes one form: development of a liking for the taste. For tobacco or coffee, it takes multiple forms.

2. Initial consumption under social pressure is maintained in adulthood, under the same motivation. That is, consumption remains in the first stage, under the explicit control of social forces: it is not internalized.

Second-Stage: Internalization
   The controlling motivation shifts from external-social to internal.
   3. Repeated and consistent use under social pressure results in inter-

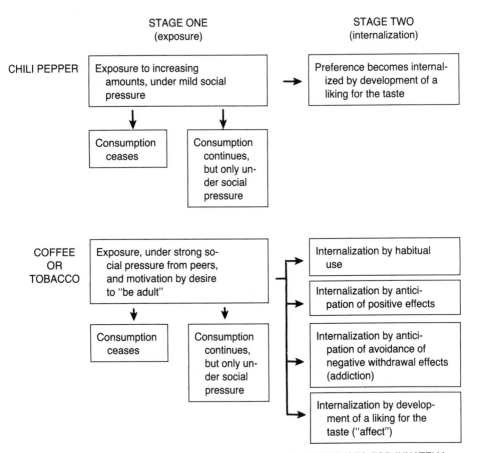

FIG. 13.8.   THE TWO STAGES OF ACQUISITION OF PREFERENCES FOR INNATELY UNPALATABLE SUBSTANCES AND THE DIFFERENT MECHANISMS OF INTERNALIZATION OF PREFERENCE
The single type of internalization (liking for the taste) for chili pepper is contrasted with the multiple types for tobacco and coffee.

nalized continuation of the behaviors, as habitual acts.

4. Consumption is maintained because the user comes to appreciate the positive pharmacological or social effects of ingestion.

5. Consumption is maintained because of addiction, as a means of avoiding withdrawal symptoms.

6. Consumption is maintained by development of a liking for the taste, flavor or other oro-naso-pharyngeal sensations produced by ingestion.

Lesson 6A
For many foods and related substances, culture acquisition proceeds

in two stages: (1) socially or culturally motivated exposure which maintains ingestion long enough for other factors to take over, and (2) development of processes within the individual that internalize consumption (or rejection). By internalization, I mean that the behavior is motivated by internal factors: it does not require the physical presence of a socializing force, although this was probably critical in the development of internalization.

Lesson 6B
The critical contrast in the comparison between chili pepper and coffee or tobacco is that consumption of some substances is internalized in only one way (sensory-affective for chili pepper, postingestional effects for gelusil) while others, like coffee and tobacco, are consumed for multiple internalized reasons. In the case of coffee, this multiple basis for use can be discovered at three levels: individual cups are often drunk for more than one reason; different cups within the same individual may be drunk for different reasons; and different individuals differ on the group of motivations that determine their coffee drinking (Rozin and Cines, 1982). In summary, the "motivational matrix," and hence the enculturation process, will vary from one food to another, and from one individual to another.

TWO PERSISTENT PROBLEMS

In this rapid and incomplete survey of contrasting pairs of foods, I find that two problems keep reappearing. These problems relate to areas of notable ignorance, or weak links, in the general scheme that I have presented.

The Problem of Historical Reconstruction

In almost all of the cases that I have discussed, the best that I could do was to provide a plausible historical scenario to explain how a food came to be used by the "first" individual, and how it then came to be incorporated in culture. For the case of innately unpalatable substances, this is a particularly serious problem. Even unrestrained by known historical sequences, it is hard to come up with a plausible story.

For the case of "first" individual adoptions of food, and to a lesser extent for earlier events in the incorporation into culture, the problem is that idiosyncratic, peculiarly circumstantial factors may be powerful determinants in the historical line. For example, one might imagine that the frequent prohibitions of protein-rich foods, which suspiciously often center on women and children (whose protein needs are surely substantial), might result from a conspiracy among politically powerful members of society (males, historically), to reserve a valuable and rare food source for themselves. Cultural "justifications" could develop later.

Small differences can have enormous historical effects. For example, corn was not adopted to a substantial degree when brought back to Europe by the early explorers and has never become a major human food in most European countries. But it is notable that Cortez and his followers probably did not bring back the tasty and more nutritious corn-based tortilla, with its cooking technology, on return to the Old World. (I suppose it is possible that they brought back some tortillas; but, knowing the tremendous deterioration in palatability that occurs within the first hour after a tortilla is cooked, one can only imagine the product of several months journey across the Atlantic Ocean.) Tortilla making is exclusively the work of women in traditional Mexico. Had Cortez a European woman with him— according to Diaz (1963), he did not—the technology might have been learned and transferred to the Old World. This could have changed the history of corn in Europe.

Hopes for historical explanations of the incorporation of individual discoveries into culture are brighter, since such events, in literate cultures, can be expected to appear in the public record. However, there are great difficulties here, too, as witnessed by interminable speculation on the reasons for the great popularity of black pepper and other spices in Medieval and Renaissance Europe. We certainly should not delay analyses of critical transitions in the straw scheme (see Fig. 13.1), as modified above, until the individual or early cultural adoption links are clarified, because they may never be. Fortunately, the nature of individual "discovery" may not influence the course of subsequent events.

The basic problem with individual discoveries also arises with individual contemporary humans. Finding out why Veronica dislikes veal is a difficult task. We can probably figure it out in most cases (though it would be helpful if we knew the laws of affect acquisition), but it would take some digging. And at least the paydirt is sitting around in the heads of some contemporaries (e.g., Veronica's or her family's).

There is another source of clues to history, at least if one believes that the culture acquisition process may mimic, in some ways, culture history. Perhaps in the generation-repeated cycle of enculturation to specific foods, we can see some of the basic mechanisms at work. At least here, we have a repeating and contemporary drama, and one that can be manipulated to some extent. What is different, and perhaps critically so, is the absence in the historical case of the cultural force that guarantees exposure and allows internal processes to take hold.

Affect and the Acquisition and Internalization of Culture

In examination of the enculturation process, the issue of affective involvement comes up repeatedly. The culture to individual transition seems to foster affective responses, through a process of exposure (Zajonc 1968). The role of affect bears further examination.

The "forced" exposure provided through culture allows a variety of mechanisms to come into play (see Fig. 13.8). In some cases, they do not, and the food is either abandoned by the individual, or continues to be used only under social pressure (as in some cases of observance of religious restrictions on eating, or cases of adults who smoke just to conform). In most cases, however, the exposure leads to internalization of culture "values:" that is, the food becomes desirable for its own sake, and the encouragement of culture is no more a major factor. Habitual use, consumption for effects (physiological or social), and liking (affect) are such examples. As indicated above, for some substances, like tobacco, the various modes of internalization can be teased apart.

We do not understand why exposure leads in some cases to affective responses (liking chili pepper or cigarettes), but not in other cases (consumption of gelusil, smoking only for effects). We do not understand why information from culture leads to affective responses in some cases (e.g., insect rejection) and not others (rejection of poisonous mushrooms or sand). It is notable that affective responses to foods (liking or disliking) almost always focus on sensations associated with the mouth (or nose). To like a food essentially means that it tastes good; to dislike it means that you are sure it tastes bad, even if you have never tried it (e.g., insects or worms—see Rozin and Fallon 1981).

The frequent appearance of affect as a result of enculturation must be explained. As I have pointed out elsewhere, strong *acquired* positive affective responses to food or other objects are rare in nonhuman animals (Rozin 1979; Rozin *et al.* 1979). In particular, the reversal of innately based rejections to foods by affective shifts, very common events in humans, are extremely rare in animals (Rozin *et al.* 1979). Affective investment seems like the best way to produce resilient enculturation: if a culturally valued food is liked, it will be sought for its own sake and be a source of pleasure. Perhaps our relative abundance of acquired positive affect in comparison to all other animals, is an adaptation to the enculturation process.

ACKNOWLEDGMENTS

Preparation of this paper was supported by National Science Foundation Grant BNS 76-80108 and National Institutes of Health Grant HD 12674. I thank Brenda Cines, April Fallon, Marcia L. Pelchat and Jonathan Schull for their contributions as collaborators in some of the research described in this paper. Thanks go to Justin Aronfreed, Ward Goodenough, Solomon Katz, Sidney Mintz, and Elisabeth Rozin for extremely helpful and constructive comments on an earlier draft of this manuscript.

REFERENCES

ANGYAL, A. 1941. Disgust and related aversions. J. Abnorm. Soc. Psychol. *36*, 393–412.

BALDWIN, J.M. 1896. A new factor in evolution. Am. Nat. *30*, 441–451; 536–553.

BODENHEIMER, F.S. 1951. Insects as Human Food. W. Junk, The Hague, The Netherlands.

CROOK, C. 1978. Taste perception in the newborn infant. Infant Behav. Dev. *1*, 52–69.

DESOR, J.A., MALLER, O., and TURNER, R.E. 1973. Taste in acceptance of sugar by human infants. J. Comp. Physiol. Psychol. *84*, 496–501.

DIAZ, B. 1963. The Conquest of New Spain. (Translated by J. M. Cohen from B. Diaz del Castillo, Historia Verdadera de la Conquista de la Nueva Espana, 1568). Penguin Books, New York.

DOUGLAS, M. 1966. Purity and Danger. Routledge and Kegan Paul, London.

GARCIA, J., HANKINS, W.G., and RUSINIAK, K.W. 1974. Behavioral regulation of the milieu interne in man and rat. Science *185*, 824–831.

GOLDSTEIN, A., and KAIZER, S. 1969. Psychotropic effects of caffeine in man III: A questionnaire survey of coffee drinking and its effects in a group of housewives. Clin. Pharmacol. Ther. *10*, 477–488.

IKARD, F.F., and TOMKINS, S. 1973. The experience of affect as a determinant of smoking behavior: A series of validity studies. J. Abnorm. Psychol. *81*, 172–181.

JOHNSON, D.C., KRETCHMER, N., and SIMOONS, F.J. 1974. Lactose malabsorption: Its biology and history. Adv. Pediatr. *21*, 197–237.

JONES, W.O. 1959. Manioc in Africa. Stanford University Press, Stanford, California.

KATZ, S.H., HEDIGER, M.L., and VALLEROY, L.Z. 1974. Traditional maize processing techniques in the New World. Science *184*, 765–773.

MAGA, J.A. 1975. Capsicum. Crit. Rev. Food Sci. Nutr. *7*, 177–199.

MAYR, E. 1960. The emergence of evolutionary novelties. *In* Evolution after Darwin, Volume 1. S. Tax (editor). University of Chicago Press, Chicago, Illinois.

MEISELMAN, H., VAN HORNE, W. HASENZAHL, B., and WEHRLY, T. 1971. The 1971 Fort Lewis Food Preference Survey. U. S. Army Natick Laboratories, Pioneering Research Laboratory, Natick Massachusetts.

MINTZ, S.W. 1979. Time, sugar, and sweetness. Marx. Perspect. *2*, 56–73.

PELCHAT, M.L., and ROZIN, P. 1982A. Memories of mammaries: the dilemma of weaning from milk. Manuscript in preparation.

PELCHAT, M.L., and ROZIN, P. 1982B. The special role of nausea in the acquisition of food dislikes by humans. Submitted for publication.

ROLLS, B.J. 1979. How variety and palatability can stimulate appetite. Nutr. Bull. *5*, 78–86.

ROZIN, E. 1973. The Flavor Principle Cookbook. Hawthorn, New York.

ROZIN, E., and ROZIN, P. 1981. Culinary themes and variations. Nat. Hist. *90*, 6–14.

ROZIN, P. 1976A. The selection of foods by rats, humans, and other animals. Adv. Study Behav. *6*, 21–76.

ROZIN, P. 1976B. Psychobiological and cultural determinants of food choice. *In* Dahlem Workshop on Appetite and Food Intake. T. Silverstone (Editor). Dahlem Konferenzen, Berlin, Germany.

ROZIN, P. 1977. The significance of learning mechanisms in food selection: Some biology, psychology, and sociology of science. *In* Learning Mechanisms in Food Selection. L. M. Barker, M. Best, and M. Domjan (Editors). Baylor University Press, Waco, Texas.

ROZIN, P. 1978. The use of characteristic flavorings in human culinary practice. *In* Flavor: Its Chemical, Behavioral, and Commercial Aspects. C. M. Apt (Editor). Westview Press, Boulder, Colorado.

ROZIN, P. 1979. Preference and affect in food selection. *In* Preference Behaviour and Chemoreception. J. H. A. Kroeze (Editor). Information Retrieval Limited, London.

ROZIN, P., and CINES, B. 1982. Multiple motivations for coffee drinking. Manuscript in preparation.

ROZIN, P., and FALLON, A.E. 1980. Psychological categorization of foods and non-foods I: A preliminary taxonomy of food rejections. Appetite *1*, 193–201.

ROZIN, P., and FALLON, A.E. 1981. The acquisition of likes and dislikes for foods. *In* Criteria of Food Acceptance: How man chooses what he eats. J. Solms and R. L. Hall (Editors), pp. 35–44. Forster, Zurich, Switzerland.

ROZIN, P. and KALAT, J.W. 1971. Specific hungers and poison avoidance as adaptive specializations of learning. Psychol. Rev. *78*, 459–486.

ROZIN, P., and SCHILLER, D. 1980. The nature and acquisition of a preference for chili pepper by humans. Motiv. Emotion *4*, 77–101.

ROZIN, P., GRUSS, L., and BERK, G. 1979. The reversal of innate aversions: Attempts to induce a preference for chili peppers in rats. J. Comp. Physiol. Psychol. *93*, 1001–1014.

ROZIN, P., EBERT, L., and SCHULL, J. 1982. Some like it hot: A temporal analysis of hedonic responses to chili pepper. Appetite *3*, 13–22.

RUSSELL, M.A.H., PETO, J., and PATEL, U.A. 1974. The classification of smoking by factorial structures of motives. J. R. Statist. Assoc. *137*, 313–333.

SASS, L. 1981. Religion, medicine, politics and spices. Appetite *2*, 7–13.

SAUER, C.O. 1970. Agricultural Origins and Dispersals. MIT Press, Cambridge, Massachusetts.

SCHULL, J., KAPLAN, H., and O'BRIEN, C. 1981. Naloxone can alter experimental pain and mood in humans. Physiol. Psychol. *9*, 245–250.

SIEGEL, P.S., and PILGRIM, F.J. 1958. The effect of monotony on the acceptance of food. Am. J. Psychol. *71*, 756–759.

SIMOONS, F.J. 1969. Primary adult lactose intolerance and the milking habit: A problem in biological and cultural interrelations I: Review of the medical research. Am. J. Digest. Dis. *14*, 819–836.

SIMOONS, F.J. 1970. Primary adult lactose intolerance and the milking habit: A problem in biological and cultural interrelations II: A cultural-historical hypothesis. Am. J. Digest. Dis. *15*, 695–710.

SIMOONS, F.J. 1979. Dairying, milk use, and lactose malabsorption in Eurasia: A problem in culture history. Anthropos *74*, 61–80.

SIMPSON, G.G. 1953. The Baldwin effect. Evolution *7*, 110–117.

SNYDER, S. 1980. Peptide neurotransmitters with possible involvement in pain perception. Assoc. Res. Nerv. Ment. Dis. *58*, 233–245.

SOLOMON, R.L. 1977. An opponent-process theory of motivation V: Affective dynamics of eating. *In* Learning Mechanisms in Food Selection. L. Barker, M. R. Best, and M. Domjan (Editors). Baylor University Press, Waco, Texas.

SOLOMON, R.L., and CORBIT, J.D. 1973. An opponent-process theory of motivation II: Cigarette addiction. J. Abnorm. Psychol. *81*, 158–171.

STEINER, J.E. 1974. The gustofacial response: Observation on normal and anencephalic newborn infants. *In* Fourth Symp. Oral Sensation and Perception: Development in the Fetus and Infant. J. B. Bosma (Editor). Publ. No. NIH 73-546, U. S. Department of Health, Education, and Welfare, Bethesda, Maryland.

STURTEVANT, W.C. 1969. History and ethnography of some West Indian starches. *In* The Domestication and Exploitation of Plants and Animals. P. J. Ucko and G. W. Dimbleby (Editors). Gerald Duckworth and Co., London.

ZAJONC, R.B. 1968. Attitudinal effects of mere exposure. J. Pers. Soc. Psychol. *9*, 1–27.

Index

A

Advertising, 139, 146–147, 158–161
Aerobic power, 21
Affect for taste, 226
Affective shifts, 238, 250–251
Africa
  restricted foods in, 205, 208–209
  use of milk in, 210–212
Alkali processing technique, 171–176
Alliesthesia, 102–103
American blacks, and lactose malabsorption, 213
American diet, 7–9, 206–207
American Indians, foods of, 171–187
American lifestyle, and foods, 153–154,
    see also Foods, convenience
Amygdala, role in feeding, 51–54
Anorexia, and brain damage, 48–49
Antitrypsin factor, 180–181
Aphagia, and brain damage, 34–35, 49
Appetite, 17, 30, 37, 67–70, 76, 78, 141,
    157–168, 225–251
  for energy, 27
  learned or conditioned, 67–68, 70–75
  in modern man, 27–28
  in primitive man, 27
Apple pie, memory of, 85, 93
Artificial sweeteners, *see* Sweeteners,
    artificial
Aspartame, 11–12
Athletics, and diet, 22
Attitudes toward foods, 139–149

B

Baldwin effect, 243
Barley, and celiac disease, 216
Bean curd, 181
Beef, cultural avoidance of, 209
Behavioral characteristics of food
    selection, 139, 171–187, 225

Behavioral effects on culture, 171–187,
    235
Behavioral testing, 9–10
Biocultural evolution, 171–187
Biological bias in food selection, 225–227,
    230
Biological factors, 1–3, 17, 68–69, 175,
    225–227, *see also* Foods, biological factors of
Biomedical factors, 205
Bitter
  evolutionary significance of, 5, 227
  and non-tasters, 136–138
Bitter manioc, *see* Manioc
Bitterness
  of PTC, 136
  of saccharin, 136–138
Black pepper, 236–237, 250
Body wisdom, 6–9, *see also* Nutritional
    wisdom
Brain mechanisms and feeding, 33–57
Brine, as preservative, 193

C

Cafeteria studies, 101–102, *see also*
    Menus
Calcium absorption, 215
Calcium deficiency, 215
Calories
  estimating, 69–70
  excessive, 28–30
  regulation of, 17–18, 23–24, 126–129
Candy, color effects of, 113–117
Cantonese cooking, 196
Carbohydrates, 8–9, 71, 161, 228–229
  as fuel, 18
Cassareep, 179
Cassava, 193
Cataracts, and diet, 217
Catecholamine pathways, and feeding,
    49–51

255

Celiac disease, 216–217
Ceviche, 192
Chemical sensing, 3–6, 88, *see also* Flavor; Taste
Cheese
    in memory formation, 95
    varieties of, 199
Chemotaxis, 3
Chewing, 77
Chili peppers, 195–196, 236–238, 246, 251
    development of preferences for, 238, 246, 251
    medicinal value, 238, 246
    varieties, 201, 230
Chocolates, variety and palatability, 113
Cholera, 215
Coffee, 246–249
    instant, 143
    memory formation of, 95
Cognition, and food selection, 74, 78–79, 147, 245
Color, effects on intake, 113–117
Completion compulsion, 75
Convenience foods, *see* Foods, convenience
Cooking, 161, 189, 194–195, 200, 202, 235
    and convenience, 143–144
    effect on flavor, 195
    open fire, 200
    as preservative, 195
Corn, *see* Maize
Cross-cultural studies, 171
Cuisine, 154, 185–186, 189–203, 225
    American, 7–9, 157–168, 162, 206–207
    Cantonese, 197
    Chinese, 182–187, 195
    Ethiopian, 207–208
    Indonesian, 196
    Italian, 197
    Korean, 196
    Mediterranean, 197
    Oriental, 196–197
    Peking, 196
    Szechuan, 196
    variety within, 230
Culinary behavior, 189–190, *see also* Cooking
Culinary techniques, 191–194
Cultural factors, 78–79, 140–141, 153–155, 165–166, 171, 190–191, 225
Cultural wisdom, of foods, 78–79, 153, 226
Culture
    and cuisine, 189–191, 199–200, 202–203
    defined by foods, 203
Curing, dry, 193
Curing foods, 193

Curry, 230
Cutting foods, 191–192
Cyclamate, 11–12, 108

D

Dairying, 243
    geographical distribution of, 210–212
Diabetic rats, experimental, 47
Diet
    and athletics, 19–21
    and cataracts, 217
    and exercise, 28–30
    and performance, 17–18
Dietary choices, 67, *see also* Food selection
Dietary imperialism, 206
Dieting, and food intake, 8–9, 14, 27, 117–120, *see also* Weight control; Calories, regulation of
Disgust reaction, to food, 79, 245
Divalent cation, 181, 184–185
Doufu, 181, 183
Drinking patterns, 124–126

E

Eating, 157–168, *see also* Feeding
    as biological drive, 3–6
    slowly, effects of, 77–78
    trends in, 27–28, 160–162
Ecosystem, human, 175
Edibility of foods, 190–191, 206–207
Egg white, in food processing, 192
Electrical stimulation, and feeding, 34
Electrophysiology, of taste, 9
Emotional homeostasis, 238–239
Energy, 2, 17–18, 69, 105
    balance, 17, 23–27
        measurement of, 25–27
    intake, 23–24
    labeling, 75
    requirements
        and diet, 23
        modern, 27–30
Ensete eaters, 207–208
Environment, effects on food use, 139
Essential nutrients, 28–30
Ethnic differences, 158, 277
    in lactose malabsorption, 213–216
Ethiopian cuisine, 207–208
Evolution, 3–6, 27, 63, 171–176, 226, 235
    of chemical senses, 3–6
Exercise
    and carbohydrates, 18–19
    and diet, 28–30
    and free fatty acids, 19–21

and metabolism, 23
prescribed, 30
prolonged, 19–21
and tissue needs, 17

F

Farming, history and geography of,
    205–207, 217
Fast foods, *see* Foods, convenience
Fats
    in diet, 17, 144, 161
    and satiety, 73–74
Fava beans, 176–179, 216
    psychological effects of, 178–179
Favism, 216
Feedback relations of foods, 185–187
Feeding, *see also* Eating; Food; Food
        selection
    behavior, 85, 90–92
    and brain changes, 35–41
    brain mechanisms, 33–57
    and catecholamine pathways, 49–51
    in child, 85, 90–92, 158, 238
    neurophysiology of, 35–41
    role of orbitofrontal cortex, 54–56
Fermentation, 194
Fish, 192
    avoidance of, 208
Flavor, *see also* Palatability; Taste
    appreciation and experience, 230
    combinations, 196–197
    duration and memory, 92–93
    familiar, 230
    importance of, 3, 65, 147–148, 194–199
    markers, 196–197
    memory of, 89–92
    novel, 92, 230
    and pharmacological value, 231
    pleasantness ratings of, 72–73
    preferences, *see also* Foods, preferences
        in adult, 6
        in infant, 5–6
    principles of, 154, 196–197, 228, 230
    quality and memory, 92, 94–95
Flavorings, 194–196
    and variety, 201
Flesh foods, avoidance of, 208
Food(s), *see also* Food selection; Food
        storage; specific food items
    accessibility, 139
    attitudes toward, 139
    attraction to, 159–160
    availability, 139
    aversion to, 7, 71, 92
    basic, 199

biological factors of, 1–2, 3, 17, 68–69,
    225
bland, 91
budgets, 142–143
central role of, 202–203
chain, 185–186
complex, 200
conditioning in humans, 72–74
and consumers, 139–140, 158–159
convenience, 143–144, 154, 158,
    206–207
cooked, 189–191
and culture, 78–79, 140–141, 153–155,
    165–166, 171, 190–191,
    225–226
distribution, 139, 185–186
enjoyment of, 85, 99, 157
extraction of, 192
ethnic, 154, 180
    American, 7–9, 153–154, 157–168,
        206–207
    African, 205, 208–209
    American Indian, 171–176
    Amerindian, 179
    Botswana bushmen, 191
    Chinese, 182–187
    Hindu Indian, 206
    Korean, 181
    !Kung bushmen, 206
fast, *see* Foods, convenience
feedback relations of, 185–187, *see also*
        Nutritional wisdom
freezing of, 194
as fuel, 17
geographical distribution of, 154,
    171–187, 205–221
habits, 8–9, 148, *see also* Foods, learning
        about
and health, 146–147
imagery, 89–90
intake, cognitive algebra of, 68
labeling of, 75
and language, 159–160
learning about, 6, 33, 41–42, 51–52,
    67–68, 86, 92–94, 96
memory for, 85, 153
neophobia, 52–54
nutritional complementarity of,
    185–186
patterns, 142–143, 206, *see also* Meal
        patterns
perception of, 74–75
and performance, 17
pharmacology of, 178–180
preference
    and calories, 72–74
    internalized, 225–226

survey of, 8
when hungry, 72–74
preferred, 7–9
by monkey, 36
by rat, 95–96
preparation, 179
and prestige, 144–145
processing, 179, 185–186, 191
production, 139, 185–186
psychological effects of, 178–179
raw, 191
restricted range of, 206, 226–227
reward, 44
and ritual, 160, 165
safe, 91, 230–231
science, 181
simple, 200
and sociability, 85, 139, 159
social factors, 68–69, 139, 226–227
and special occasions, 85, 144, 164–167
staple, 118, 142
and symbolism, 146, 157, 165–166
taboo, 79, 207–210
texture of, 85, 163, 192
time saving, 158–159, see also Foods,
  convenience
transforming of, 191–195
variety of, 101–120, see also Variety
Food selection
Americans restricted, 206–207
analysis of, 68–70
and availability, 190–191
and culture, 190–191
and price, 141–144
and religion, 205, 207–210
behavioral characteristics of, 225
biological bias, 225, 230
cognitive factors in, 245
environmental effects on, 139
genetic factors in, 205
individual, 225
limits of, 205–207
non-Western, 206
pleasure in, 250–251
range of, 205
role of flavor, 147–148
social determinants of, 139
values in, 250–251
Food storage, 139, 185–186
Foraging errors, 91–92
Free fatty acid utilization, 19–21
Freezing foods, 194
French cooking, 197

G

G-6-PD deficiency, 176–179, 216

Genetic markers for celiac disease, 217
Genetics
and celiac disease, 216–217
and food selection, 205–221
and G-6-PD deficiency, 176–179
and lactose malabsorption, 214–215,
  242–243
and milk selection, 214–215, 242–243
and PTC taste, 136
Geography
and foods, 205–221
and lactose malabsorption, 214–216
Ginger root, 195
Gluconeogenesis, 22
Glucose
in blood, 17–18
and brain response, 39–41
Glucosidases, 179
Gluten enteropathy, 216
Glycogen stores, 17, 22
Glycogen loading, 21–22
Goats, as food, 209
Gymnema sylvestre, 13–14

H

Habits, eating, 8–9
Health beliefs, 146–147
Health foods, 146–147
Hedonic conditioning, 67–68
Herbs, adaptive role of, 180
Hindu Indians, foods selected by, 206
Historical reconstructions, problems of,
  249–250
History of milking, 210–212
HLA-B8 antigen, and celiac disease, 217
Horse bean, 216
Hot peppers, 201, see also Chili peppers
Human ecogenetics, 155, 171, 216–221
Human information processing, 86–90,
  175
Hungarian cooking, 197
Hunger, and palatability, 67, 102–103,
  110, see also Meal patterns;
  Satiety
Hyperinsulinemia, 47
Hyperphagia, experimental, 45–48
Hypothalamus, feeding control, 34–35

I

Illness
and food memory, 93–94
and food preference, 7, 51–52, 71, 93
Incorporation, food process, 192
India, beef avoidance in, 209

Individual's role in culture, 226–228
Indonesian cuisine, 196
Infant taste preferences, 5–6
Inherited flavor preference, 90–91
Insects, as food, 227, 245, 251
Italian cuisine, 197

J

Jerky, 193
Jewish cooking, 197

K

Korean cuisine, 196

L

Labeling, energy of foods, 75, *see also*
    Foods, labeling of
Lactase, 242
Lactase activity, 214–216
Lactose
    consequences of ingestion, 213–214
    malabsorption, 213–216
    tolerance, 242
Lactose absorption, and calcium
    absorption, 215
Latent inhibition, and memory, 96–97
L-Dopa psychological effects of, 178–179
Leaching, 193
Learned food aversions, 7, 51–52, 71,
    92–93
Learning, *see also* Foods, learning about
    about flavor, 7, 230
    and brain response, 41–42
Licorice, 6–7
Lime, in tortilla technology, 234
Lipogenesis, 45–47
Liquid diets, palatability of, 119
Long-term memory for foods, 87, 89
Low energy consumers, 28–30

M

Magnesium, 181, 184
Maidu Indians, foods of, 198
Maize, 171–176
Malaria, 176–179
Malnutrition, and obesity, 28
Manioc, 179–180, 193, 207, 231–233
Marathon runners, diet, 22
Marination, 192–193
Meal patterns, 69–70, 158–160, 166–167

Meals, 69–70, 103–105, 166–167
    sedation effects, 76–77
Meal size
    control of, 77–78
    and fullness, 76–77
Meat, taste of, 190
Memory, 85
    development of, 91–92
    for flavor, 89
    inherited, 90–91
    long-term, 87, 89
    sensory, 87–88
    short-term, 87–88
    working, 87, 88, 92
Menus, 7–8, 68–69, 118–119, 160–161,
    see also Cuisine
Metabolic adaptation, 25
Metabolic rate, 23–24, 69
    and muscular activity, 23
Metabolism, 17–30, 69, 225
Milk
    and cataracts, 217
    human usage of, 210, 242–243
Milled grain, 192
Milling foods, 192
Miraculin, 12–13
Mixing sweeteners, effects of, 123–134,
    129–131
Mixtures, sweet, 64
Monotonous diets, 27, 117–120
Motivation
    to eat, 226
    effects on brain, 37
    in sweet intake, 131–133
Mushrooms, 243–244, 245

N

Neophobia, food, 52–54, 230
Nigari, 184
Nonmilking, and geography, 210–212
Novel flavors, 52–54, 92, 230
Nutrients
    in blood, 17–18
    essential, 28–30
Nutrition
    and cuisine, 171, 185–186
    effects on choice, 67
Nutritional anthropology, 232
Nutritional complementarity, 185–186
Nutritional education, 78, 146
Nutritional hedonic conditioning, 67, 70,
    see also Feedback relations
Nutritional requirements, 146, 226–227
Nutritional wisdom, 64, 67–68, 70, 78,
    146, 153, 185–186, 232, *see also*
    Body wisdom

O

Oats, and celiac disease, 216
Obesity, 28–30, 48, 75, 77–78, 101,
    117–120, see also Weight control
    and brain damage, 33
    and brain tumor, 48
    control
        through energy labeling, 75
        through surgery, 49
    and hyperinsulinemia, 48
    and insulin, 45–48
Odor, and food enculturation, 231
Olfaction, 71, 88
Olive oil, 197
Oral factors, in rats, 129–134
Orbitofrontal cortex, role in feeding,
    54–56
Oriental cooking, 196–197
Overeating
    and brain damage, 33
    effects of, 76–77
Oxidization, and ATP production, 18–19

P

Palatable foods, 67, 85, 91, 101–109,
    118–120, 198, see also Taste;
    Flavor
Palatibility
    changes during meal, 103–105
    and energy, 105–107
    and hunger, 67–69
    ratings of, 103
    and sweet intake, 129–131
Particulation of foods, 191–192
Pemmicans, 193
Pepper, see Chili pepper; Black pepper
Performance, see Foods, and performance
Pharmacological value of flavor, 6–7, 231,
    236, 246
Phenyl-thiocarbamide (PTC), taste of, 136
Pickle, food curing, 193
Pigs, and pork avoidance, 208–209
Poisonous mushrooms, 243–245
Politics, and pork avoidance, 209
Polydipsia, 123–134
Pork, avoidance of, 208–209
Portion sizes, 75
Post-ingestion, 92–94
Post-ingestional factors, 76, 123–124, 249
Post-ingestive consequences, and palat-
    ability, 70, 107–108
Preference reversals, 102

Preferred foods, 7–9, 160–161, 228
Preferences, sweet, 6
Preservatives, spices, 198
Prolamins, 216
Protein
    as fuel, 18, 29
    and satiety, 73–74
    selling of, 147
Psychobiology, 221, 225–226
Psychological effects, 178–179
Psychological factors, 63–65, 68–69
Psychophysics, 9
    of sweets, 134–135
Pureeing foods, 191–192

R

Repetitive diets, effects of, 118–120
Recipes, and culture, 202
Religion, and foods, 79, 191, 210, see also
    Culture; Symbolism
Reward centers, in brain, 44–45
Rice, varieties, 200
Rickets, 215
Ripe food, 194
Rotten food, 194

S

Saccharin, 11–12, 228–229
    bitterness of, 136–138
    preference of rats, 93–94
Saccharin/glucose mixture, 123
Sacred cow, 209
Saffron, 197
Salads, 7, 198
Salt, as preservative, 193
Sandwiches, variety and palatability,
    110–111
Satiety, 64, 67–68, 70–71, 101–109, see
    also Post-ingestional factors
    centers in brain, 34–35
    learned, or conditioned, 67–68, 70–71,
        76
    sensory specific, 64, 101–109
Seafood, 192
Seasoning agents, 196, 198–199
Seasonings, 198–199, 228, see also
    Flavorings
    and climate, 199
    historic use of, 198–199, 236
Sedentary man, 17, 28–30, 69

Self-selection of foods, 6–7, 101–102, 119
Self-stimulation, reward, 45
Senses, 3, 87
Sensory memory, *see* Memory, sensory
Sensory receptors, 4–6
Sensory specific satiety, 33, 39, 101–109
Sickle cell anemia, 179–180
Sleeping sickness, and dairying, 210–212
Slimming, *see* Dieting
Snacks, 6, 70, 143–144, 160–161, *see also* Foods, convenience
Soaking foods, 193
Social determinants, 139–149, *see also* Foods, social factors
Social factors, *see* Foods, social factors
Sociocultural factors, 139–149, 153–155, 205–221
Sour, taste of 12–13
Soybeans, 180–185
 history of, 182–183
 non-food usage, 183
 use in China, 182–187
Soysauce, 181, 194, 196
 varieties of, 201
Spices
 adaptive role of, 180, 230–231, 236
 as luxury item, 198
 as preservatives, 198
Staple foods, 118, 142, 238
Starch, 8–9
 and satiety, 73–74
Sucrose, *see also* Sugar; Sweeteners
 memory for, 97–98
 as stabilizer, 162–164
Sugar, 5, 8–9, 73, 123–138, 157–168, 228, 236, *see also* Carbohydrates
 and culture, 6, 8, 164–165, 228
 in diet, 161–165
 as preservative, 163, 167
Survey, food preferences, 8
Sweet sense, in man, 5, 228
Sweet-sour flavor, 197
Sweet taste
 effect on technology, 228–229
 in humans, 134–135, 228
Sweeteners, 10, 123–138, 157–168
 additive properties, 134–135
 artificial, 11–12, 123–138
 magnitude estimation of, 134–137
 natural, 12–13
Sweetness, chemistry of, 10–14
Sweets
 adaptive, 231
 biological origin for, 8–9
 innate liking for, 5, 8–9, 228–229
 maladaptive, 8, 231

predictor of energy, 228
Symbolic nature of flavors, 146, 196
Synergism, and sweeteners, 123–130, 136–138
Szechuan pepper, 196

T

Taboo foods, 207–208
Tapioca, 193
Taste, *see also* Flavor; Palatability
 aversion conditioning, 51–52, 92
 and brain response, 36
 and food selection, 147–148, 194, 198
Taste blindness, 136
Taste buds, 5, 88
Taste
 cues nutrients, 71
 dominant role of, 6–7, 65, 194–198, 225
 human, 5–6, 9–10
 inherited, 90–91
 in insects, 4
 liking for, 226
 in mammals, 5
 in man, 5–6, 9–10, 134
 in rat, 92–98, 123–134
 of saccharin/glucose, 123–124
Taste modifiers, 13–14
Taste nerve impulses, 10
Television advertising of foods, 139, 146–147, 158–160
Tempeh, 181
Temporal patterns, mixing sweets, 123–134
Texture, *see* Food, texture of
Tobacco, 246–249, 251
Tofu, 181, 183
Tomato, as flavoring, 197, 201
Tortilla technology, 234
Toxins in foods, 7, 230
Training, effects, *see* Exercise

V

Variety
 effects of
  on feeding, 101, 109
  on sandwich intake, 110–111
  on yogurt intake, 111–113
 and obesity, 101, 117–120
 through flavors, 201–202
 within cuisine, 230

Vinegar, as curative, 193
Vitamin D, 215–216

Wheat, and celiac disease, 216
Work, and foods, 17, 27

W

Weight
  gain, 8, 17, 24–27
  loss, 3, 8, 17, 25–26, 101, 119
Weight control, 8–9, 101, *see also* Dieting

Y

Yeast, adaptive role of, 180
Yogurt
  and cataracts, 217
  variety and palatability, 111–113